Memory and Imagination

Or
From Remember to Create

DAN MANOLESCU

Published by Book Writing Experts

ISBN (paperback): 978-0-578-26232-1
ISBN (hard copy): 978-0-578-26263-5
eISBN: 979-888589512-5

In loving memory of my first English teacher,   Valeria Magda

An ESL teacher's self-preparation core of memory, imagination, and creativity

A treasure trove of useful information for ESL instruction

> Creative learning is the combination of memory and imagination.

Everything we learn

    has a meaning

        eventually

            if it is shared.

There are certain things that cannot be learned easily or quickly. Time, our most precious possession, will require a life-long journey so we can fully grasp its meaning and purpose. Such simple things, like perception, belief, and reasoning, are at the root of our mental processes. Nonetheless, if life has a purpose and if we want to grow, every little bit of novelty that we acquire when we delve into **our memory, imagination,** and **creativity**, may likely be priceless. Through **recollection, discovery, and invention**, we should be able to find our way to **knowledge**.

Table of Contents

Acknowledgements

I am trying to make this a pleasant reading of discovery after benefitting from the generosity of my students, my fellow teachers, and trusted colleagues who helped me find a way to share what I learned from them. Inquisitive students may pose questions you don't expect, but versatile teachers are those who will have to provide an answer.

The memory of my first project finalized and published in 2019 brought me back to my former supervisor at LIFE in Rutherford, New Jersey, to whom I am gratefully indebted: Rosemary Rowlands. In the spring of 2021, she provided her analysis of the manuscript of my second project and, among other valuable recommendations, with a major contribution: She suggested adding a proficiency level and a Bloom's Taxonomy Level to the worksheets and the lesson plans included in the book.

While I was working on the much-needed revision, I sent a working draft to my former supervisor at New Jersey City University, Dr. Anne Mabry, who discovered other issues related to verbiage, consistency, clarity, and volume. It took me several months to address all her concerns, but now I think they were absolutely necessary. Along the same lines, I must thank Dr. Clyde Coreil for his unflinching support and his original approach to the subject of asking questions.

This book is, in large measure, an expression of gratitude to those who shared with me worksheets and lesson plans, which I duly incorporated in the general framework and made their contributions an essential part of our collaboration.

Though all those who gave generously of their time compose a substantial list, I will first recognize Peter Campisi, who helped me almost from the outset with several contributions, including his concept of motivation as well as ideas about using students' imagination, but also practical exercises from his own toolbox of lesson plans and magical approaches to the ESL classroom. Next, I thank Burgel Rosa Maria Levy, who added a lesson plan and helped me review, proofread, and edit the whole section devoted to creativity. Along the same lines, my gratitude also goes to Rhianna Weber for her exquisite addition and critique. I am equally indebted to Evina Baquiran Torres, who submitted a captivating lesson about using pictures and thus helping students develop their own creativity. Next, I thank John Artise and Ralph Herman, who gathered together the Business English section.

A special word of gratitude will go to John Egan. I am indebted for his enormous effort in reading my two books, *TIPS* in 2018 and *Memory and Imagination* in 2021, with additional comments regarding word usage, vocabulary choices, and formatting suggestions.

Particular thanks go to Bill McBride for his original lesson plan, his critical constructive view and much needed encouragement, to Paul Serrato for his advice on using poetry in the classroom, to Alexandra Story for her challenging exercise in observation, to Thomas Seo for his lesson plan incorporating music in teaching irregular verbs, to Elina Yasinov for her innovative lesson in teaching vocabulary in stories, to Enikő Szondi for her well thought grammar lesson, to Lateef Ferguson for his wonderful combination of vocabulary and grammar that can be used in activities involving several academic skills, to Jason Chase for his original lesson plan on creativity and artistic license, to Tom Shandorf for his fascinating Culture Capstone Project – Florence, Guidance and Support Materials for Trainers and Course Managers, to Tammy Johnson, Ph.D. for checking substantial parts of the project and for her advice regarding TPRS, i.e. Teaching Proficiency through Story-Telling, and to Ed Friedel for his lesson plans in giving directions.

My heartfelt gratitude goes to our esteemed colleagues of BRAC Institute of Languages, BRAC University, Bangladesh for their extremely valuable lesson plans about life lessons from autobiographies, travel brochures, and human rights. Their contribution will definitely provide a glimpse into the unique approach to teaching English in Bangladesh, in which culture and language are combined in a remarkable instructional sample they shared for all of us to enjoy.

I extend my thanks to Rupert Johnstone, a good friend and collaborator, who joined us from Down Under with his enchanting lessons about Australia, its language and its inhabitants.

I am also grateful to Amanda Kennedy for her understanding and patience with my manuscript in its various stages before printing and publication.

Last but not least, my gratitude goes to the wonderful staff at Clarence Dillon Public Library in Bedminster, where most of this project was done.

Foreword

L ouis Leakey, a famous anthropologist and paleontologist, was looking for a scientist to go to Africa and study the chimpanzees in the wild. The requirements were quite simple: he was looking for somebody with an open mind, a passion for knowledge, and monumental patience. The person who was chosen for the job was Jane Goodall, who did not have a college degree but managed to convince Leakey that she was the right person for the job. Her accomplishments and the results of her studies proved that she was gifted with skills beyond anybody's imagination.

While watching the documentary entitled *Jane* tracing the work and the research accomplished over the years by Jane Goodall, I came to realize that the same simple requirements would hold for an ESL teacher: **an open mind, a passion for knowledge,** and **monumental patience**. I would humbly add that an open mind **should be trained to absorb and retain** as much information as possible by **doing research.**

The many facets of teaching an ESL class are set before the instructor, and the key to success lies in the knowledge and the preparation of every detail. We all assume that students and learners of all ages willingly go for a journey into the unchartered maps of **language, culture**, and **communication skills.**

Rationale

When I started teaching ESL in 1984, although I thought I had accumulated enough knowledge to go into the classroom, I was not sure my college professors would approve of my performance - not because I was not ready to reconstruct the best moments retroactively of our methodology classes. I was looking for a collection of every conceivable piece of information that would allow me to recover bits and pieces from every nook of my memory (and add my imagination) to communicate with my students in a way that they would benefit from our exchange of ideas.

I was trying to find the best way to get ready for my first classroom assignments. However, the frightening realization came that I could not find all this information in a book. Deep down in my heart, I judged myself unprepared for the uphill battle, and indeed I was groping in the dark with no palpable solution in sight.

One thing I knew for certain: Somewhere along the way, I was going to collect, from my own experience, what I thought would be best for my students. The intensity and scope of my perceptions led me nowhere, only to realize that Toni Morrison was right when she said that if you can't find the book you want to read, you must write it yourself.

What my instinct was telling me, I surmised, was the basic idea that I would continue to be a student and at the same time grow into an educator. Then I had to acknowledge that I had to work around one BIG concept – the **fusion of learning and teaching**.

Following the unavoidable moments of silence and reflection, I started a list of questions, not because I knew what I was looking for, but because I was going back to what learning meant to my fellow fledglings and me: "Ask questions," I was told, "And in time one question will beget another one." Eventually, I "submitted them to a book as you might to a dream." And I needed those questions to find the best way to **communicate with my students.**

We should never forget that **language is a means of communication among people.** According to Dor (2015), language is "dedicated to the systematic instruction of imagination: we use it to communicate directly with our interlocutors' imaginations." He argues that when we communicate with each other, the language we use goes beyond sharing experience. In his opinion, language "allows speakers to intentionally and systematically instruct their interlocutors in the process of imagining the intended experience – instead of directly experiencing it. […]

Language is thus the only system that allows for communication that bridges the experiential gaps between speakers." (p. 2)

Teaching is a journey, and we need to wrap the cloak of knowledge around the **concept of memory and imagination.** This will open the mind and help us organize and articulate our thoughts, communicate better with ourselves and the people around us, and discover the unexplained and the unknown.

How do we combine advice and lifetime observations so we can better communicate with our students?

I was lucky and blessed to work side by side with teachers of exceptional talent and dedication for many years. We sometimes find ourselves between the known and the unknown, and the best way out, in my opinion, is to analyze **how we gather lifetime observations and share our knowledge and experience with our students**.

Overwhelmed by the huge volume of information teachers have to absorb, interpret, and deliver to their students, we need to remember "our knowledge of the outside world depends on our modes of perception." (Bronowski, 1978, p. 5) Transplanted in the classroom, this idea reverberates in our minds as we prepare to tackle various facets of the teaching process. In doing so, we are reminded that **what we perceive is not what our students perceive**. We should accept this seemingly insurmountable obstacle.

Following the example and advice I got over the years from my dear colleagues, I learned lessons not taught in books, journals, or even in the best methodology classes. I also realized that we share the same or similar perceptions in mind more than in the heart because the mind is an instrument for understanding the nature of natural language both as a tool and as a behavioral goal.

When our students' curiosity challenges us, we find ourselves in the position of mediators between the students' inquisitiveness and our reliance on structured systems of already established knowledge. And suppose we want to empower our students. In that case, we need to accept that **information** given to our students should be **followed by practical examples**.

We have at our disposal a wide array of good stories or *bon mots* to attract our audience's attention. However, we also need to establish a **distinction between information and instruction**. While information can be defined as things, we know about something, the **instruction** would be **teaching that information**.

Some of us lay the grounds of a structured language. Others prefer to let students play with the language freely. Does this imply the **act of discovery** and the **challenge of creativity**?

Sifting through many valuable sources of information, I found these words which one of my esteemed colleagues shared with me:

I have found that minimizing the structures presented in a lesson is essential in the student's growth. Less is more. Most of the lessons, I believe, should take the form of some kind of creative task that gives the students time to play with a few different forms to complete a task like the situational tasks you shared. I also like to ask them to create interviews with pre-set language they must creatively incorporate into the dialogue. This forces them to be creative to accomplish a task. I believe they are making connections in their brain more naturally because they are free. In short, I think that best language learning comes from solving problems.

(Peter Campisi, 2019)

To continue along the same lines, and to paraphrase Peter, I must say that when we communicate with our students and help them answer challenging questions, we can guide them towards the process of discovery. That can be done through **curiosity and creativity.**

Curiosity and Creativity

What is the value of curiosity and creativity?

Curiosity and **creativity** have produced thousands and thousands of inventions and discoveries. While it is impossible to tell when or where they all took place, we must admit we don't even know where invention ends, and discovery begins.

> Whatever they are, few inventions or discoveries are made overnight. There is usually a period of preparation before they emerge. Even then, they take time to act. An invention may take years to displace existing methods. A discovery may take generations to change the habit of thought. (Bridgman, 2006, p. 4)

Teachers learn from books, journals, magazine articles, and other sources of information. Humans also learn enormously from each other and share everything we discover because exchanging **messages, ideas, opinions, questions, and answers eventually provides enjoyment**. They are all an integral part of our mind at work. When we create new learning situations, our students are invited to question themselves, and in turn, to be inspired and empowered. New information will **satisfy their thirst for knowledge**, practical hints will **stimulate their curiosity**, and in time, new skills will **make them better thinkers, better speakers, and better writers**.

We open our minds whenever our everyday life shocks us with new challenges because necessity is the mother of invention. Students and teachers are the ones who know how to create, especially **when their curiosity is aroused and stimulated by new knowledge.**

Our students will assimilate the new information if we approach them with a **rich and abundant treasure trove of ideas**. The historical concept of **merger and acquisition** that built many contemporary languages will also foreground English as a Second Language of the 21st century. Ostler (2005) takes his readers into what he calls "an inquiry into the Language Prestige, defined as the propensity to attract other users." *(Empires of the Word. A Language History of the World*, p. 19)

Borrowing from other similar researchers, Ostler argues that several new linguistic approaches have tried to explain or at least give a tentative answer to a difficult question:

Under what conditions do languages have the power to grow?

Not an easy task, considering the value and relevance of a language like English.

> World powers make world languages ... The Roman Empire made Latin, the British Empire English. Churches too, of course, are great powers ... Men who have strong feelings directed towards the world and its affairs have done most. What the humble prophets of linguistic unity would have done without Hebrew, Arabic, Latin, Sanskrit and English, it is difficult to imagine. Statesmen, soldiers, sailors, and missionaries, men of action, men of strong feelings have made world languages. (Ostler, 2005, p. 20)

The English language of the 21st century has a unique function in the **process of communication**. Primarily because in these days' cultural, political, and economic context, we need to improve our overall skills necessary to navigate through the wealth of opinions and ideas, at home and work, on a local and an international level.

This exchange of opinions, rich and diverse but always relevant will start from what we **already know** and take us into what we **would like to know.**

Teachers and students usually enter a class with abundant knowledge from previous activities where certain skills have already been engraved in the learners' receptacle of mental perceptions. We always build on **prior experiences,** which gradually become **the building blocks** that **create new knowledge.**

How do we create new knowledge through communicative competence?

To facilitate what linguists call "successful communication "(Hymes 1989, Kumaravadivelu 2006), several factors (shorted into an acronym SPEAKING) are taken into consideration:

Setting refers to the place and time in which the communicative event takes place.

Participants refers to speakers and hearers and their role relationships.

Ends refers to the stated or unstated objectives the participants wish to accomplish.

Act sequence refers to the form, content, and sequence of occurrence.

Key refers to the manner and tone (serious, sarcastic, etc.) of the utterance.

Instrumentalities refers to the channel (oral or written) and the code (formal or informal).

Norms refers to conventions of interaction and interpretation based on shared knowledge.

Genre refers to categories of communication such as lecture, report, essay, poem, and so forth.

(Adapted from http://www.languageinconflict.org/how-language-works/context-of-situation.html Source Hymes, 1974)

After a quick analysis of these factors, which Hymes describes as basic "for determining the rules of language in a given context," the conversation about language communication may very well continue and pose the question: What do we do with language? Austin (as cited in Kumaravadivelu, 2006)) answered in his book entitled *How to Do Things with Words*: "We perform speech acts."

> By speech acts, he refers to the everyday activity of informing, instructing, ordering, threatening, complaining, describing, and scores of other such activities for which we use our language. In other words, language is an activity that we do in myriad situations and circumstances. (p. 1745)

Speech acts may vary from culture to culture, and language teachers are the ones who will take all these relevant ideas into the classroom. When classroom activities are organized around , teachers raise the standards to a higher level of benefit for the language learners. A good class is perceived as a **structure** in which **every detail** derives its **meaning** only from its place in the **whole**. Is there any place in our instruction where we can improvise? Of course, but improvisations do not replace the big game of exchanging ideas, playing with the tremendous force of learning through **articulate arguments**.

Teacher's self-check for effective communication:

1. Are students aware that classroom activities have a learning purpose?
2. What is it that motivates students to accomplish each task?
3. Do we have enough classroom interaction so students can question each other?
4. What skills are students learning and/or enhancing in the classroom that can be used in the real world and applied to the workplace?
5. How do we facilitate effective language use without too much teacher intervention?
6. Do we take notes of common misunderstandings, expectations, and beliefs that may hinder classroom management?
7. How do we mediate when cultures present opposing views?
8. What can be gained from one class that can be used and developed in another class?
9. Can we guess what questions students may have during and after class?
10. Do students leave the classroom with a feeling of accomplishment?

To make students aware of the intricacies of each task, teachers resort to examples. Too many rules create abstractions and cannot be understood without an example. We may want to **let the students give us the rules**, but we should always present examples first.

One quick suggestion would be to make comparisons and inspire our students to follow the best examples we can provide.

> My memory is like a film. That is why I am good at remembering things, […] what people were wearing, what they smelled like because my memory has a smell track which is like a soundtrack. And when people ask me to remember something, I can simply press **Rewind** and **Fast Forward** and **Pause** like on a video recorder. But more like a DVD player because I don't have to Rewind through everything in between to get to a memory of something a long time ago. And there are no buttons, either, because it is happening in my head. (Haddon, 2003, p. 76)

Curiosity and **creativity** can be developed if our students know that one of the most important treasures is a rich vocabulary that can be used to articulate thoughts. We communicate with ourselves and with the world around us. In doing so, we look for what is meaningful, for things that, by and large, determine our lives, that most often shape who we are and what we can accomplish. The **value of our ideas** and the **eloquence of expression** depends on how we resort to the power of the written word that will be an asset in combining what we **discover** (because we are curious) with things and concepts that we can **create** with them.

For further reading, please check:

Beghetto, R. A., & Kaufman, J. C. (2016). *Nurturing Creativity in the Classroom.* United Kingdom: Cambridge University Press.

Harris, A. (2016). *Creativity and Education.* United Kingdom: Palgrave Macmillan UK.

Brainstorming creativity

Students can interview each other.

Do you think creativity is a good thing? Why?

How can people be creative?

Do you consider yourself a creative person?
               If the answer is *Yes*, please explain.

Can you give an example of something creative that you have done?

What are some creative ways to develop reading skills?

What creative questions can you ask to find the best solutions to major issues?

Does the education system in your country encourage creativity?

Do people become creative or are they born with this ability?

Do you think creativity can be taught in the classroom?

What creative activities do you think are necessary to make a class more interesting?

Can classes be made more motivating if the teacher is more creative?

If you had enough time and money, what do you think you could do with your creativity?

Let students use their creativity

> "Creativity is the process of bringing something new into being.
> Creativity requires passion and commitment. It brings to our
> awareness what was previously hidden and points to new life.
> The experience is one of heightened conscience: ecstasy."
> (Rolo May, *The Courage to Create*, 1994)

Creative ESL learners usually progress faster because, when they create, they also develop **better communication skills** in reading, writing, and speaking.

Being creative in the classroom also allows students to develop a greater sensitivity to problem resolution. By resorting to their own intuition and resources, creative students will set a good example to the whole class and, in time, gain confidence in themselves and empower others to do the same.

What makes an ESL student creative?

Curiosity?

Motivation?

Flexibility?

A need for novelty?

Originality of thought?

Self-reliance?

Undaunted courage?

The ability to pose unique questions?

Looking for and finding a better solution?

How do we motivate our students?

According to Dörnyei (2001), "teacher skills in motivating learners should be seen as central to teaching effectively." (p. 116). To increase student motivation, teachers will have to create the necessary conditions in all the classroom activities, thus positively affecting the overall student performance and at the same time attaining their learning objectives.

If we include the students' specific needs and learning preferences, we may find Dörnyei's *Ten Commandments for Motivating Language Learners* (1998). The best way to approach this challenging issue:

1. Set a personal example with your own behavior.
2. Create a pleasant, relaxed atmosphere in the classroom.
3. Present the task properly.
4. Develop a good relationship with the learners.
5. Increase the learners' linguistic self-confidence.
6. Make the language classes interesting.
7. Promote learner autonomy.
8. Personalize the learning process.
9. Increase the learners' goal-orientedness.
10. Familiarize learners with the target language culture.

(p. 131)

Can we activate all the motivational components in every class every day? **Motivation** – this critical force that works miracles – can be used daily if we encourage pair work and group work, if we remember that learners have differences in mastering skills, that they learn more from their peers, and if we help them build confidence.

For further reading, please check:

Chambers, G. N. (1999). *Motivating Language Learners*. United Kingdom: Multilingual Matters.

International Perspectives on Motivation: Language Learning and Professional Challenges. (2013). United Kingdom: Palgrave Macmillan.

How do we start, develop, and sustain student motivation?

- Find more opportunities for cooperative learning.
- Switch from goals to viable vision so learners can see the benefits of practical knowledge.
- Write 'motivation' on the board and try to get the students to give you a definition.
- Ask students to work in pairs or in small groups and give examples of activities from 'useful' to 'most useful' they would really enjoy and therefore get motivated.
- Encourage students to draw pictures, sketches, or cartoons of a story while you read that story in the classroom.
- Give them a couple of minutes to write down as many words as possible that can be related to a topic like 'music' or 'fun.'
- Challenge them to choose an object that represents them.
- Make classrooms interactions meaningful by pairing reticent students with other students who display patience and natural leadership qualities.

How do we use student motivation in the process of learning?

"After reflecting on my teaching and my experience as a student, I have come to embrace the gradual release of responsibility (I do, we do, you do) model. It supports learning and encourages engagement in tasks because the students have a responsibility to their group members. It is more than that, though; it puts students in a situation where they are working in small groups to create a product while also demonstrating their own learning. As students become more independent while also having the space to play with the language to communicate their ideas, they are developing an interest in learning the language.

This model is in direct contrast to the lecture style of teaching that only allows for students' receptive skills, not their innate preference toward interaction and language production in activities connected to their lives, which encourages creativity.

I have come to believe that, while standardized tests are common, the inherent nature of the test runs counter to how the human brain is built to function. They are motivation killers because right and wrong answers encourage the students to focus on the end product, not the learning process. The gradual release of responsibility model design focuses on the process."

(Peter Campisi, 2021)

Can guessing games stimulate motivation?

Guessing games can be **good motivators** and should be used as ice breakers or as warm-up exercises. Ask questions that students may be able to answer individually or while working in groups. Points are given for each good answer and tabulated for end-of-class prizes.

For example: What is it?

1. Can't stop running. – Can be analogical or digital. – Tells you the time.
2. Locks and unlocks doors. – Thieves don't need it.
3. The king of the animals. – Lives in Africa but can also be found in zoos.
4. Keeps food cool. – Usually found in the kitchen. – Uses electricity.
5. Can be used to measure things. – Also good for drawing a straight line.
6. Found in the kitchen. – Can be filled with water – Boils when heated.

Conversely, you can use objects in the classroom and challenge students to create clues.

(Adapted from
https://games4esl.com/guessing-games-for-kids/
https://www.twinkl.com/resource/t-s-892-what-am-i-guessing-game-cards)

> "Creativity is intelligence having fun."
> – Albert Einstein

According to Jones and Richards (2015), there are a few principles regarding creativity in language teaching. First, creativity is not an "optional" component. Instead, "creativity is seen as central to successful teaching and learning." For teachers and learners alike, real creativity "brings about valuable and concrete outcomes that are linked to the pedagogical knowledge and plans of teachers and the goals of learners." (p. 5)

According to the same authors, the second principle will take creativity in language teaching beyond "creative language." While acknowledging the value of the old concepts of creating literary, poetic, or dramatic texts, they are also focusing on "*using* language in creative ways to solve problems, to establish or maintain relationships, and to get people to act, think or feel in certain ways." (p. 5)

The fact that creativity in language teaching cannot be accomplished alone brings us to the third principle, as presented by Jones and Richards. They also argue that creative teaching skills cannot be developed in isolation. Pennycook (2007) is also mentioned to assert that "creative language use and creative language teaching are often a matter of refashioning, re-contextualizing, and building upon the words and ideas of others." (p. 7)

Do we need to explain creativity?

Creativity is not only important to classroom learning but also to the critical informal learning that occurs in the pre-school years – how to speak a first language, how to behave at the dinner table, how to make friends and engage in group play (Sawyer, 1997).

Explaining creativity provides more than intellectual satisfaction; it will lead to a more creative society, and will enhance the creative potential of our families, our workplaces, and our institutions (Sawyer, 2006).

Creativity worksheets and lesson plans

Teachers and students can use the following samples as they are, or, if necessary, adapt, revise, or re-design the worksheets, and the lesson plans to meet the requirements of the classroom activities.

This section begins with short worksheets of one or two pages and will develop into more extended lesson plans.

In worksheets, the format follows the idea that an activity should have a task, an example to follow, and collocations or idioms that might be learned in context. Commonality may function as context. Lesson plans should have a learning objective, one or more group activities, and a learning outcome.

Keeping these worksheets together is one **topic** that should attract the **students' attention** and encourage their **participation** without correcting them too often.

Students can be assigned to work in pairs, small groups, or even larger groups.

The following section is designed to help teachers challenge their students with interesting and attractive topics and at the same time help them hone their skills to a point where **originality, creativity, and imagination will prevail.**

Worksheets and lesson plans in this book are organized according to the students' proficiency level and Bloom's Taxonomy of six levels of learning.

Proficiency levels:

Beginning
High Beginning
Low Intermediate
Intermediate
High Intermediate
Low Advanced
Advanced
High Advanced

Bloom's Taxonomy Levels

Remembering	Level 1
Understanding	Level 2
Applying	Level 3
Analyzing	Level 4
Evaluating	Level 5
Creating	Level 6

Looking for creative uses of common objects?

"Marilyn Oppezzo, a Stanford University psychologist, used to walk around campus with her Ph.D. advisor to discuss lab results and brainstorm new projects. One day they came up with an experiment to look at the effects of walking on creative thinking. Was there something to the age-old idea that walking and thinking are linked?

Oppezzo designed an elegant experiment. A group of Stanford students was asked to list as many creative uses for common objects as possible. A Frisbee, for example, can be used as a dog toy, but it can also be used as a hat, a plate, a birdbath, or a small shovel. The more novel uses a student listed, the higher the creativity score. Half the students sat for an hour before they were given their test. The others walked on a treadmill.

The results were staggering. Creativity scores improved by 60 percent after a walk."

https://lithub.com/on-the-link-between-great-thinking-and-obsessive-walking/

Suggested classroom activities:

1. Select one or two objects in your classroom and ask your students to find as many creative uses for the objects as possible—for example, maps, photos, pictures, etc.
2. Let students choose one of their favorite objects they carry around daily and list as many creative uses they can think of—for example, cell phones, backpacks, plastic bottles, etc.
3. Share the information with the whole class and summarize the findings on the board.

Proficiency Level: Low Advanced – Bloom's Taxonomy Level 2

Food

What people eat tells you a lot about them – whether they are greedy, picky, friendly or unfriendly, young, old, or middle-aged.

What they eat will also tell you what part of the world they come from or what part of the country they grew up in. Certain foods or meals may seem to go with specific occasions, like birthday parties, anniversaries, weddings, etc.

1. **Imagine a room** with a table and some chairs. Decide who will be eating and what the occasion will be.
2. You may want to **arrange the students in pairs** and start with a brunch or an afternoon snack.
3. **Now imagine setting the table,** and don't forget to choose the right **tableware**, plates, and decorations.
4. Another suggestion would be **a picnic in the local park** or **a holiday party.**

Select items from the following list and add your own:
plastic cups and plates – flower centerpiece – white linen table cloth – coffee mugs – silver forks, knives, and spoons – fish sticks – fruit cake – potato chips – napkins – garlic bread – paper hats – meat loaf – pretzels – hot dogs – mints – cinnamon rolls – salt shaker – pepper mill, etc.

You may want to use some of the collocations below:

gourmet food	*fresh market*
low fat diet	*steak and baked potatoes*
staple food	*pancakes and maple syrup*
ready-made	*peanut butter sandwiches*
wholesome food	*genetically modified foods*
daily food intake	*vegetarian/vegan*
food allergy	*food processing*
take-out food	*nutritious food*

Proficiency Level: Intermediate - Bloom's Taxonomy Level 2

Do we know any stories about cooking?

"Some days in the kitchen are good, and some are bad. Sofia was *on a roll* the other day when she made pumpkin soup as an appetizer, chicken and rice as the main meal, and then chocolate for dessert. Not only did she *cook up a storm*, but everything was *done to a T*. However, that isn't always the case in the kitchen. Last week she tried to make a simple scrambled egg and overcooked it. Then she tried to make some toast and burned that, too. It is *like she jumped out of the fire into the frying pan*. Well, at least she knew that it was just a bad cooking day and not a problem where there were *too many cooks in the kitchen*. Fortunately, she knows that happens to everyone, so she has not given up cooking." (Martinez-Alba, 2017, p. 34)

Challenge your students to **tell or create their own stories about cooking**. Encourage them to use some of the following collocations related to cooking:

good to the last drop
a flash in the pan
too many cooks spoil the broth
to butter someone up
to bring home the bacon
gourmet cooking
stirring the pot
leftovers
home cooking

For example: "So I was baking a chocolate cake for a dinner party that my family was having. My first step, before even starting the batter, was pre-heating the oven. After about 20 minutes, I noticed there was a weird smell. When I opened the oven, I realized that I melted a blender that my mom put in there to make more counter space for food prep. My mom was so pissed off, but the cake was the most decadent and moist chocolate cake I have ever made." – Olivia (https://spoonuniversity.com)

Proficiency Level: Intermediate – Bloom's Taxonomy Level 2

How would you describe a happy day in your life?

Excerpt from *My Antonia* by Willa Cather:

"I sat down in the middle of the garden, where snakes could scarcely approach unseen, and leaned my back against a warm yellow pumpkin. There were some ground-cherry bushes growing along the furrows, full of fruit. I turned back the papery triangular sheaths that protected the berries and ate a few. All about me giant grasshoppers, twice as big as any I had ever seen, were doing acrobatic feats among the dried vines. The gophers scurried up and down the ploughed ground. There in the sheltered draw-bottom the wind did not blow very hard, but I could hear it singing its humming tune up on the level, and I could see the tall grasses wave. The earth was warm under me and warm as I crumbled it through my fingers. Queer little red bugs came out and moved in slow squadrons around me. Their backs were polished vermilion, with black spots. I kept as still as I could. Nothing happened. I did not expect anything to happen. I was something that lay under the sun and felt it, like the pumpkins, and I did not want to be anything more. I was entirely happy. Perhaps we feel like that when we die and become a part of something entire, whether it is sun and air, or **goodness** and **knowledge.** At any rate, that is happiness; to be dissolved into something complete and great. When it comes to one, it comes as naturally as sleep." (p. 16) [NB: author's emphasis]

What makes you happy? Can you buy happiness? Ask the students to prepare a short passage about a happy day that brought them **goodness and knowledge**. Some of the following collocations may be useful:

to find/ achieve happiness	*lasting happiness*
pursuit of happiness	*supreme happiness*
a feeling of happiness	*to radiate happiness*
happy as a clam/lark	*to deserve happiness*
perfect/ultimate happiness	*to spread happiness*

Proficiency Level: High Intermediate – Bloom's Taxonomy Level 3

Paraphrasing computer vocabulary

Teachers can make a list of vocabulary words. Instead of giving the students any explanations or definitions, they may let them prove they **understand** the verbiage properly by paraphrasing computer vocabulary.

For example:

a (computer) geek   an enthusiast or expert

to navigate a website _____

to archive documents _____

to bookmark a site _____

to download (music) _____

to run software _____

to cut and paste _____

to forward a message _____

social networking _____

memory stick _____

search engine _____

an email bounces back _____

remote access _____

Proficiency level: Low Intermediate – Bloom's Taxonomy Level 2

For further reading, please check:

Alajmi, M. (2019). *Paraphrasing Student Guide: '7 Simple Steps.'* (n.p.): Independently Published.

Story fill-in

Here is an incomplete story about a UFO – an unidentified flying object – for the students to finish. They are free to use any word they want, but everybody will create a **different story.**

I Saw a UFO

    Late one afternoon I was _____ing through _____. I crossed the _____ and entered _____. Twilight had come, and it was very _____ there. All at once, I heard _____. I looked up, and there was a _____ coming straight down. It landed with a _____. I was _____. "I'm seeing a _____!" I thought.
    I_____ closer. I tried to touch the _____ with my _____, but my _____ bounced off a _____ that surrounded the UFO. Then a _____ opened its side. A _____ was lowered. Out came a _____. It had a _____ like that of a _____. In two of its hands it carried a machine that looked like a _____. I think it took my _____. Then the _____ was taken up again. There was a _____ and the UFO shot up. The it changed course and hovered over _____. Suddenly, it was gone! On the ground where it had been was a _____. I _____ home and told my neighbors about the _____. They said, "_____! You've been reading too many _____!" But I decided to report the UFO to _____.

Moral: Don't go _____ in _____, or you may have your _____taken by a _____ from _____.

(Mueller & Reynolds, 1992, p. 29)

Proficiency Level: Intermediate – Bloom's Taxonomy Level 3

Developing your own description skills

Invite your students to use some of the following collocations and describe their hometown.

residential area
cobbled streets
road signs
conservation area
pedestrian crossing
local amenities
cycle lanes
cul-de-sac
shopping arcades
sprawling city
imposing buildings

For example:

If you are on route 287 in New Jersey, halfway between Morristown and Somerville, you can look to your right, and you will see some *quaint old buildings* in a *sparsely populated area* at the bottom of Somerset Hills. The *winding streets* can easily be mistaken for a *meandering branch* of the Raritan River, which crosses the west-central parts of New Jersey. When the *volume of traffic* gets too congested, you can take the first exit and get to a *car park* adjacent to the *first traffic light*. Step out of your car, and you will be enchanted by several *upmarket shops* with names that will remind you of old movies.

Proficiency Level: High Intermediate – Bloom's Taxonomy Level 4

For further information about description, please check:

Elbourne, P. (2013). *Definite Descriptions*. United Kingdom: OUP Oxford.

Using descriptive adjectives

Ask your students to list their **favorite types of activities.**

For example:

kayaking,   snowboarding,   listening to music,

playing outdoor games,   jogging,

mountain climbing,   surfing,   swimming,

drawing,   crossword puzzles, etc.

Provide a list of descriptive adjectives:

dazzling,   attractive,   .   enjoyable   awesome,

inspiring,   astonishing,

challenging,   funny,   relaxing,   breath-taking, etc.

Students are then asked to **find adjectives to match the activities:**

For example:

great game,   fierce football,

easy exercise,   rough race,

harmless hockey

Proficiency Level: Low Intermediate - Bloom's Taxonomy Level 2

Associations of "a beautiful character"

"Aristotle says that everything we do voluntarily seems to aim at some good, and hence it has been beautifully said that the good is that at which all things aim. The word good is ἀγαθοῦ – agathoú. And the word beautiful is τἀγαθόν – tagathón. And beautiful is the highest form of the good. And so this statement that everything seems to aim at some good, the statement that the good is that at which all things aim, Aristotle calls a beautiful statement."

(https://www.hughhewitt.com/dr-larry-arnn-makes-it-through-the-first-paragraph-of-aristotles-ethics)

Students should be encouraged to use one of the following adjectives and associate/match the personality with the name of the person. They can refer to a **beautiful character trait** of the person they are going to describe:

agreeable	affectionate	ambitious
approachable	articulate	artistic
brave	calm	cautious
charming	confident	clever
competent	considerate	dependable
dazzling	discreet	dynamic
easy-going	efficient	enthusiastic
faithful	flexible	humble
imaginative	intelligent	likeable
loving	loyal	mysterious
passionate	reasonable	reliable
romantic	resourceful	sensitive
sincere	sociable	tactful
trustworthy		

For example: *Dazzling Diana*   *Lovely Lavinia*

Your example: _____

Proficiency Level: Low Intermediate – Bloom's Taxonomy Level 1

My favorite teacher

I remember our first day in sixth grade when our new English teacher walked in. The previous year we had fallen in love with a young teacher with a bubbly, effervescent personality. This time, however, the new teacher was different. Not better or worse, just different. From day one, she overwhelmed us with her generous, warmhearted, and lovable approach, and she made all of us intensely happy. No need to add that she left us mesmerized and wanted to know more about everything in English.

Worksheet

Ask your students to **describe their favorite teacher** using adjectives and match them with one of the emojis below. They should explain why or how they found the teacher and focus on the effect their classes had on the students. Or, if they prefer, how they felt at the end of each class.

Students may want to use adjectives like *exciting, happy, curious, annoying, dedicated, motivated, embarrassing, affectionate, monotonous, creative, caring, innovative, brilliant, amazing, patient, thoughtful, reliable, understanding, compassionate, appreciative, supportive, inspiring, gracious, unique, wonderful, wise, funny, confusing, etc.*

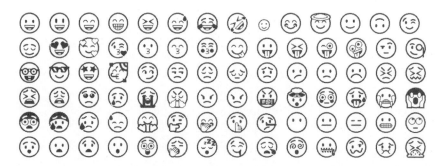

Proficiency Level: Intermediate – Bloom's Taxonomy Level 2

Necessary job skills

Ask your students to make a list of occupations and mention what skills these people must have to function in their jobs.

For example:

Accountant
    teamwork ability
    communication and interpersonal skills
    proficiency in IT

Bank teller
    _____
    _____
    _____

Flight attendant
    _____
    _____
    _____

Football coach
    _____
    _____
    _____

School principal
    _____
    _____
    _____

Pharmacist
    _____
    _____
    _____

Travel agent
    _____
    _____
    _____

Proficiency Level: High Beginning – Bloom's Taxonomy Level 1

Using art in the ESL classroom

Draw it out
Instead of asking our students to summarize, we can have them **write a simple story** and then switch or rotate their papers and **draw out** what they like or understand. The drawings could be slapped on the chalkboard, and the students will have to guess what happened in those stories. This can also be a follow-up to writing practice or reading comprehension exercises. The same activity may also incorporate vocabulary and grammar taught previously in another class.

Descriptive writing
Students are asked to describe an **object**, an **event**, or a **character** of their choosing. Then, another student will draw it out to see how accurate the description is.

Visit an art gallery
A quick **list of vocabulary words** can be presented before going in person or visiting an art gallery online.

Each student will have to choose a painting or any other work of art and describe it, in summary, using some of the following words and collocations:

portrait	*landscape*	*artwork*	*arts and crafts*
watercolor	*decorative*	*visual*	*abstract art*
exhibit	*pottery*	*still life*	*sketch*

(Adapted from How to Use Art Activities to Illustrate ESL Vocabulary by Sarah Li Cain)
https://www.fluentu.com/blog/educator-english/art-vocabulary-esl/

Proficiency Level: High Beginning – Bloom's Taxonomy Level 2

Writing an imaginary biography of a movie character

Choose a movie that can be watched together with the students. For example: *12 Angry Men*

Short summary

In a New York Courthouse, an 18-year-old boy is on trial for stabbing his father to death. The 12 members of the jury begin deliberations in what looks to be an open-and-shut case. From the start, it is quite clear that the jurors have already decided that the boy is guilty. Consequently, they plan to return their verdict without taking time for discussion. Only one member (Juror 8) disagrees because he says that, in such cases, when a guilty verdict will be accompanied by a mandatory death sentence, the jurors should at least check all the details first. They look at the defendant's alibi, analyze the witnesses and their accounts, and consider the knife that the boy claims to have lost but is found at the murder scene. Carefully sifting through the evidence presented in court, the other jurors finally decide that there is enough reasonable doubt of the boy's guilt. Juror 8 is, therefore, able to convince the other jurors that a non-guilty" verdict might be appropriate in this special case.

Some **vocabulary** may be used to facilitate the assignment:

testimony	*preliminary vote/tally*	*secret ballot*
to deliberate	*to abstain*	*to testify*
arrogant	*prejudiced*	*merciless*	*wise*

Classroom assignment:

Students are asked to choose one juror, describe him, and write a short **imaginary biography**. For example: Who is Juror Number 8, and what is his profession?

Proficiency Level: Intermediate - Bloom's Taxonomy Level 3

Learning life lessons from autobiographies

Materials: Steve Jobs video and small pieces of paper for each student.

Introduction (5 minutes)
The teacher greets the students and then asks them to review the last class. She/he tells them to think and to come up with one idea from the last class that was new or interesting. Then the students share their points.

Step 1 Intro to Autobiography (25 minutes)
Suggested preliminary questions:

Do you know anything about autobiography?
What is an autobiography?

The teacher encourages students to share their ideas. If the students are not familiar with the concept, the teacher explains with examples.

Then the teacher tells the students that they are going to learn about someone by watching a video. His name is Steve Jobs. The teacher may ask them who Steve Jobs is and listen to their responses.

The teacher plays the Steve Jobs video. After watching the video, the teacher may ask the following questions:

What was interesting about this video?
How has this video inspired you?
What were some of the important autobiographical points that were included about his life?

Again, the teacher gives the students time to think and provides positive reinforcement for their ideas.

Step 2 Activity – Naming (15 minutes)
The teacher asks the students to write down the name of an object on a piece of paper that they think represents them.

For example:
"I chose the bird as my symbol because I love freedom."
The teacher may give them 3 minutes to think and provide the answers. Afterward, they may randomly choose two or three students and ask them about the objects:
So what object did you pick, and why does it represent you?

Step 3: Drawing Activity (35 minutes)

After listening to a few students, the teacher asks everyone to draw themselves as they see themselves in ten years. The teacher may give an example to make the idea clear.

After the students finish their work, they will come in front of the class to show the picture and share in a minute how this picture represents the future of him/her.

Conclusion:

Students share the life lessons they learned from watching the video and discussing its content.

Proficiency Level: Advanced - Bloom's Taxonomy Level 5

(Adapted from BRAC University/BRAC Institute of Languages, Bangladesh, 2021)

Tell me, where is fancy bred.
Or in the heart or in the head,
How begot, how nourished?
Reply, reply.

William Shakespeare, T*he Merchant of Venice*

What do we need to write a good story?

Good ideas

"If one idea in particular seems attractive, and you feel you could do something with it, then you toss it around, play tricks with it, work it up, tone it down, and start writing it. That's not nearly such fun – it becomes hard work." (Christie, 1970, p. vii)

Interesting characters

Whether they are taken from real life or invented, they will come alive in the story's narration.

The setting

If ideas and characters come from inside the author's mind, "the third is outside – it must be there – waiting – in existence already. […] So, in a sense, you don't invent your settings. They are outside you, all around you, in existence – you have only to stretch out your hand and pick and choose." (Christie, p. x)

"…one knows – of one's own knowledge – how much goodness there is in this world of ours – the kindnesses done, the goodness of heart, the acts of compassion, the kindness of neighbor to neighbor, the helpful actions of girls and boys." (Christie, p. xii)

Students should be asked to find an example from their own lives and make up a story that can be shared with the whole class.

Proficiency Level: Low Advanced – Bloom's Taxonomy Level 4

Writing a story using target vocabulary

- "Give students a list of target words (generally the new important vocabulary from today, this week, etc.). There should be at least 20 words for students to choose from. Ten will do in a pinch.

- Divide students into groups (3 students per group might be best).

- Each group needs to choose a writer.

- Each group needs to write a connected story using a certain number of items from the list. (I recommend that students use at least ten words from the list unless the list only has ten items. In that case, it should be eight words that need to be used.)

- Set a time limit.

Notes on the topic:

- You can leave the topic up to students; however, this may be difficult, especially for lower-level students.

- Another option is to require a topic related to the current class topic.

- Special challenges:

  – Students need to retell a story (a well-known fairy tale or movie, for example) using the target vocabulary.
  – Students should try to include as many of the target words as possible in one grammatically correct sentence.

Other notes:

- Decide whether different word forms (e.g., noun if the word on the list is a verb) are acceptable.
- I recommend doing this group activity as a non-graded practice activity (e.g., a practice for a similar activity that students will do individually for a grade).

- Let students know that the sentences they create must illustrate that they understand the meaning of the target vocabulary. For example, an unconnected sentence in the story like "This is very X" does not show that the students understand the meaning of X.
- Sometimes it can be very difficult for students to get started, especially if this is the first time they are doing this activity. In that case, it can help to provide a first sentence."

(Maria Levy, 2021)

Proficiency Level: Intermediate – Bloom's Taxonomy Level 3

What makes you proud?

Collins English Dictionary defines 'pride' in two ways:

1. Satisfaction in one's own or another's success or achievements
    the sense of pride in a job well done.
2. A sense of dignity or self-respect
    Her rejection was a severe blow to his pride.

People say that somebody who is *as proud as a peacock* is excessively proud.

"Every morning, punctually at nine o'clock (it is strange how birds and animals have an accurate sense of time), the peacock would stand on the leads outside my mother's bedroom, waiting for me to come and say good morning to her. When he saw me, he would let out a harsh shriek of welcome. He would wait until I left my mother's room, and then, with another harsh shriek, would fly down into the garden to wait for me. We would walk round and round the large garden, not arm in arm, since that was impossible, but side by side, with my arm round his lovely shining neck. If it hadn't been for his crown, which made him slightly taller than me, we would have been of exactly the same size."

(Sitwell, 1962, p. 18)

What is it that makes you proud? Write a short paragraph and use your own choice of words or some of the following:

to take pride in	*my pride and joy*
to do something out of pride	*to swell with pride*
to swallow one's pride	*a strong feeling of pride*
a source of pride	*a sense of pride*
to salvage one's pride	*a matter of pride*

Proficiency Level: Low Advanced – Bloom's Taxonomy Level 4

Perseverance and determination

Take a quick look at the word *perseverance*. You will notice it is made of the prefix *per-* meaning "very" and the Latin word *severus* meaning "serious, grave, strict." *Perseverance* is used to mean "doing something despite obstacles." People who *persevere* usually show an unusual ability to do something no matter how hard it is. History is full of people who managed to become successful through hard work and determination.

Bill Gates and his friend Paul Allen created a device called *Traf-O-Data* to read and interpret traffic data. The whole project was a failure, but the two friends tried again, and this time Microsoft was born. **Henry Ford** tried out several types of businesses but failed and went bankrupt five times before becoming successful with Ford Motor Company. **Benjamin Franklin** only went to school until the age of 10 because his parents could not afford to support him. A self-made man, Franklin taught himself determination. After reading books at the library, he discovered (among other things) the lightning rod and the bifocal glasses. Eventually, he became one of the Founding Fathers of the United States of America, together with John Adams, Alexander Hamilton, John Jay, Thomas Jefferson, James Madison, and George Washington.

How can we build perseverance in the classroom?

1. Build a mindset to persevere.
2. Encourage positive self-talk and mindfulness.
3. Praise effort and process, not intelligence.
4. Put failure and mistakes into a growth perspective.

(www.connectionsacademy.com)

Students can write a short paragraph and describe a moment when they **overcame failure** by showing sheer **determination through hard work and perseverance**. They may want to use some of these words and add their own:

to set one's mind to do something   *to pay off*
to display perseverance   *resolution*   *to persist*

Proficiency Level: High Intermediate – Bloom's Taxonomy Level 4

Do you have any phobias?

We are told that **phobias** are illogical **fears of perfectly ordinary things.**

But are they real?

"Phobias are real," says Jerilyn Ross, a licensed clinical worker, President of the Anxiety Disorders Association of America, and director of the Ross Center for Anxiety and Related Disorders Inc. in Washington, D.C. "People should not feel ashamed. For some reason, their bodies do this. Phobias are serious -- and can be treated."

Ross is familiar with phobias from two vantage points: as a medical expert and as a patient. She overcame a severe phobia of being trapped in tall buildings.

> "The experience of phobia is so unlike what most people know as fear and anxiety. If you try to tell them there's nothing to be afraid of, that just makes the person feel more alone and distant," Ross tells WebMD. "People with phobias are always aware that their fear doesn't make any sense. But they cannot face it."
>
> "An adult with phobia does indeed recognize the fear response is exaggerated," says Richard McNally, PhD, a Harvard psychology professor. For example, "they recognize that this is not a poisonous spider but can't help but react with disgust and aversion to any spider they see. So these people cannot go into their backyard for fear of spiders." (www.webmd.com)

Among the most common types of phobias, you will find *claustrophobia* (people feel uneasy in closed places, like elevators), *acrophobia* (the fear of high places), *agoraphobia* (the fear of open spaces), and *arachnophobia* (the fear of spiders).

Literature has very good examples:

Peter Pan suffers from **gerascophobia** (fear of growing old), in *Harry Potter*, Ron Weasley suffers from **arachnophobia**, in *Great Expectations*, Miss Havisham suffers from **metathesiophobia** (fear of changes), the narrator of Edgar Allan Poe's *The Premature Burial* suffers from **taphephobia** (fear of being buried alive), and Damien from *The Omen* is struck with **hierophobia** (fear of priests or sacred things).

Questions for classroom discussion:

1. How does fear become extreme or unreasonable?
2. Can you give a personal example of the fear that turned into a phobia?
3. Should phobias be taken seriously? Why or why not? Please defend your choice.
4. What symptoms or behaviors might indicate a phobia?
5. Do you think people with phobias can recover through therapy?
6. What sort of fear do you regard as real or legitimate?

Your questions:

_____
_____
_____

For further reading, please check:

The Little Book of Phobias: An Unflinching Look at Our Deepest Fears, with More Than 250 Quotations from Life and Literature. (1994). United States: Running Press.

Proficiency Level: Intermediate – Bloom's Taxonomy Level 2

Newspapers and magazines

Acta Diurna ("Action Journal"), first published in 59 B.C., seems to be the first regular publication for spreading the news. The paper was begun by Julius Caesar, who posted it in the major cities in places where the people congregated and wanted to be informed about social and political events, criminal trials and executions, as well as the sports and theater events of the day. In China, the T'ang Dynasty started to circulate what they called *Pao* ("report"), which was a government-controlled circular that ran continuously until the end of Ch'ing Dynasty in 1911.

However, the first "true newspaper" that could be recognized today was the Dutch *Nieuwe Tijdinghen,* published in 1605, focusing mainly on trade news and containing social and political commentary, the first international news of the day. In England, Nathaniel Butter obtained a license to disseminate the news. On September 24, 1621, he printed the English translation of a Dutch paper as *Corante, or newes from Italy, Germany, Hungarie, Spaine and France.* In 1690, *Worcester Postman* was launched, but in 1709, it started publication as Berrow's Worcester *Journal*, the oldest surviving English newspaper. The same century saw the birth of newspapers in many other countries: Austria (1634), Italy (1636), Sweden (1645), and Poland (1661).

In the United States, the newspapers came to exemplify the freedom of the press, starting with the publication of *The New York Herald* (1835), the first one that operated independently, without government restrictions or outside pressures. (Adapted from Charles Panati, 1984, pp. 144-146 and www.newsmediauk.org/History-of-British-Newspapers)

Ask the students to write a short paragraph about their ESL experience or a letter addressed to a good friend that might be published in the school newsletter or a local newspaper in their native country.

Proficiency Level: Low Intermediate – Bloom's Taxonomy Level 3

ESL Newsletters

Would you like to see how your students practice their language skills and at the same time become creative? What is the best way to find out who excels in writing and, in doing so, teach their peers to develop their own skills? How do you start?

1. Get all the students in your class to create a list of topics they would like to write about in their newsletter.

2. Encourage your students to share anything that makes their culture unique.

3. Select the most interesting and the most attractive topics that would involve as many students as possible.

4. Allow them to work in pairs or small groups, depending on their common interests.

5. Invite your students to share their articles with friends and family members.

6. Every separate group should have its own writers, editors, spell checkers, and graphic designers.

7. Motivate your students to find common grounds and teach each other.

8. Whenever possible, include new vocabulary, sayings, and collocations that might be used in their articles.

9. Avoid making too many corrections and emphasize originality and creativity.

10. Bring the class together and ask your students to share their articles with each other and the whole class.

For further reading, please check:

Resource Guide to Newsletters of Interest in Adult ESL Literacy. (1990). United States: Center for Applied Linguistics.

Our island – applying *would* + infinitive

1. Tell your students you have just won the lottery and you would like to buy an island for them and need their help.
2. Students are assigned to work in small groups (3 learners per group would be ideal). Tell them to discuss the questions, write down their answers on a sheet of paper which would be placed later on the board so that everyone could read them, and vote which island they consider to be the best.
3. Each group should choose a writer.
4. Put down the following sentences on the board and tell them to write at least ten lines that start like this:

We would ... / (Name) would .../The island would ...
Questions:
Where would the island be?
What would be the weather like?
What kind of animals would live there?
Would the island have any mountains/fields/sandy beaches?
Who would build our houses? What would our houses look like?
What would we eat? Who would cook?
What would we wear? Who would work?
What would we do in the evenings? How would we travel?

5. Tell them they can use a dictionary. Suggested vocabulary might include:

Collocations:
go skiing/cycling/swimming/sailing/surfing/fishing
sunbathe on the beach   do the washing/washing-up/shopping
make lunch   tidy the rooms   take out the rubbish/garbage

Adjectives:
comfortable, luxurious, sunny, warm, cold
6. Set a time limit. (15 minutes)
7. Ask your students to share the compositions and choose the best island.   (Enikő Szondi, 2021)

Proficiency Level: Low Intermediate – Bloom's Taxonomy Level 3

Creativity and artistic license

Learning Objective:

- To challenge students' imagination and creativity by analyzing a poem written by Lewis Carrol.
- To widen their vocabulary knowledge.
- To improve their oral and reading skills.

Tasks/classroom activities:

- Pair work/small group.
- Quick exercises and discussions about word definitions, parts of speech, and onomatopoeic vocabulary.

Assessment:

Teachers can empower their students to critique each other and to share their personal opinions.

Learning Outcomes:

Students will be able to use their imagination and discover new words by looking at context and enriching their vocabulary by creating their own paraphrases, their own word definitions, and associating nonsense with potential meaning.

The following information may be given to the students:

Jabberwocky is a nonsense poem written by Lewis Carroll about killing a creature named "the Jabberwock." It was included in his 1871 novel *Through the Looking-Glass*, the sequel to *Alice's Adventures in Wonderland* (1865). This poem turns up in our pop culture; students may be familiar with it from *Alice Through the Looking Glass*, a 2016 fantasy film produced by Tim Burton, starring Johnny Depp.

This poem is especially famous for its use of made-up words. Nonsense words are a feature of "artistic license." If you are familiar with "artistic license" (also called "creative" or "poetic" license), try to write a definition below. Consult with your partner(s) and compare definitions (try this before looking at the explanation below). If you have no idea, move on!

Creative   License   (your   definition):

_____

_____

The actual definition can be paraphrased, but generally, it means "deviation from fact or form for artistic purposes"; i.e., an artist gets to break the rules because that's what artists do.

Exercise 1: Read *Jabberwocky* and underline the nonsense words.

Jabberwocky
by Lewis Carrol

"Twas brillig, and the slithy toves
    Did gyre and gimble in the wabe:
All mimsy were the borogoves,
    And the mome raths outgrabe.

"Beware the Jabberwock, my son!
    The jaws that bite, the claws that catch!
Beware the Jubjub bird, and shun
    The frumious Bandersnatch!"

He took his vorpal sword in hand;
    Long time the manxome foe he sought—
So rested he by the Tumtum tree
    And stood awhile in thought.

And, as in uffish thought he stood,
    The Jabberwock, with eyes of flame,
Came whiffling through the tulgey wood,
    And burbled as it came!

One, two! One, two! And through and through
    The vorpal blade went snicker-snack!
He left it dead, and with its head
    He went galumphing back.

"And hast thou slain the Jabberwock?
    Come to my arms, my beamish boy!
O frabjous day! Callooh! Callay!"

He chortled in his joy.

'Twas brillig, and the slithy toves
    Did gyre and gimble in the wabe:
All mimsy were the borogoves,
    And the mome raths outgrabe.

Exercise 2: Classify the following words as nouns, verbs, or adjectives. What do you think they might mean?

Brillig : _____

Slithy: _____

Toves: _____

Gyre: _____

Gimble: _____

Wabe: _____

Mimsy: _____

Borogroves: _____

Mome: _____

Raths: _____

Outgrabe: _____

Onomatopoeia

Another literary device is *onomatopoeia*. Consider "snap," "crack," "sizzle," "thud," "buzz," "crunch," etc.... It's easy to see how these words originated, as they try to imitate the literal sound of the thing or action described. The word "chortle" in *Jabberwocky* exists in today's dictionary as a "joyful, somewhat muffled laugh" and appears to have been invented for this poem. What started out as a nonsense word has now become an actual word.

Exercise 3: What other examples of *onomatopoeia* can you find in *Jabberwocky*?

——————————————————   ——————————————————

Exercise 4: In Exercise 2, you were asked to provide a possible definition for certain nonsense words used in the poem. This relates to art and creativity in that it is *subjective*. There is no right answer. This exercise is a conversation practice in which you are to discuss with your partner(s) why you associate the nonsense word with a potential meaning.

For example: "I think 'slithy' maybe means something underwater that's mysterious or dark because it sounds sort of like 'slimy' or 'sly' or 'slither,' like a snake. But that's just me. What do you think?"

Exercise 5: "Every child is an artist. The problem is how to remain an artist once he grows up." - *Pablo Picasso, Spanish artist (1881-1973)* [N.B.: Author's emphasis]

For discussion: What do you think Picasso meant by this? Why do some adults consider themselves (and are considered by others) to be "artists" while others are not?

(Jason Chase, 2021)

Proficiency Level: Advanced – Bloom's Taxonomy Level: 6

Using pictures to enhance the students' imagination and creativity

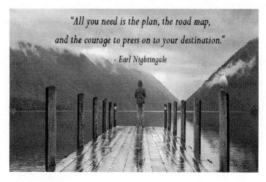

"All you need is the plan, the road map, and the courage to press on to your destination."
- Earl Nightingale

Learning Objectives:

- To enhance the students' imagination and creativity through photos.
- To develop their storytelling ability.
- To widen their vocabulary knowledge and contextualize them.
- To improve their oral/writing skills using accurate grammar.

Tasks/classroom activities

- Small group/pair work.
- Quick discussions about the content of the pictures.
- Short presentations of vocabulary related to the pictures.
- Questions about possible events that happened before, during, and what will happen afterward. For example, is there an event or a story behind the pictures?
- Integration of useful grammar points to match the content.
- Oral and/or written descriptions with a focus on narration.

Assessment

- Students can offer their own critiques and grade each other.
- Teachers can assess the students' ability to create original stories.

Learning Outcome

- Students will be able to share their ability to create original stories by looking at various pictures, enriching their vocabulary, and practicing correct grammar.

From my mind to my notes

Students can start by making a list of words they would like to use for this picture.

Suggested questions:

Who are these two people?
How are they dressed?
Time of day? Season?
Where are they going?
What do you think will happen next?

Make up or share a story about a young couple getting married.

Describe the picture with the five senses in mind

Students should be encouraged to focus on their feelings using adjectives.

Suggested questions:

What is the first thing that impresses you?
What words would you use to describe the freshness of the air?
Is this a quiet or a noisy place?
How does the sun help the viewer?

Your question(s):

_____
_____
_____

Make up or share a story about a day in winter.

Why did I choose this picture?

Grammar activity: Present Continuous vs. Present General

Suggested questions:

How does it relate to you, the viewer?
What happened before the picture was taken?
Who are these people?
Where are these people going?
What is the attraction?
Your question(s):

_____
_____
_____

Make up a dialogue about an evening with friends.

An activity that makes you happy

Describe an activity that makes you happy. Show why – don't tell!

Sample Picture Story

Ask the students to arrange the pictures in chronological order and then write a story.

Sample Story: Charlotte and George's Journey

In the Rockies in Southwest Colorado, there lived two cats named Charlotte and George. They were born sick, and their owner had little hope that they would live past their infancy, but they did. They grew into beautiful playful teenage kittens in a loving home in the countryside. During their fourth year, tragedy struck as their human parent passed away. The cats were then assigned to the nearest animal shelter. One night, they escaped and began a long journey to their human owner's daughter, who lived in a big city in the east. Most of their journey was along a long black highway that stretched as far as they could see into the horizon.

The cars and trucks zoomed by them, but they continued slowly and steadily on their way. One day, suddenly, a mountain loomed in front of them. Charlotte and George realized that this journey was far from over and that this was about to get more difficult. But they were determined to get to their destination, so they carried on. As they climbed through the mountain pass, they came across a small cabin and a couple who had moved to the mountain to get away from the hustle of the big city. The couple took pity on them and took them in, giving them food and a place to sleep away from the elements. Just before they went to sleep, the couple began to talk about and describe the big city with all its shining lights, people, and buildings.

That night, Charlotte and George dreamt of the big city and what it would be like for them. They hoped that the daughter of their owner would take care of them as their owner had. The next day, the cats were on their way again, walking through the countryside towards the big city. The countryside was big, and so they got lost. They walked and walked until they couldn't walk anymore. Suddenly they came across their grandfather, the tiger. The tiger took the cats under his wing and told them about the dangers of living in the city and why he now lived in the country with plenty of food and freedom. Charlotte and George thought about their lives and decided that they wanted to live free with their grandfather Tiger Joe and gave up on their journey to the city. Grandfather Tiger Joe welcomed them, and they lived happily ever after in the beautiful mountainous countryside of Colorado.

(Evina Baquiran-Torres, 2021)

Proficiency Level: Low Advanced – Bloom's Taxonomy Level: 6

For further reading, please check:

Lambert, M. D. (2015). *Reading Picture Books with Children: How to Shake Up Storytime and Get Kids Talking about What They See*. United States: Charlesbridge.

Show me a Story! Why Picture Books Matter: Conversations with 21 of the World's Most Celebrated Illustrators. (2013). United States: Candlewick Press.

The *Carpe Diem* 3-D vocabulary lesson

"Warm-Up Exercise: View the 'Carpe Diem' scene from *Dead Poets Society,* where Robin Williams first introduces the notion of 'Carpe Diem' to the students. The objective is to get students to appreciate the importance and power of their role in developing vocabulary. Explain that *Carpe Diem* means 'Seize the day.' The teacher, Robin Williams, is challenging students to look for the opportunities in life and make the most of them--making the best of situations and creating chances to excel. A challenge is to seize this time to make their lives and their language extraordinary. The best way to make the most of your time in life is to be creative and original.

Also, mention that 3-D means three-dimensional. The lesson will focus on three dimensions of their creativity – Diction, Dialogue, and Discourse.

CARPE DIEM DICTION

The first dimension is diction. To find the vocabulary for diction, students are asked to use a notebook to record at least five unfamiliar words that they encounter in the day. You can give them this list of questions to help record the words.

1. What is the image or word you have encountered?
2. How do you say or pronounce the word? (You can mention that dictionaries are created by lexicographers who have recorded what people say.)
3. When was the first originally used in English? (The online source *etymonline.com* is valuable for this answer.)
4. What is an example of a sentence using the word from your experience?
5. What other word from your vocabulary lessons can you associate with it? Have students present each word to the class with complete sentence answers to these five questions. The presentation might begin in the following way:

These are the words I met yesterday. Let me introduce them to you today. _____ is a word I encountered yesterday. It is pronounced _____.

CARPE DIEM DIALOGUE

You might note that dialogue reveals character. In other words, what you say tells us a lot about who you are. Have students create a dialogue using their five words. The words can be expressed in whatever form of the word is important to the dialogue. You can challenge students to use collocations, idioms, or expressions created in the class in developing a relevant and revealing dialogue. With dialogue partners, students present their dialogues. You can improve engagement by having listeners in teams note the new vocabulary words they remember from the dialogue.

CARPE DIEM DISCOURSE

Use the word to shape questions about the use of the word in the context of topics of importance in their lives. Remind the students that discourse is a public way to expand on the importance of the words to advance the discussion of the topic. Also, emphasize that the international dimension of their class creates a sense of universal public discourse. Challenge them to avoid no-brainer questions and clichés and create discussion questions for the class to think about using the new vocabulary words. Students present their questions in a small group. The person who presented the particular words and questions leads the group discussion."

(William McBride, 2021)

Proficiency Level: High Intermediate – Bloom's Taxonomy Level 2

An exercise in observation

"Bring to class some household item whose function may be unfamiliar or difficult for most people to identify. This could be a cooking implement, a highly specialized tool for some craft, a cosmetic tool, or any interesting item from your kitchen drawer or tool chest. Do not select anything that has sharp points or blades. Bring this item to class in brown paper so that no one else can see it. Do not discuss what you have brought with anyone else.

Step 1 – I will ask you to exchange your bag with someone else. Sitting at your desk and with your eyes closed, put the bag on your lap under your desk and take the object out of the bag quietly. Spend a couple of minutes exploring your subject with your hands, getting to know its shape and texture by touch. Set aside your concerns about how to label it. Your perceiving mind will want to categorize it immediately according to some mental stereotype. 'Oh,' it will say, 'that is just a can opener. All can openers are the same. I know what this looks like already.' When this happens, just notice what your mind is doing and go on exploring the object as though you were a child, enjoying its touch, its smell, temperature, and taste (If you dare*!). Remember, this is not a guessing game whose purpose is to label an object but an exercise in gaining information about an object through your senses.* Get all the data you can without looking. Try to guess its color. Take notes as you go along.

Step 2 – When the instructor gives the signal, put the tool on your desk and open your eyes. Notice and write down your first reaction. Now spend at least fifteen minutes observing the visual details of your object and taking more notes. Gather all the information you can from seeing the object.

Step 3 – After class, put your information together and write a one-page typed description that enables readers to imagine the object. (You can also provide a drawing.) Organize your information so that the reader can follow your process of exploration. In a final paragraph, or as you go along, describe what it felt for you as you worked. Were there different stages in your process? Did you have different stages of interest and concentration? At what point did you become bored? Excited? Angry? Impatient? Lost in daydreams? Did you feel frustrated if you couldn't label your object? Acknowledge these distractions by writing them down as you bring your attention back to the task of observing your object.

Describe the item as you experienced it with all your senses and describe your personal process as well – the journey of discovery, insights, reactions, and stages."

(Alex Story, 2021)

(Adapted from Mayfield, M. (2014). *Thinking for Yourself*. United States: Cengage Learning, pp. 28-29)

Proficiency Level: Low Advanced – Bloom's Taxonomy Level 3

Teaching subordinating conjunctions

"I like to call these the **cousins of the adverbial conjunctions**; they need another full sentence piece to make them whole. These activities involve reading, speaking, conversation/discussion and writing. Part 1, read the passages taken from the famous love advice column Dear Abby. Part 2 After reading, discuss with a partner what the problem is and what your feeling is after reading them. The final part is to then use the conjunctions to help the person and give them advice!

Questions to think about before and after reading.
1. What is the main problem in the passage you chose?
2. How would you feel if this passage were about you/your relationship?
3. What advice would you give to this person? (Group Discussion)
4. What does a good relationship have? (Group Discussion)

Vocabulary/collocations/idioms
to run into – to cheat on /violate the relationship – to break up
to express emotion/show feelings that can be seen
to put a wedge between – to settle for
to work it out /end the relationship – in the long term

Dear Abby conjunctions (linkers)
After reading the Dear Abby stories and thinking about the general advice they are asking, choose one or two stories and use the linkers to make sentences, give advice and help them. Use at least 3-4 linkers. Give bonus for more linkers used correctly. Be prepared to read and share your advice! We will present our advice to the class.
since/while/although/even though when/whereas/whenever/wherever
even if/as long as/because/in order to/unless
as soon as/before/after – in order to

For example:

Dear Adam,
Even though you are no longer living with your wife, I think your differences can be worked out.
What advice would you give these people?

70

1. DEAR ABBY: I have just found out I'm 10 weeks pregnant. Both sets of parents are overjoyed – it's their first grandchild – and I'm happy because this was the plan all along. My husband wants kids, and this is our first baby. My husband isn't the kind to wear his heart on his sleeve. I have tried to involve him in appointments and classes, but he seems uninterested. He has *expressed no emotions*, even when he saw our first sonogram. It makes me feel sad and lonely. When I ask him if he is happy about the pregnancy, he says yes, but it's hard to tell.

What can I do? His feelings do not feel genuine. This is supposed to be a milestone, the next chapter of our lives.

2. DEAR ABBY: I was recently told by a friend that my husband had sent her texts of an inappropriate nature. My husband didn't deny that he sent them and refused to tell me what he sent. This woman is envious of my husband and jealous of our relationship. She often comments about how she'd love to have a man like mine, etc. *My concern is*, he admits he texted her, but I don't understand why. My intuition tells me she told me the truth, but I want to trust my husband. Now I'm suspicious. I check him a lot, especially his texts. I always want to check his phone and analyze every aspect of our life and marriage. I feel this has *put a huge wedge* between us, and I no longer feel the same love and passion for him. I don't trust him anymore. Please help. What do I do now? Is my marriage over?

3. DEAR ABBY: I am 29 and need advice on what to do. My 32-year-old boyfriend of a year and a half, "Aiden," proposed while we were in Europe last month. Aiden is a sweet guy who would do anything for me. I waffled and said I had to think about it. He bought a lovely engagement ring that he still has in his possession. We do not live together. Aiden says he's certain he wants to spend his life with me. My problem is, I don't want to marry him. Aiden is a tradesman with no money. Even though he *kisses the ground I walk on*, I don't think I'd be happy *in the long term* with him and would always wonder if I could have done better. On the other hand, I am almost 30 and want children. It seems that nice guys who want to commit are in short supply. Should I *settle for* Aiden? *Breaking up* with him, as I did a few months ago for a couple of weeks, would crush him. But he has little social life and no hobbies, just me.

4. DEAR ABBY: I am a 13-year-old girl in middle school. There are two boys I like. One of them is someone I've known for two years and is a really good friend. The other boy I don't know anything about. I like

him because he's cute. What I like about the first guy is that he's funny, smart, looks good, and we like the same things. I don't know which to pick. Please help!

5. DEAR ABBY: After 26 years of marriage, I recently left my husband. We live only a few blocks away from each other, so we run into each other often at the store, the gas station, everywhere. My problem is more about *running into* some of the women he cheated on me with. One of them always ends up at the same shopping center or restaurant I happen to be at. She thinks I don't know who she is. At first, I didn't want to say anything to her, but now it has really gotten to me. What can I tell her the next time she meets up with me? I want to keep myself from yelling at her and *work it out*. Please help.

6. DEAR ABBY: I know if a girl ends the engagement, she's supposed to return the ring to her ex-fiancé. Does the situation of a wife filing for divorce fall under the same set of rules?"

(Lateef Ferguson, 2021)

Proficiency Level: High Intermediate - Bloom's Taxonomy Level 3

Traveling

"We have all traveled somewhere at some point in time – maybe across the world or even just to a neighboring town. Sometimes we travel a short distance, and sometimes we go far. In this exercise, you will discuss your memories of traveling and then imagine your dream vacation.

1. What are some reasons you travel?

2. What are some reasons other people travel?

3. Do you enjoy traveling? Why or why not?

4. Where did you go on your first vacation?

5. Where did you go on your last vacation?

6. Choose one memorable trip you've taken. Discuss the following:

    a. Where did you go?
    b. When did you travel?
    c. How long were you away?
    d. What was your first impression of the place and people?
    e. Were there things that were different than what you were used to?
    f. Did you experience culture shock?
    g. What did you do on this trip?
    h. Why do you think you remember particular aspects of your trip and not others?
    i. Did you learn anything new on this trip?
    j. Would you return? Why or why not?

7. Now use your imagination. Imagine your dream vacation and discuss the following:

    a. Where would you like to go? (It can be imaginary)?
    b. What activities would you like to do?
    c. What does your ideal vacation day look like?

d. What is the climate like?
e. How would you feel?
f. Would you want to return home? Why or why not.

Common phrases:

to make travel arrangements

to travel for leisure

itinerary

sightseeing

a day trip

a business trip

a pleasant journey

travel bug

jet lag

time zone change

trip of a lifetime"

(Rhianna Weber, 2021)

Proficiency Level: Intermediate - Bloom's Taxonomy Level 2

Aussie (Australian) English

"G'day, mate! Can you speak 'Strine?! (Australian)

Welcome to the wonderful land 'Down Under,' where the local language celebrates the unique, charming Australian wildlife.

Did you know?

Australians are the masters of abbreviation! To follow a conversation in Sydney, Melbourne, or in any outback restaurant or tavern, you will need to be familiar with the most common Australian abbreviations and slang words.

Can you guess the meaning of the 12 common Australian English abbreviations below? In pairs or small groups, talk to your classmate and write down two possible meanings for each abbreviation:

Abbreviation	Meaning 1	Meaning 2	Correct definition
G'day			*Good day*
Ambo			*Ambulance*
Arvo			*Afternoon*
Avo			*Avocado*
Barbie			*Barbecue (BBQ)*
Choccy biccy			*Chocolate biscuit*
Cockie			*Cockatoo*
Cuppa			*Cup of tea (or coffee)*
Kookie			*Kookaburra*
Postie			*Postman*
Roo			*Kangaroo*
Servo			*Service station*

Now watch the following YouTube video from the popular "Hi Josh" channel and try to find the meanings. List these in the "correct definition" column.

https://www.youtube.com/watch?v=yDb_WsAt_Z0

Did you find them all? (If not, try finding the definitions in YouTube, Google, or another search engine using "Aussie English abbreviations" or a similar search phrase.) Did you learn any other popular slang expressions or abbreviations?

A true story: If you have watched the famous Australian movies 'Crocodile Dundee' or 'Australia,' you will know that the common Australia pronunciation of 'G'day' or 'today' sounds more like 'good die' and 'to die.' During my first month in Australia, I was horrified when my friend told me that 'I have to go to the hospital today'!!

Australian wildlife

Everybody knows the famous Australian kangaroo (or wallaby), and of course, the cuddly koala bears... But do you know what the other animal on the Australian coat of arms (see below) is?

That's right; it's an emu!

Visitors to Australia are always enchanted by the unique wildlife – perhaps excluding the deadly snakes and venomous spiders! They soon learn that Australians' love of their abundant nature is deeply embedded in their language.

Animal proverbs and idioms

Have you heard any of the following expressions?

1) *He's mad as a cut snake!*

2) *That guy is as mad as a box of frogs!*

3) *Stop acting like a galah!*

4) *She's got a kangaroo loose in the top paddock!*

5) *Stone the crows!*

What do you think they mean? (Clue: The English word 'mad' can mean both 'angry' and 'crazy'!)

1) _____

2) _____

3) _____

4) _____

5) _____

Now work with your classmate to present three animal idioms/expressions from each other's country. Write the meaning in English below:

Student 1

1) _____

2) _____

3) _____

Student 2

1) _____

2) _____

3) _____

(Rupert Johnstone, 2021)

Proficiency Level: Low Advanced – Bloom's Taxonomy Level 3

Discussing travel brochures

Learning Objectives: By the end of the class, students will be able to:

- Analyze reasons for an opinion.
- Identify the different stereotype ideas.
- Describe different aspects of a particular place through travel brochures.
- Demonstrate creativity while designing their own travel brochures.

MATERIALS: Pictures, sample brochures, whiteboard, markers, etc.

TIME: 80 minutes

Step 1: 15 minutes (Introduction)

The teacher (T) will tell the students to come up with corresponding adjectives that can represent the different attributes of the male and female gender. T will write them up on the whiteboard. To help students find the appropriate examples, T can suggest the following adjectives:

Table of adjectives / **(T can use other relevant words/examples)**

humorous	hardworking	nationalistic	romantic
tolerant	sad	generous	emotional
lazy	happy	miser	sociable
talkative	arrogant	hospitable	punctual
quiet	serious	sophisticated	crazy

After they agree on the right adjectives, T may tell the students to identify the reasons for attributing the genders with those specific adjectives. T will again write their responses on the whiteboard.

Step 2: 10 minutes (Stereotype)

Regarding the basics of how we form different perspectives about a different group of people, T may provide several pictures and then ask the following questions:

1. How do we form a general perspective of a particular group?
2. Are those perspectives formed based on any valid reason?

Then T will write the word "Stereotype" on the whiteboard and ask students if they know the word's meaning. T can also elicit the vocabulary meaning by relating it to the previously shown pictures.

Step 3: 10 minutes (Group formation and presentation)

The teacher will divide the class into five groups, and each group will choose one country or culture as their discussion topic. T may also encourage the students to select one stereotype idea and the reasons behind those stereotypes. One representative from each group will present the stereotypes and their reasons. T will approach each group and challenge the students to provide their own constructive input.

Step 4: 20 minutes (Travel brochure)

After the students finish their presentation, T will ask them what other aspects regarding that particular country or culture they want to present besides these stereotypes.

T will also elicit different major aspects of those cultures like historical places, language, stereotype beliefs, popular food items and write them on the whiteboard. Students are then assigned the task of doing travel brochure presentations. T will also write and elicit the following points on the whiteboard to show the students the detailed structure of an ideal travel brochure.

- **Introduction**
1. Greeting
2. Group Introduction
3. Brief introduction of the country
- **Historical background**
1. Overall history
2. How the country evolved
- **Historical/tourist places**

1. Historically significant places
2. Natural beauty
3. Architecturally famous places
- **Popular Food items**
- **Culture**
1. Language
2. Festivals
3. Dresses
- **Famous people**
- **Transport and accommodation**
- **Stereotype beliefs**
1. Positive stereotype belief along with reasons
2. Negative stereotype belief along with reasons

The teacher will also encourage the students to work in groups. Each student of the group will take at least one of the above sub-topics and present it during the assigned day of presentation.

Step 5: 25 minutes (Sample travel brochure)

Finally, students get a chance to analyze sample Travel Brochures and their structures. They will also divide and distribute the sub-topics and roles of their presentation among themselves.

Students discuss their plans for preparing the brochure and share their creative ideas. Teacher's help might include:

- Encouraging group work and empowering collaboration.
- Eliciting responses from shy and less active members.
- Paying undivided attention while listening to students' opinions.
- Reaching a consensus or agreement on the topic.

Proficiency Level: Advanced – Bloom's Taxonomy Level 6

(Adapted from BRAC University/BRAC Institute of Languages, Bangladesh, 2021)

Culture Capstone Project – Florence
Guidance and Support Materials for Trainers and Course Managers

Project Management

Trainers and/or the Course Director will be required to undertake the following tasks:

1. Provide all trainees with information about the project (objective, overview, organization, management, project tasks, templates, deadlines, evaluation process, and rubric). This may be achieved by arranging a 30 minute on-site or virtual briefing session and by distributing the trainee guidance and support materials.
2. Establish groups (2-3 trainees per group).
3. Provide ongoing advice and support as required.
4. Evaluate assessment submissions through reference to the rubric.
5. Provide feedback to trainees.
6. Provide an opportunity for all trainees to share their experiences in a managed real-time or virtual forum.
7. On an ongoing basis, evaluate the effectiveness of the project and modify as necessary.

Project objective

The Culture Capstone Project provides trainees with an opportunity to:

- become more familiar with the city;
- focus on the development of intercultural communication skills;
- experience what makes Florence such a unique city.

Project overview

Trainees will be required to work as part of a small team in order to complete several tasks. Each task will require them to:

- visit a particular location in the city;
- respond to a set of questions;
- reflect on the experience;
- gather a visual item (e.g., a photograph, a video, a drawing, a postcard, an information leaflet, etc.).

Global citizenship and Cultural Awareness

A significant aspect of one's training as a language teacher with Via Lingua relates to developing cultural awareness and the trainee's role as a global citizen.

Cultural awareness allows us to challenge cultural barriers, build cultural bridges, and develop greater awareness. It also helps us understand ourselves, our own cultural background, and the background and experiences of cultures that are different from our own. Hopefully, this results in enhanced cultural connection and less misunderstanding and conflict.

Greater cultural awareness enables us to become familiar with and understand why differences exist in values, beliefs, and behavior and not automatically assume that 'we are right and they are wrong.' It allows us to value our own experiences without being uncritically judgmental or prejudiced about the experiences of others. We also become more aware of behaviors that might be considered inappropriate or offensive to ourselves or others.

A good starting point is to reflect on similarities and common needs, how different communities meet these, and the reason for the differences. For example, we all need food, whichever cultural background we come from. The food we eat and how it is prepared differ from community to community, choices being influenced by climate, local availability of produce, religion, history, taste, and tradition.

Project Organization

- Each team should **jointly** select three of the twelve tasks listed below and complete them as a group.
- Each team member should complete an individual recording template, as set out below, when visiting the sites.
- On completing the three tasks, team members should **jointly** share their reflections, discuss them, and prepare and submit an overall response using the template provided below.

Project evaluation

Once trainees have completed their assigned project, they are required (as a team) to submit a one-to-two-page detailed written *reflection* (single-spaced) as well as one visual exhibit. A template for this reflection is provided below. The visual exhibit may be a photograph or photographs, a video, drawings, postcards, informational flyers, etc.

The depth of reflection will be a vital part of how this project will be evaluated. An evaluation rubric is provided below.

The Tasks and Individual Recording Templates

Task One. Visit the Tepidarium Roster at the Horticultural Garden, near Ponte Rosso.

1.1. Find out:

a	When were the building and gardens built?	
b	What was the Tepidarium Roster originally built for?	
c	What is it used for now?	
d	When was the Serpent Fountain (above the garden) built?	
e	Who built the Serpent Fountain?	

1.2. Record your reflections on the experience (e.g., I noticed ..., I felt ..., I experienced ...., I wondered ...., I hope ...., I would like ....)

1.3. Attach a visual exhibit from the visit.

Task Two. Check out the vast array of door knockers in Florence. Choose your favorites.

2.1. Find out:

a	Which historical period are they from?	
b	An example of a lion's head knocker.	
c	What is the significance of the lion's head?	

2.2.   Record your reflections on the experience (e.g., I noticed ..., I felt ..., I experienced ...., I wondered ...., I hope ...., I would like ....)

2.3.   Attach a visual exhibit from the visit.

Task Three.   Take a trip to the Marucelliana Library.

3.1. Find out:

a	What is the historical significance of the library?	
b	Who was the library originally intended to serve?	

3.2. Record your reflections on the experience (e.g., I noticed ..., I felt ..., I experienced ...., I wondered ...., I hope ...., I would like ....)

3.3. Attach a visual exhibit from the visit.

Task Four. Visit Piazza del Limbo and discover its history! Find Via dell'Inferno and the Porta al Paradiso at the Battistero! You will experience Dante's *Divine Comedy*, rolled into one walk around Florence!

4.1. Find out:

a	What is the history of Piazza del Limbo?	
b	What is the significance of Via dell'Inferno?	
c	What is the history behind the Porta al Paradiso?	

4.2. Record your reflections on the experience (e.g., I noticed ..., I felt ..., I experienced ...., I wondered ...., I hope ...., I would like ....)

4.3. Attach a visual exhibit from the visit.

Task Five. Go to Piazza SS. Annunziata and find the 'baby' window.

5.1. Find out:

a	Why was the baby window installed?	
b	Who was it originally intended for?	
c	What is the history of the square?	

5.2. Record your reflections on the experience (e.g., I noticed ..., I felt ..., I experienced ....,
I wondered ...., I hope ...., I would like ....)

5.3. Attach a visual exhibit from the visit.

Task Six. Go to the Farmer's Market at Piazza della Liberta' (Parterre) on Friday morning.

6.1. Find out:

a	What are the seasonal fruit and vegetables sold at the market? (ask a farmer)	
b	What would be a typical recipe for the time of year? (ask a farmer)	

6.2. Record your reflections on the experience (e.g., I noticed …, I felt …, I experienced ….,
      I wondered …., I hope …., I would like ….)

6.3. Attach a visual exhibit from the visit.

Task Seven. Take the number 7 bus to Fiesole. Learn about the Roman Amphitheater.

7.1. Find out:

a	Who built this theater and why?	
b	What is it used for now?	

9.2. Record your reflections on the experience (e.g., I noticed …, I felt …, I experienced ..., I wondered …, I hope …)

7.2. Attach a visual exhibit from the visit.

Task Eight. Walk from the center to S. Miniato al Monte for Vespers. Explore the cemetery behind the church.

8.1. Find out:

a	Why is this cemetery so fancy?	

b	Can you find monuments dedicated to any famous people with whom you are familiar?	

8.2.   Record your reflections on the experience (e.g., I noticed ..., I felt ..., I experienced ...., I wondered ...., I hope ...., I would like ....)

8.3.   Attach a visual exhibit from the visit.

Task Nine.   Find the commemorative plaques dotted around Florence showing the level of water from the great flood of 1966.
9.1. Find out:

a	What happened?	
b	Who were the 'angeli del fango'?	
c	How many different countries did they come from?	
d	What did they do?	

9.2. Record your reflections on the experience (e.g., I noticed ..., I felt ..., I experienced ..., I wondered ..., I hope ...)

9.3.   Attach a visual exhibit from the visit.

Task Ten. Study the replicas of Michelangelo's David statue in the city
10.1.   Find out:

a	How many replicas were made?	
b	What is the history of these copies?	
c	Where is the original?	
d	Why were the copies made?	

Record your reflections on the experience
(e.g., I noticed …, I felt …, I experienced …, I wondered …, I hope …,
I would like …)

10.2.   **Attach a visual exhibit from the visit.**

Task Eleven. Check out the amazing park at the Stibbert Museum. Find the Egyptian temple.

11.1.   **Find out:**

a	What do you know about this park?	
b	Who was it built by?	
c	Which other temples can you find?	
d	What is contained in the museum?	
e	Why was this collection made?	

11.2.   **Record your reflections on the experience** (e.g., I noticed …, I felt …, I experienced …., I wondered …., I hope …., I would like ….)

11.3.   **Attach a visual exhibit from the visit.**

Task Twelve. Go to the church of Orsanmichele. Originally built in 1336 as a market and grain store, it contains statues of the Patron Saints of each Florentine guild.

12.1.   **Find out:**

a	What were the historic guilds?	
b	How many guilds are there?	
c	Where else can we see plaques or statues of the guilds?	

12.2.   **Record your reflections on the experience** (e.g., I noticed …, I felt …, I experienced …., I wondered …., I hope …., I would like ….)

```
┌─────────────────────────────────────┐
│                                       │
│                                       │
└─────────────────────────────────────┘
```

12.3.   **Attach a visual exhibit from the visit.**

Evaluation Rubric

Project submissions that meet requirements will exhibit the following characteristics. They will:

- Be submitted on time.
- Comprise two elements: a reflective component (maximum two pages) and a visual component.
- Indicate evidence that all members of the group have contributed to the end product.
- Exhibit evidence of enhanced cultural awareness and insight.
- Be reflective in nature.

Group Project Submission Template

Your joint assessment submission should be reflective and comment on some or all of the following:

- Your experience as a group when working together and completing the project.
- Insights gained about Florence's culture, language, history, and traditions and how they are similar to/ different from your own experience.
- How local and regional history, climate, and geography have shaped Florence's present-day traditions and customs.
- How history has shaped cultural pluralism, integration, and diversity.
- The role of class, economic status, and gender in the historical development of Florentine culture.
- An awareness of behaviors that might be considered inappropriate or offensive to others.
- The way in which the project has influenced your behavior, attitudes, cultural awareness.
- Aspects of Italian culture, language, history, and values that you plan to explore in more depth.

- Personal actions that you plan to take as a result of the insights gained as part of this project.

Your joint assessment submission should be accompanied by a visual exhibit, with a brief indication of why you have chosen this item.

(Thomas Shandorf, Via Inlingua, 2021)

Human Rights

Learning Objectives: Students develop general awareness of Human Rights and their principles and building blocks through class discussion and a project that requires group work.

Learning Outcomes: By the end of this lesson, students (Ss) will be able to:

- interpret the concept of HR from the video and the UDHR (Universal Declaration of the Human Rights).
- identify and analyze specific cases related to Human Rights (HR) from the local and global context.
- analyze causes, effects, and solutions related to specific cases where Human Rights are being denied or violated.
- design a poster paper with their project findings.
- demonstrate communicative competence through presenting an organized, well-supported presentation.

Materials: a video titled *The Story of Human Rights* (www.youthforhumanrights.org), poster papers, markers, booklet (text entitled "Child Marriage" (http://www.iheu.org/child-marriage-a-violation-of-human-rights), UDHR and the presentation rubric), instructions for presentation, guidelines for academic poster

Time: 80 minutes

Class-1: Discussion on Human Rights
Introduction: 5 minutes
The teacher takes attendance and asks Ss to review what they feel were the most important points from the previous class and then answers any questions that might be brought up.

T tells Ss that they will discuss a project work on Human Rights and plan a Human Rights project. T writes the topic "Human Rights" on the board and asks Ss – *"Why do you think we are doing a class on this topic?"*

Step 1: Elicitation (15 minutes)
T elicits Ss' responses on the following questions:
- What is the concept of "Human Rights?"
- Could you mention some of the Human Rights?

- What are the Rights that you enjoy?
- Are you being denied any Rights? What are those?

T tells Ss that they will watch a video titled *The Story of Human Rights* and encourages them to take notes of the important ideas while watching it. T plays the video **ONCE** only.

After Ss have watched the video, T asks them two concept-checking questions as follows:
1. What is UDHR?
2. According to the video, which Human Rights are still denied in today's world?

Step 2: Reading and whole-class discussion on Causes, Effects, and Solutions (10 minutes)

T divides the class into groups (preferably five members in each group). In order to help Ss understand a specific example of Human Rights, T asks the groups to **skim** the text "Child Marriage: A Violation of Human Rights" from the booklet. After five or six minutes, T asks random groups to respond to the following questions:
- **Causes:** What are the causes for this Right being denied?
- **Effects:** How do the victims of child marriage suffer?
- **Solutions:** What needs to be done so that this right is ensured all over the world?
- Do you know of any other specific case where this Right to Marriage and Family is being denied?

Step 3: Presenting a Human Rights Tree using the UDHR (40 minutes)

Students are assigned group work for a presentation based on the UDHR (Ss will also be in the same group for their poster presentation on the project findings the following week). T asks Ss to skim through the UDHR from the booklet and select any two Rights that they are interested in. **(5 minutes)**

In the meantime, T draws a tree on the board with two branches and two roots.

- After 5 minutes, T gives each group 1 chart paper and a marker and instructs Ss to draw a similar tree on the chart paper.
- T asks Ss to write any two Human Rights from the UDHR on the branches that all people need in order to lead a life of dignity and justice. (For example, all people need a decent place to live, sufficient food and water, education, etc.)

- T then asks Ss to choose two cases/examples related to those 2 Rights that are being denied (with examples).
- T explains that the tree needs roots to grow and flourish. So, T asks the groups to think of two solutions or prerequisites that make Human Rights flourish: the rule of law, a healthy economy, etc. For example, a prerequisite for the Right to Life is ensuring the rule of law. T then asks the groups to write down those two solutions on the two roots of their tree.

Ss will get **10 minutes** to draw the Human Rights Tree. For effective time management in the group work, T encourages Ss to divide the tasks among the members, e.g., two members can draw the tree while the other members select the two Rights, two examples, and two solutions to be written on the tree.

T closely monitors the group discussion and guides them in selecting specific examples of any enjoyed and denied Right.

When students finish drawing the tree, T gives them ten more minutes to discuss the following points for the 2-min presentation:

1. Who is/are the victim(s) in this case or example? Which Human Right from the UDHR is being denied to them?
2. How do the victims suffer because of this denied Right? (one effect only)
3. How can the points on the roots ensure the victims their Rights?

T informs Ss that any randomly selected S might do the presentation, so everyone should participate in the group discussion. One student from each group is chosen to explain any one Right on the tree. **Presentation of all 5 or 6 groups may take up to 15 minutes.**

Note for Teachers: T should instruct the later groups to explain any other Right that the previous group(s) did not explain.

After each presentation, T invites the audience to share their feedback on the relevance of the examples provided and the presenters' body language. **(5 minutes)**

Step 4: Instructions on project work (10 minutes)
To help Ss understand the project work and group presentation the following week, T gives each group one copy of the instructions for Poster Presentations.

T asks the Ss to read these instructions thoroughly, discuss them in the group for **5 minutes** and then ask questions for further clarification. The instructions are as follows:

1. All the groups will design their posters with two specific real-life cases or examples (of a person or a community in any country or culture) related to two different Human Rights.

2. To explain each Denied Right, Ss will answer the following questions:

- Who is/are the victim(s) in this case or example? Which Human Right from the UDHR is being denied to them?
- Why is this Right still being denied today? (Explain two causes only.)
- How do the victims suffer due to this denied Right? (Explain two effects only.)
- How can this Right be ensured? (Explain two solutions only.)

3. All the cases must be taken from reliable local or international newspapers or magazines. Each group will mention their sources in their presentation.

4. The posters will be designed with **pictures and relevant information** (in bullet points only) of those selected two cases or examples from newspapers. Students should also write the specific Rights and the article numbers from the UDHR for those cases. Ss may select a picture of one such report from any reliable newspaper/magazine and answer the four questions above in their presentation.

5. Each group will get 12-15 minutes to present their findings using the poster. Every member in the group will get 2-3 minutes for their presentation. The groups have to ensure equal distribution of time and content among their members.

T asks Ss to skim through the rubric and answer any pertinent questions. T writes down the date of the presentation on the board. **(5 minutes)**

Conclusion: (5 minutes)

After Ss discuss these instructions in groups, T invites questions and clarifies all confusions. T thanks the class for their enthusiastic performance and encourages them to come during consultation hours for further information or any other questions or concerns.

Class-2: Group presentation on Human Rights

Instructions

- T asks all the groups to keep their posters against the wall in front of the class.

- Next, T tells the class to take another look at the rubric for the project presentation on human rights that was discussed in the previous class.

- T tells the audience that after each group's presentation, any random groups from the audience will be asked to provide feedback using the points on the rubric. They will evaluate both strengths and could-improve points of the group.

Presentations (70 minutes)

T sits at the back of the class, takes notes, and writes feedback and marks on the rubrics for all the groups. After each presentation, T asks any one group to share any two strengths of this presentation, while another group may share suggestions for further improvement.

Conclusion: Providing feedback (5 minutes)

At the end of all the presentations, T gives Ss general feedback on their performance and significant learning points. T ends the class appreciating Ss for their hard work and insightful presentations.

Human Rights

Instructions for poster presentations

1.   All the groups will design their posters with two specific real life cases or examples (of a person or a community from any country or culture) related to two different Human Rights.

2.   To explain the 2 Denied Rights, Ss will answer the following questions:
- Who is/are the victim(s) in this case or example? Which Human Right from the UDHR is being denied to them?
- Why is this Right being denied still today? (Explain two causes only.)
- How do the victims suffer due to this denied Right? (Explain two effects only.)
- How can this Right be ensured? (Explain two solutions only.)

3.   All the cases must be taken from reliable local or international newspapers or magazines. Each group will mention their sources in their presentation.

4.   The posters will be designed with pictures and relevant information (in bullet points only) of those selected 4 cases or examples from newspapers. Students should also write the specific Rights and the article numbers from the UDHR for those cases. They may select a picture of one such report from any reliable newspaper/magazine and answer the four questions above in their presentation.

5.   Each group will get 12-15 minutes to present their findings using the poster. Every member in the group will get 2-3 minutes for their presentation. The groups have to ensure equal distribution of time and content among their members.

Proficiency Level: Advanced - Bloom's Taxonomy Level 6

(Adapted from BRAC University/BRAC Institute of Languages, Bangladesh, 2021)

> "*Imagination* is a word which derives from the making of images in the mind from what Wordsworth called *the inward eye*."
>
> (Bronowski, 1978, p. 10)

What is creative learning?

In an interview with Professor Loren Frank conducted by April Cashin-Garbutt in December of 2017, this question came up followed by a detailed explanation:

"Are **memory and imagination** two sides of the same coin?"

Yes, to a degree. Imagination depends critically on memory, in that it is hard to imagine things that aren't at least made up of elements that you know. Memory provides the building block for things to be imagined. Memories of things that have happened before also provide the building blocks of imagining possible futures. For example, was this a good idea or not, this worked well the last time and so forth. So memory is certainly critical for imagination.

(https://www.sainsburywellcome.org/web/qa/memory-and-imagination-two-sides-same-coin)

Each has its own value and relevance, but they function together. **Memory** would be the first step, followed by the use of **imagination**. We certainly remember collocations and structures, but when it comes to communicating in speaking or writing, we automatically switch on our imagination button and build on what we already know. What transpires at the end would be our own ideas and thoughts based on definite **structures already existent in our knowledge reservoir.**

Learning a second language involves the types of activities designed to improve our memory, how we process, register, and store new information.

Learning is concerned with registering and storing information. Given that information is stored, however, its efficient use must depend on access in the right form at the right time. There is nothing more frustrating than having a name or a word on the tip of one's tongue, something that you know but simply cannot produce at the crucial moment. Having good, flexible, efficient retrieval is as important as having good information storage. (Baddeley, 1997, p. 5)

Brainstorming the concept of registering and storing information

1. How do students acquire new information when they read, listen, or converse?
2. Do we encourage learners to underline and/or highlight when they read?
3. How does context become relevant if teachers and students focus on meaning?
4. What techniques are more efficient in registering information: alliteration, word puns, word games, jokes, etc.?
5. How important is taking notes?
6. Is practice in speaking or writing the best way teachers can reinforce the relevance of good vocabulary?
7. How do teachers set an example of storing any kind of information that might become useful in another classroom activity?
8. How can word families, collocations, set phrases, and idioms improve and enlarge our students' vocabulary?
9. How do we empower our students to use their own imaginations and find ways to store and retrieve information?

In the opinion of many linguists, **the mingling of the two concepts** – memory and imagination - might be called "creative learning." (Rajamanickam, 2007; Runco and Pritzker, 2020)

Drawing upon past knowledge will help us find the best solutions to whatever problems we may face in the future. Teachers can create lesson plans, and students can devise plans of action using this fundamental element – imagination -which is always available. We can all just let our thoughts wander freely and let our unconscious part of the brain tap into our imagination.

Teachers are quite aware and know instinctively what their students expect from them**: to educate, inform** and **assign tasks**, but also **to entertain** and, in doing so, create an atmosphere conducive to learning. Good instruction makes students absorb but also process information. Giving them something to do is not enough; giving them **something to**

think about will eventually release the **power of imagination**. If they find pleasure in what they do, language learners will definitely find new ways of expression that will enrich their mental abilities and develop their own ideas.

One example should suffice: **reading** broadens our imagination by stimulating the right side of our brain. Reading will help students practice what they already know and, at the same time, **improve brain function**. When we read, the left side of our brain will make a connection between the written word and its spoken equivalent. One side of our brain **analyzes words,** while the other side **recognizes meaning**.

To recap:

From curiosity and creativity to memory and imagination, students will discover new information that will **satisfy their thirst for knowledge**, practical hints will **stimulate their curiosity**, and in time new skills will **make them better thinkers, better speakers, and better writers.**

For further reading, please check:

Thomson, P. (2010). *Researching Creative Learning: Methods and Issues.* United Kingdom: Taylor & Francis.

Memory and Imagination

The two sides of the coin can be easily exemplified by the following two quotations:

"Of Mem'ry's use, the endless might,
No wit nor language can expresse:
Apply and try both day and night,
And then this truth thou wilt confesse."
John Dee (1527-1608)

"Where beams of warm imagination play,
The memory's soft figures melt away."
Alexander Pope (1688-1744)

> "The richness of our memory [...] emerges through a biological cascade of timescales. New information builds upon the old, fitting into constraints offered by previous experience. [...] With each new thing you learn, the better you're able to absorb the next related fact."
>
> (Eagleman, 2020, p. 231)

Is memory related to imaginative creativity?

Teachers need to develop an **active imagination** to succeed in communicating effectively with their students and provide them with a platform where creativity is encouraged and supported until it becomes boundless.

According to Kirkpatrick (1920), imagination is not only about what is untrue and unreal. "Imagination may concern itself either with what has existed or may exist in the future, or it may represent what never has been and perhaps never will be experienced by any human being in exactly the form pictured." (p. 4) Kirkpatrick goes on to propose that we can distinguish three rather distinct types of imaginative creativity.

1) **Reproductive imagination**, in which the past is presented to **the** mind with the images arranged just as they were in the original experience.
2) **Constructive imagination**, in which the separate images are combined not according to some particular experience but in accordance with their more usual arrangement or as directed by descriptions.
3) **Creative imagination** in which the images are freely arranged in **accordance** with one's own feelings and purposes. (p. 7)

For further reading, please check:

Gregory, D. (2006). *The Creative License: Giving Yourself Permission to Be the Artist Your Truly Are.* United Kingdom: Hyperion Books.

Brainstorming the idea of imagination

Create a dialogue with your students and invite them to tell you and the whole class what they think about **imagination**.

Give your students a chance to define what they mean by imagination and/or active imagination in their own words.

Identify daily experiences that stimulate their imagination. Is the morning a better time to imagine, or is it the afternoon? How about an evening with friends and loved ones?

Invite them to visit a place in their imagination: a street, a store, a beach, a mountain trail, etc. Why did they choose that place?

Challenge every student in your class to find the best classroom activities that stir their imagination. Anything they find inspiring or worth discussing?

Organize small groups in which they imagine an interview with a famous personality. One student asks questions, and another student pretends to be that well-known person. Challenge all the other students in the group to come up with a list of questions they should ask.

Record the main points of the conversation or everything you consider relevant and share the information with the whole class.

Collect the best main points of each class and display them all on the board or anywhere visible in the classroom. At the end of the semester, these points might set a very good example of what students can accomplish or imagine in such a short period of time.

Quick overview of memory and imagination

The following presentation is adapted from *Great Ideas* (1984).

We do not remember objects we have never perceived or events in our own lives, such as emotions or desires, that we have not experienced. The imagination is not limited in the same way by prior experience. However, we can imagine things we have never perceived and may never be able to.

Memory and imagination are usually regarded as belonging to **the same general faculty as the external senses**. The generic power of sense can be divided into the exterior senses such as sight, hearing, and touch, and the interior senses such as memory and imagination. However, memory and imagination are not to be confused with sense perception or with rational thought.

Without memory and imagination, man would live in a confined and narrow present, lacking past and future, restricted to what happens to be actual of the almost infinite possibility of being. Without them, man would be impeded in all the work of science if memory and imagination did not extend the reach of his senses.

The analysis of memory leads us to separate acts or phases. **Recollection is distinct not only from retention but also from recognition**. The illusion known as déjà vu consists of the experience of intense familiarity with a place or scene that has never been witnessed before so far as one can recall. In contrast, normal recognition depends on previous acquaintance with the object being cognized again, i.e., *recognized*.

Whereas recollection is remembering through the recall of images, **recognition consists in remembering at the very moment of perceiving**. Both, however, depend upon what seems to be memory's fundamental act – retention. In describing the capacity of memory to hold the innumerable things which are not now in mind but can be recalled, the ancients speak of memory as *the storehouse of images*. "Every variety of thing which can be perceived can be 'stored up in memory,'" says Augustine, and "called up at my pleasure … When I speak of this or that," he goes on, "the images of all the things I mention are at hand from the same house of memory."

[…] In the tradition of the great books, we also find a more traditional and, perhaps, less familiar conception of **memory as the chief source of knowledge.**

This is Plato's doctrine of reminiscence, in which all learning is a kind of remembering of knowledge already present in the soul. All teaching takes the form of helping the learner recollect things he may not know by reminding him through **a process of questioning, which awakens the knowledge latent in him.**

Though he differs from Plato in his conception of the soul and the origin of the knowledge it innately possesses, Augustine seems to hold a similar view. As he examines his own **memory**, it appears to contain much that has not been implanted there by sense experience. Certain things, referred to by words he understands, he says, "I never reached with any sense of my body, nor even discerned them otherwise than in my mind; yet in my memory have I laid up not their images, but themselves. How they entered into me, let them say if they can, for I have gone over all the avenues of my flesh but cannot find by which they entered." If the seeds of learning are in the soul at its creation, memory can draw from these 'seminal reasons' the full fruit of knowledge."

"Imagination," writes Aristotle, "is different from either perceiving or discursive thinking, though it is not found apart from sensation or judgment without it. For **imagining lies within our own power whenever we wish** (e.g., we can call up a picture, as in the practice of mnemonics by the use of mental images), but in forming opinions, we are not free; we cannot escape the alternative of falsehood or truth." Aristotle holds that imagination is "incapable of existing apart from sensation." He also holds that **rational thought**, which is quite distinct from imagination, **cannot exist apart from imagination**.

Aristotle is, in addition, insisting that the act of **understanding is always accompanied by imaginative activity.** The kind of thinking that depends upon the abstraction of ideas from imagery also depends upon the presence of images when the thinking occurs. "The faculty of thinking," says Aristotle, "thinks the form in the images"; or, as Aquinas expresses it, "for the intellect to understand actually, not only when it acquires new knowledge, but also when it uses knowledge already acquired, there is need for the act of imagination."

Augustine refers to things "which we know within ourselves without images." When we consider numbers, for example, "it is not their images which are in [our] memory, but themselves." The question of **imageless thought** – of thinking abstractly without the use of images – seems to be peculiarly insistent in science like **mathematics, metaphysics,** and **theology**, in which the conceivable may not be imaginable. The objects peculiar to these sciences seem to require the scientist to do without imagery, or, as Aquinas says, "to rise above his imagination."

[NB: author's emphasis]
(Adapted from *The Great Ideas*, 1984, pp. 133-139)

How do we work with knowledge?

Whatever we know, whatever we think, cannot exist without **the power of our imagination**. Many linguists claim that the best teaching empowers learners to develop **cognitive skills**, question everything, and in doing so, awaken the **knowledge latent in them.**

How do we develop cognitive skills?

Benjamin Bloom created Bloom's Taxonomy in 1956 in an effort to classify learning outcomes and objectives. The cognitive skills originally included **Knowledge, Comprehension, Application, Synthesis, and Evaluation.**

Bloom's Taxonomy is a hierarchical ordering of cognitive skills that can, among countless other uses, **help teachers teach and students learn**.

For example, Bloom's Taxonomy can be used to:

create assessments

plan lessons

design curriculum maps

develop online courses

plan project-based learning

self-assessment

(Adapted from https://www.teachthought.com/learning/what-is-blooms-taxonomy-a-definition-for-teachers/)

For further reading, please check:

https://www.cambridge.org/elt/blog/2014/04/18/teaching-critical-thinking-using-blooms-taxonomy/

From **Remember** to **Create**

In 2001 an eclectic group of linguists revised *Bloom's Taxonomy* and came up with *A Taxonomy for Teaching, Learning, and Assessment.* They used these "action words" to describe the **cognitive processes** by which thinkers encounter and work with knowledge:

- Remember
    - Recognizing
    - Recalling
- Understand
    - Interpreting
    - Exemplifying
    - Classifying
    - Summarizing
    - Inferring
    - Comparing
    - Explaining
- Apply
    - Executing
    - Implementing
- Analyze
    - Differentiating
    - Organizing
    - Attributing
- Evaluate
    - Checking
    - Critiquing
- Create
    - Generating
    - Planning
    - Producing

(Adapted from https://cft.vanderbilt.edu/guides-sub-pages/blooms-taxonomy/)

How do we get from **Remember** to **Create**?

Whr hen we approach the concept of teaching vocabulary, for example, we may find ourselves dealing with a list of principles that will involve the use of memory. Tejera (2017) asserts that there are five principles that need to be considered:

1. **The Principle of Cognitive Depth**: "The more one manipulates, **thinks** about, and uses mental information, the more likely it is one will retain that information." (Schmitt, 2000: 120)
2. **The principle of Retrieval**: "The act of successfully recalling an item increases the chance that the item will be remembered." (**Baddeley**, 1997: 112)
3. **The Principle of Association**: "The human lexicon is believed to be a network of associations, a web-like structure of interconnected **links**. When students are asked to manipulate words, relate them to other words and then to their own experiences, and then to justify their choices, these word associations are reinforced." (Sökmen, 1997: 241-2)
4. **The Principle of Re-contextualization**: "When words are met in reading and listening or used in speaking and writing, the generative of the context will influence learning." (Nation, 2001:80)
5. **The Principle of Multiple Encounters**: "Due to the incremental nature of **vocabulary** acquisition, repeated exposures are necessary to consolidate a new word in the learner's mind." (Schmitt & Carter, 2000: 4)

(Adapted from Yoanis Ulloa Tejera, "The Five Guiding Principles of Vocabulary." *The EFL Magazine*, 10/11/2017)
(https://eflmagazine.com/the-five-guiding-principles-of-vocabulary-learning/)

Memory in the classroom

What is memory, anyway, and how is it related to learning?

According to Bailey and Pranksy (2014), there are five core memory and learning concepts. Based on how the brain works, the authors identify five elements that can help us understand human learning in the early 21s century context.

1. **Learning means the efficient functioning of the memory system.**
   Bailey and Pransky argue that "without memory, learning would be **impossible**" (p. 11). In their opinion, the process of learning consists of accumulating knowledge stored in long-term memory and then retrieving it for practical purposes.

2. **Memory is a physical process.**
   "When we learn, a physical change takes place in our brain" (p. 12). When we encounter new information, instinctively, we stick to what is easily remembered.

3. **Our brain learns best through multiple pathways.**
   The neural interconnections of our brain allow us to take "visual information and integrate it with our language system so we can talk about what we see" (p. 16). When we stimulate several senses with information, more brain connections become available. "For example, having students listen to a video of a scientist talking about a concept, and then having them read about the same topic along with visual representations (such as pictures, graphic organizers, or charts) provides three pathways to learning the new concept and helps to build networks that facilitate long-term storage and retrieval" (p. 17).

4. **We do not experience reality directly.**
   "Learning comes from a deeper understanding of the connections between raw input from our environment – a thunderclap, un utterance from a teacher, a sentence from a book – and the 'knowledge representation' we store in memory" (pp. 17-18). However, we process all this new information through our senses and develop opinions based on our own feelings and perceptions; in other words, "student learning is fundamentally

determined more by what goes on inside the learner than our instruction pouring in from the outside" (p. 18).

5. **Honoring the limbic system.**
Human emotions like joy or fear help us transfer information from the environment through our limbic system, "which draws on the knowledge representations we've stored in long-term memory to make sense of context and come to a conclusion about what our priorities for action should be, based upon how we are feeling" (p. 20).

Practical grounding ideas

Inferencing   We could ask students, "Have you ever done something your parents asked you not to do, and just by looking at them, you know just how they feel about it?"

Multiplication   We could ask students how many of them eat cookies or chips or how basketball shots turn into points. There are many examples of things that kids know well that come in packages or groups, or that are calculated more than one time.

The scientific method   We could ask students how they figure out how to beat levels in a video game. Kids hypothesize and make adjustments to what they do through what they've experienced throughout their lives.

(Adapted from Bailey and Pransky, *Memory at Work in the Classroom*, 2014)

> "When I was younger, I could remember anything whether it happened or not."   – Mark Twain

Perceiving and remembering

If the lesson is interesting, students will use their senses of sight, hearing, smell, taste, and touch to register the incoming information. An overview of human memory would definitely include tracing how such stimuli are processed and remembered.

According to Lanir's (2020), this is what happens:

> This brief registering process – less than a second for visual sensations and about 4 seconds for auditory sensations – is fragile. Information processing at this first stage is influenced significantly by three essential factors: attention, meaning, and emotion.

In other words, a **good lesson is remembered** if students find the **new information** to be **interesting.** If there is **meaning** attached to what we present, the whole class reacts well because we managed to stir their **emotions.**

Although already overloaded ESL/EFL teachers might think they don't have time to deal with sensory channels and memory lanes, adapting lessons does not have to be too time-consuming. It's possible that English teachers are already being eclectic without realizing it.

Easy memory card games can convince our students that, for example, ten target vocabulary games might be quite easy to process, digest, and remember. Simple games and activities may involve **writing new words**, **drawing pictures** that match these words, **saying and repeating** them, and finally **matching** the words with the **pictures**.

In order to make sure that new material settles permanently in our students' memories, language instructors should ask themselves the following questions:

1. How do our students find the new material?
2. Do we relate concepts to students' background knowledge?
3. Do we encourage our students to refer to personal and/or past experiences, likes, interests, hobbies, and concerns?
4. Do we explain to the students the real benefits of the lesson?
5. Do we provide stimulating, comprehensible information broken down visually and verbally into manageable chunks?

Three essential factors that govern student memory, mainly short memory, are **attention, meaning,** and **emotion**. In other words, language teachers should be aware that communication is effective if students pay enough **attention**, if we attach **meaning** to the subject matter being taught properly through the sensory **perceptions.**

(Adapted from Leslie Lanir, "Teachers: Are Your Teaching Methods Stimulating the Senses?")

(https://languagelearningdifficulties.com/2020/09/30/)

Are there any general techniques for improving memory?

Mastropieri and Scruggs (1993) touched on the value of mnemonic devices that can be used to **improve memory** in students who might have problems remembering things. Here are some of their suggestions:

- Increase attention.
- Promote external memory.
- Enhance meaningfulness.
- Use pictures.
- Minimize interference.
- Promote active manipulation.
- Promote active reasoning.
- Increase the amount of practice.

To be more specific, many things that need to be remembered can be written down, a practice known as "external memory." By the same token, the content of a meaningful class should be related to the students' prior knowledge and their own lives. When students make a mental effort and think about the subject matter, **reasoning will help them remember better**. Still, the best piece of advice, according to Mastropieri & Scruggs, would be to include lots of **reviews** with a focus on **practicing previous information frequently.**

(Adapted from Mastropieri, M. A., & Scruggs, T. E., "Enhancing School Success with Mnemonic Strategies")
(http://www.ldonline.org/article/5912)

So, where does **imagination** fit in?

> "Novelty in ideas has nearly always been connected with the powers of imagination to 'see' solutions to problems." (Egan, 1992)

"In my mind, imagination is a precursor to applying a creative solution to a problem. We have to use our imagination to envision the ideas that we want to test. When we create the environment where we are stimulating our students' imaginations, we are creating space for our students' minds to consider new ideas or develop hypotheses related to a classroom task. However, I believe that imagination does not mean that your mind is wandering aimlessly, it just means that they just have not arrived at the final solution or idea that they want to apply.

Furthermore, active imagination seems to imply that the students are willing participants or that the teacher has created a situation that requires their imagination. In my experience, students want to use their imaginations to complete a task when it is just beyond their current proficiency level or when they don't feel overly self-conscious or concerned about being embarrassed. I believe that it is essential to find the right balance between these two ideas for imagination to flourish in a classroom setting.

To stimulate the students' imagination, you could give them something specific to focus on. For example, imagine what your dream house looks like and explain it to a partner. I have done similar mental exercises where the students are given 1-2 minutes to close their eyes and imagine their dream house. Descriptive language works really well for this (adj/adjective clauses/appositives). I could also see using the students' imagination in design. You could use conditions in the conversation. If you did this, you could…

I also like asking my students to create a dialogue where they interview a famous person. One student is the interviewer and the other student is a famous person. Depending on your class you can require them to use vocabulary, and grammar that they must include in their dialogue. To spark their imaginations, I give the students the freedom to play with the language because I explicitly tell them that they do not need to be perfect. Mistakes are good! The exercise is more about making an effort to communicate for meaning while challenging yourself to use the new language you have learned. It is also an opportunity to get feedback.

To conclude, imagination supports language learning because it can help the students relax and engage with the language. You can worry about being perfect and use your imagination at the same time!"

(Peter Campisi, 2021)

For further reading, please check:

Imagination in Educational Theory and Practice: A Many-sided Vision. (2010). United Kingdom: Cambridge Scholars Publisher.

Imagination and its images

Instead of talking about the importance of imagination in education, students should be assigned several tasks that involve the **personal use of images** and their **effects** on the students.

1. Decide which of the **images** aroused by the italicized words are more vivid and why:

   > The *dog* is one of the most useful animals.
   > At breakfast, we only had *oranges*.
   > Of all flowers, I like *roses* best.

2. To test **control of images**, form as vivid images as you can of the following:

   > The *taste* of sugar/the *smell* of violets
   > The *feeling* involved in running upstairs
   > The *color* and *shading* of an apple
   > The *pitch* and *quality* of a friend's voice
   > The exact *color* of a friend's eyes

3. Decide which **sensation** is **more powerful** and why:

   If the ocean is represented, I actually see its motion, smell the salt breeze, the fish.
   If the country is pictured, I smell the pine woods and hear the murmur of the wind in its branches.

4. The word "coffee" brought to my mind a cup of coffee standing on a table, and then I thought of the odor. The first image was *visual,* and the second was of *smell.*

   What images and smells do these words bring to your mind: banana – mountain – chocolate?

(Adapted from Kirkpatrick, *Imagination and Its Place in Education,* 1920, pp. 23-25)

Proficiency Level: Intermediate – Bloom's Taxonomy Level 2

Imagination – a balance of memory and forgetting?

A quick answer and an elaborate explanation come from the pen of Jorge Luis Borges as quoted in Lewis Hyde's *A Primer for Forgetting*:

> A lively imagination requires a balance of memory and forgetting. "You should go in for a blending of the two elements, memory and oblivion," says Jorge Luis Borges, "and we call that imagination." Because Mnemosyne is the mother of the Muses, all arts require her double power, her ability to record or erase as the need may be. There are then two ways for memory to destroy imagination: by retaining too many abstractions […] and by retaining too many details.
>
> (Hyde, 2019, p. 39)

If we talk about imagination, we should also consider the origins of the word *literature*. We get it from the Latin word for *letter*, meaning "writing." What we have accumulated over the centuries is the connection between writing, speech, and reason created by those who used their **imagination** to leave us the works that preserve things and values for the future.

In other words, there is a difference between, let's say, **history**, which relates to **facts** or what already happened and can be verified, and **literature**, which is **the product of our imagination**.

To recap:

Memory as the chief source of knowledge and the use of **imagination** can help teachers teach and empower learners to develop cognitive skills, question everything, and in doing so, awaken the **knowledge** latent in them.

> "Judge a man by his questions, rather than by his answers." – Voltaire

Why do we ask questions?

Linguists like Dewey (1906), Krashen (2002), and Pinker (2003) have tried to ascertain the values and the intrinsic qualities of language, and some of them have even come up with remarkable theories. One such approach is that English, like some other languages, is based on structures.

In 1985, while teaching in Saudi Arabia, Clyde Coreil, Professor Emeritus at New Jersey City University, was asked to write a textbook for his students. After some thought, he chose one subject of common interest among his students: **Asking Questions.**

The author called his method *Structure-Based Acquisition* and described his idea in his introduction:

> By memorizing and manipulating sentences of increased grammatical complexity, students learn the abstract patterns underlying those sentences, internalize them, and become more able to generate and understand the language (foreword, p. iii).

While discovering the necessary tools of the language, students learn how to use certain structures, practice them in various contexts, and finally apply them in writing and speaking. Coreil also suggests that "although extensive reading and listening exercises are not central to Structure-Based Acquisition they are indeed very strong supporting elements." After a short but very convincing plea for the advantages presented by what he calls 'complex' tenses and structures, the author delves into the values presented by the importance of the knowledge regarding verbs. From here, there is just a short step towards asking questions.

Questions Socrates asked

Why is that happening?

How do you know this?

Can you give me an example of that?

What was the point of asking that question?

What exactly does this mean?

Why are you saying that?

How does this relate to what we have been talking about?

What do we already know about this?

What is the nature of this?

On what authority are you basing your argument?

How could you look another way at this?

Who benefits from this?

Why do you think I asked this question?

Am I making sense? Why not?

(adapted from www.changingminds.org)

Questions philosophers ask

What is truth?

How do words refer to reality?

What is meaning?

What is the foundation of knowledge?

What is real?

Is our universe real?

What am I?

Do we really have free will?

What is the mind?

What is moral virtue?

What are the moral principles we should follow?

Is our society a just one?

What is justice?

(Adapted from www.quora.com)

Ask your own questions:

_____

_____

_____

Questions you could ask your students

Who(m) do you trust and why?

What made the homework assignment so challenging?

When do you feel most confident at school?

Do you find that your challenges get in the way of your friendships?

You're too upset to concentrate at the moment. Do you want to take a break?

Do you feel like you have enough downtime to see your friends and have fun?

Is it ever acceptable to lie to a partner?

What's the difference between physical attraction, a crush, and love?

If someone tried to gossip with you, how could you change the topic?

How does it feel when you can tell you've hurt someone's feelings?

What do you think you'd do differently if you found yourself in this situation again?

(Adapted from Fagell, 2019)

Your question(s):

_____
_____
_____

I Keep Six Honest Serving-men
                    By Rudyard Kipling

"I keep six honest serving-men;
          (They taught me all I knew)
Their names are What and Where and When
          And How and Why and Who.
I send them over land and sea,
          I send them east and west;
But after they have worked for me,
          I give them all a rest.

I let them rest from nine till five,
          For I am busy then,
As well as breakfast, lunch, and tea,
          For they are hungry men:
But different folk have different views;
          I know a person small –
She keeps ten million serving-men,
          Who get no rest at all!
She sends'em abroad on her own affairs,
          From the second she opens her eyes –
One million Hows, two million Wheres,
          And seven million Whys!"

                    (Kipling, 1978, p. 83)

Nota Bene: The "small person" is the author's daughter.

> "Experience is the hardest kind of teacher. It gives you the test first and the lesson afterward." – Oscar Wilde

What is arching?

Innovative teachers can always use their experience and therefore resort to lots of tricks of the trade to encourage students to be inquisitive and, in doing so, have access to unlimited sources of the mind.

What better way to sharpen the keen students' imagination than to encourage them to challenge themselves as well as their partners? Not only do we train our students to use the correct grammatical structure, but we also let them practice good vocabulary, and of course, advance original ideas. With practice, they will gradually go **from words** to **phrases** and then to **complete sentences.**

> Arching is a strategy in conversation whereby a person responds to a question with another question. Arching, as a strategy, serves several functions. First, in answering a question with a question, a speaker may be making a negative comment on the initial question. Second, the use of arching may be a way of avoiding the substance or content of the initial question (especially if the question is embarrassing to the person responding). Finally, arching sometimes functions to signal a change of topic.
>
> (Findlay, 1998, p. 12)

Here are some ideas that teachers can use to get their students to be creative and use their imagination.

Remember ... and then use your imagination.

This is a good exercise that can be used to encourage our students to be **inquisitive**. Remember that certain questions are Yes/No questions, whereas others can be looking for information. Keeping in mind that questions usually follow a pattern, students also have a chance to resort to their imagination and come up with ingenious types of questions to test themselves and to challenge their peers.

Step I. Students are reminded that questions starting with Wh- (what, where, when, etc.) and How (How long, how much, etc.) are usually followed by an auxiliary verb.

For example: **Where** *did* you buy the laptop?
How long *have* you *been* living here?

Step II. Ask them to work with a partner and ask each other one question, followed not by an answer but by another question about the same topic. All the questions should be information questions, although some YES/No questions may be accepted:

For example:
A: *How long have you been studying English?*
B: *Why do you want to know?*
A: *Are you afraid you might make a mistake?*
B: *How would you know if I made a mistake?   etc.*

Proficiency Level: Low Advanced – Bloom's Taxonomy Level 2

Remember … and then use your imagination.

Step I
Remind the students to focus on **the use of the Present Perfect**. A quick review of the structure and usage might come in handy.

Step II
In small groups of three, the students are assigned the following task: Use the Present tense, the Past Tense and then connect them using the Present Perfect.

1. Student A provides an original sentence using the Present or Present Continuous.
For example: *I am studying English in New York.*

2. Student B continues the same idea and uses a sentence in the Simple Past.
For example: *I started my English studies three years ago.*

3. Student C makes the connection and provides his/her own idea by using the Present Perfect.
For example: *I have been studying English for three years.*

Rotate and start again with Student B but following the same format.

Step III
Students work in pairs and are assigned another task: asking questions.

1. Student A: Where are you living these days?
   Student B: Possible answer:
   (*I am living in New York.*)
2. Student A: When did you come to New York?
3. Student B: Possible answer:
   (*I came here last year.*)
4. Student A: How long have you been here?

Proficiency Level: Low Intermediate – Bloom's Taxonomy Level 2

Remember … and then use your imagination.

Start with a quick review of IF.

1. If I have enough time, I will go to Boston next weekend.
   Future Possible
2. Water freezes if/when the temperature goes below 32 F.
   Present general
3. If I were you, I would buy that car.
   Present Unreal
4. If I had known, I would have told you.
   Past Unreal
5. If he was here yesterday, he would have met her.
   Past Real Conditional
6. If/Since/Because you were here yesterday, you remember we read a nice story together.
   Past Real
7. If you had listened to your mother's advice, you wouldn't be sick now.
   Mixed type
8. If I liked him at first, now I think he's boring.
   Contrast

Ask your students to use their imagination and finish the following sentences:

1. If I get a chance, _____.
2. Water boils if/when _____.
3. If I had a million dollars, _____.
4. If you had come to our party, _____.
   Past Unreal
5. If you saw the movie last night, _____.
   Past Real Conditional
6. If you were here last month, _____.
   Past Real
7. If I had eaten my breakfast this morning, _____.
   Mixed Type
8. If I liked the food at first, now _____.

Proficiency Level: High Intermediate – Bloom's Taxonomy Level 3

Remember … and then use your imagination.

Step I. Provide a short **list of collocations** re: giving directions.

For example:
>*Go straight. Go straight ahead.*
>*Continue/Continue on First Avenue.*
>*Go left/turn left/make a left.*
>*Go right/turn right/make a right.*
>*Go left at the next intersection.*
>*Turn right at /Make a right onto (Second Avenue).*
>*Bear right/bear left onto …*
>*North/south/east/west*
>*Continue north/south/east/west.*
>>>>*(adapted from Ed Friedel, 2020)*

Step II. Quick **review of question word order** in conversation.

Step III. Students are assigned **several tasks and teach other**:

From your house, how do you get to the airport?

From where you are right now, how do you get to the bus stop?

Where is the nearest subway station? How do you get there?

When your friends come to visit you, how do you give them directions?

Proficiency Level: High Beginning – Bloom's Taxonomy Level 2

Remember … and then use your imagination.

Remember the language we use daily has a basic structure.

Ask your students to **imagine a conversation with or about an old friend** they haven't seen for a while. No matter what the subject of their conversation is, let them try to use as many of the following collocations as possible:

When he recognized and greeted me, _____.

The main thing is _____.

This is an attempt at _____.

I thought it advisable to _____.

There is no one in the world for whom _____.

I grasped the significance of _____.

It would make me very happy if you could _____.

I imagine you would not mean _____.

Are you admitting to me that _____?

One explanation of course is the fact that _____.

It amazed all of us that _____.

I was at least able to _____.

I am cordially inviting you to _____.

That gesture seemed to me _____.

I could not make out whether _____.

Proficiency Level: High Intermediate – Bloom's Taxonomy Level 3

Remembering the irregular verbs with music

Introduction

ESL students should be encouraged to remember grammar structures by singing popular songs. Some students may have trouble memorizing irregular verbs because, unlike regular verbs, there are no rules to follow. However, music may be just another way to help students practice and at the same time have fun singing.

Guided practice

Provide each student with a sheet of the **Irregular Verb Chart** containing the most common irregular verbs. Teach them how to divide the verbs into four different categories on their notes.

1. **A-A-A**: cut-cut-cut
2. **A-B-A**: come-came-come
3. **A-B-B**: bring-brought-brought
4. **A-B-C**: fly-flew-flown

Practice activity

AAA: cut-cut-cut

bet	bet	bet
burst	burst	burst
cost	cost	cost
cut	cut	cut
fit	fit	fit
hit	hit	hit
hurt	hurt	hurt
let	let	let
put	put	put
quit	quit	quit
set	set	set
shut	shut	shut

Use the song 'Twinkle, Twinkle, Little Star.'

Bet bet bet (twinkle twinkle)
Burst burst burst (little star)
Cost cost cost (how I wonder)
Cut cut cut (what you are)
Fit fit fit (up above the)
Hit hit hit (world so high)
Hurt hurt hurt (like a diamond)

130

Let let let (in the sky)
Put put put (twinkle twinkle)
Quit quit quit (little star)
Set set set (how I wonder)
Shut shut shut (what you are)

ABA: come-came-come

become	became	become
come	came	come
run	ran	run

Use the song, 'London Bridge Is Falling Down.'

Become became become (London Bridge is falling down)
Come   came   come (Falling down)
Come   came   come (Falling down)
Become became become (London Bridge is falling down)
Run   ran   run (My fair lady)

ABB: bring-brought-brought

bend	bent	bent
bind	bound	bound
bring	brought	brought
build	built	built
buy	bought	bought
catch	caught	caught
creep	crept	crept
deal	dealt	dealt

Use the song 'Happy Birthday to You!'

Bend bent bent (happy birthday)
Bind bound_____ (to you)
Bring brought brought (happy birthday)
Build built_____ (to you)
Buy bought bought (happy birthday)
Catch caught caught (dear 'Angela')
Creep crept crept (happy birthday)
Deal dealt_____ (to you)

131

ABC: fly-flew-flown

blow	blew	blown
break	broke	broken
choose	chose	chosen
do	did	done
draw	drew	drawn
drink	drank	drunk

Use the song 'If you are happy and you know it.'

Blow blew blown (If you are happy and you know it, clap your hands)
Break broke broken (If you are happy and you know it, clap your hands)
Choose chose chosen (If you are happy and you know it)
Do did done (Then, your face will surely show it)
Draw drew drawn (If you are happy and you know it)
Drink drank drunk (Clap your hands)

After class:

With some encouragement, students might use music while learning difficult structures and even turn this pleasant activity into a regular habit - humming and singing along to popular songs.

Suggested assignment:

Find your favorite songs to match any of the above four irregular verb patterns. Please check the Appendix for a complete list of irregular verb.

(Thomas Seo, 2021)

Proficiency Level: High Beginning – Bloom's Taxonomy Level 2

For further reading, please check:

Cafuta, J. (2016). *The Use of Music, Songs and Song Lyrics in an ESL Classroom and Their Motivational Impact on the Learners:* Master's Thesis. Slovenia: J. Cafuta.

Grünert, R. (2010). *Teaching English Through Songs*. Germany: GRIN Verlag.

Definitions

Start the lesson with a quick review of adjective clauses and then ask your students to define the following nouns using

WHO, THAT, WHICH, WHERE, WHEN

For example:

An architect is someone *who* designs buildings.

A customer _____.

A website _____.

ATM machines _____.

A coward _____.

A burglar _____.

Memes _____.

A couch potato _____.

A sitcom _____.

Rain forests_____.

Twilight _____.

Busybodies _____.

Ecofriendly cars _____.

Your examples_____

Proficiency Level: Low Intermediate – Bloom's Taxonomy Level 2

> "Words are only the outer clothing of ideas."
> – Agatha Christie

From structures to collocations in conversations

When we talk, especially when we are taking part in **challenging conversations**, we find ourselves looking for the fastest and the best verbiage.

Students can learn a lot by using certain structures they may have heard in previous conversations with similar subjects. **Collocations**, for example, are easier reproduced, and then the imagination will only add the necessary 'fill-in the-blanks.'

Structures work extremely well if they are presented in a familiar context, and if the activities differ depending on **the level of English proficiency** and if they are **not repeated but varied**. When the answers are correct, there is no need to ask for definitions. However, for the sake of precision, teachers may want to ask students to provide their own explanations or definitions, followed by the general consensus of the class.

We always want to express our own ideas and thoughts, argue a point, defend a choice, explain reasons, describe, define, classify, analyze, etc. For each task, we need a separate or **specific choice of collocations.**

A word of caution: **collocations,** like idioms, are **NOT FLEXIBLE**. They must be remembered as they are, and changes in the wording may make the communication stilted or difficult to follow. Not only that, a collocation might be a better way because it is a synthesis, not a succession of words. For example: Instead of saying that our team is successful and winning game after game, you might say that *our team is on a winning streak*. It even sounds better!

In 2019, after writing a little masterpiece entitled *Between You & Me*, Mary Norris produced another example of **intellectual curiosity** (turned into entertaining writing) when she published her highly informative work entitled *Greek to Me. Adventures of the Comma Queen.*

Among the plethora of facts and curiosities, the author makes the connection between the word "letter," as **a letter in the alphabet**, and the word for a collection of letters, as in **a letter to a friend**. As for **the alphabet**, Mary Norris argues that "… [it] is the greatest invention of humankind because it gave us **the means to communicate** with both the past and the future." (p. 22) [NB: author's emphasis] When it comes to self-expression, we are reminded that every time the English language

134

needs to coin new words, it resorts to an ancient language. For example, many words come from Greek: *ocean, dolphin, peony*, etc. mostly because some of them are for exotic creatures: *octopus* comes from the Greek words that mean *eight+foot*. In Mary Norris's opinion, another fascinating concept that interests everybody who loves words is the difference between a **lexicon** and a **dictionary**. She emphasized how valuable a lexicon could be when she defined it as "a collection of words occurring in the work of a given group of authors, with citation and definitions." (p. 80)

In a nutshell, Mary Norris is articulating the argument that the alphabet – "the greatest invention of mankind" – has been a **tremendous force in the way we communicate** with each other across centuries. As for the **English vocabulary with its own collocations**, this huge **accumulation of knowledge**, as it is now, is still growing and developing because it can absorb new words and create new ones. While **lexicons** may be recognized and appreciated by researchers and linguists for their intrinsic value in general, **dictionaries** may be useful tools for learners of all ages who want to improve and even perfect their oral and written skills.

What is essential about **motivating** students to discover? In other words, **is motivation somehow related to something else?**

How is motivation related to learning?

One very important step in our **students' motivation** springs largely from the **frame of their minds**. While they rely on their own background and culture, students will firmly transform into successful learners **if they understand** why certain activities are necessary to cultivate **knowledge**.

Role-Plays in ESL

"**Role-play** is an effective technique **to** animate the **teaching** and learning atmosphere, arouse the interests of learners, and make the **language** acquisition impressive. Incorporating **role-plays** into the **classroom** adds variety, a change of pace and opportunities for a lot of **language** production and also a lot of fun!" (https://www.teachingenglish.org.uk/article/role-play)

If we want to take our students out of the monotonous and rigorous classroom environment, **role-plays** can be a very **attractive transition from imagination to real-world situations.** Several ideas might come in handy to manage effective classroom activities:

1. Students feel more **comfortable** acting out real-life situations in which they might have been involved or may be tempted to try to better prepare for similar **learning experiences**.
2. There are cases when the teacher can assign students to perform tasks when-in which they assume **a different personality**.
3. To make such **role-plays memorable and engaging**, we must remember that students will usually resort to **previous knowledge** from their own culture or general background.
4. If students can use their own personalities, we only need to **encourage and empower** them without making too many adjustments or corrections.

Imagination is the beginning of creation.

Practical knowledge   Use your imagination

1. **At the Post Office** – Create a dialogue referring to the
    following items and collocations:

    postage stamps – tracking number – junk mail – postcode
    first-class – registered mail – certified mail – express
    media mail – overnight delivery – second-day mail
    confirmation receipt

2. **At the bank** – Create a dialogue using the following items
    and collocations:

    open an account – order checks – endorse a check
    deposit money – withdraw money – cash checks
    savings account – checking account – monthly statements
    money transfer – deposit slips – withdrawal slips
    outstanding balance

4. **At the travel agency** – Create a dialogue using the following
    items and collocations:

    make a reservation – book a ticket – ask for a brochure
    rent a car – make travel arrangements – travel on business
    traveling tips – traveler's checks – hotel accommodation
    one way/round trip ticket – bonus mileage
    holiday destination

4. **At the airport – ask for information**

    airport lounge – departures – arrivals
    lost luggage – overnight flight – airport shuttles
    delayed flights – unattended luggage – terminal B
    check-in gate – boarding time – aisle seat – window seat

Be prepared to answer the following questions:

1. *Anything to declare?*
2. *What is the purpose of your trip?*
3. *Did you pack this bag yourself?*
4. *May I see your passport?*

5.   Shopping

Build on the following questions and create original dialogues:

How can I help you?
Are you being helped?   *What can I do for you?*
Anything else?   *Should that be all?*
Cash or charge?   *Debit or credit?*

The following collocations may also be helpful:

   to find a bargain   *gift voucher*
   to place an order   *to ask for a discount*

How do we empower our students to use collocations and idioms?

"When it comes to teaching collocations, I like to tell my students that it is important to think of vocabulary learning as really learning chunks of words together. It is more efficient. This works especially well with verbs because they basically have 4 collocations after the verb: no object, a prepositional object, 1 object or 2 objects (direct and indirect).

I run.
I spoke to the author.
I stole your cookie.
I gave him a new helicopter.

Multiple exposures in listening, speaking and writing help build that connection with the word and the collocation. I believe that it is essential students say the word with the correct collocation at least 10 times and have an opportunity to perform a creative task that encourages them to use the collocations. Like creating a dialogue that is performed for the class or writing a short story. The other students could provide feedback or act as the teacher to correct them when appropriate."

(Peter Campisi, 2021)

How much do students need to remember?

Some linguists dislike the idea that students should resort to memorization. They also think ESL students should be included in the same category. Others argue that ESL students might surely benefit from the vast field of grammar structures, expressions, or set phrases they need to accumulate (and therefore memorize) so that they may **cross the threshold between accuracy and fluency** and **speak like a native.**

How does memory work?

In his essay entitled *Imagination and Memory: Friends or Enemies,* Earl W. Stevick (1993) delved into the highly controversial debate about the two concepts of imagination and memory:

> … very important to the way I'm guessing memory works, is the place of purpose and the place of emotion. What we call a *memory* contains many kinds of information – most obviously, visual and auditory information, and the information from the rest of the so-called *five senses*. But a **memory** also contains information about time (remoteness and duration), and about the purposes we had in connection with the experience, and the emotions that went along with the experience. (p. 11)

These are some suggested activities, **bearing** in mind that ESL students **remember** vocabulary and specially set phrases, idioms, or collocations if they can somehow relate them to an experience in their past, a moment or an event that triggered an emotion, a sentiment of pleasure, fear or anything completely different or unique. From my own experience as an ESL student and teacher, I might stretch it and propose the idea that such structures can be retained easier and faster if they are all **related to something similar** (time, place, etc.), **or if they have something in common** (idea, context, spelling, etc.).

Sports

When it comes to our favorite sports, we should remember that metaphorical expressions can be hard to understand. However, students should be encouraged to try their best. The truth is, most students can only guess what these words mean, but teachers should be able to create at least one or two situations to generate context and to exemplify word usage.

Ball games   **keep your eye on the ball**   'pay attention'

Baseball   **to step up to the plate**   'assume responsibility'
to touch base 'contact, in order to communicate'
ballpark figure   'rough estimate of a number'

Basketball   **slam dunk**   'an inevitable success'
out of someone's league   'A person is too good for his team'

Football   **spiking the ball**   'showing off about a success'
It's a game of inches.   'Progress towards a goal comes in small increments'

Golf   **par for the course**   'normal or to be expected'

Races   **on the home stretch**   'nearing completion'

Horse races   **neck and neck** 'in exactly the same position'

Swimming   **sink or swim**   'either succeed or fail'

Tennis   **The ball is in your court**. 'It's someone's turn to take action'

For further reading, please check:

Chetwynd, J. (2016). *The Field Guide to Sports Metaphors: A Compendium of Competitive Words and Idioms.* United States: Clarkson Potter/Ten Speed.

Teaching Business English

"English has become a lingua franca for global business activities around the world. As a result, more English is used by non-native speakers of English than native speakers, and English is used in an exceptionally broad range of professional contexts, both in speaking and writing.

When we think about the characteristics of successful business professionals, effective communication skills and keen listening skills come to mind. Many can underestimate how important it is to be a good listener, and of course focused listening is even more critical for those who are English language learners. In order to digest the relevant information imparted by speakers, these individuals often need to make sense of vocabulary and idiomatic expressions which are unfamiliar to them. By becoming a keen listener, an English language learner can start absorbing the collocations and idioms that they hear, as well as remembering and internalizing the expressions used frequently in their particular business contexts. Further, they can hone their listening skills by watching business news and talks.

Part of being a good listener is the ability to come up with a range of initial and follow-up questions. Even advanced English learners can struggle with question formation. In a business environment, the stakes can be very high for correct English usage compared to other more casual situations. Business professionals need to build relationships with colleagues, managers, clients, partners and many others. Impressions are set at an early stage, and fluency in asking questions and listening actively will foster positive impressions.

As in other areas of English, there are many idiomatic expressions that we use in question formation, particularly to "soften" language and convey more politeness. For example, it would come across as rude to ask a retail customer "What do you want?" even though the grammar is correct and the speaker's intent is to be helpful. Instead, we might ask "Is there anything I can help you with?" If you were to meet a fellow attendee at an industry conference, it would be natural to find out the other person's reason for attending. A typical question to ask in this situation would be "What brings you to the conference?" On the other hand, while the question "Why are you here?" may seem logical for a non-native speaker to ask, it may well be interpreted as rude and judgmental by a native English speaker. For business professionals, it can be as important to know what <u>not</u> to say as well as what to say, so as to not unintentionally damage a relationship. Business English teachers can create focused lessons for their students to practice the Dos and Don'ts of question formation and usage, and engaged BE students will see the benefits of becoming effective communicators in English."

(Ralph Herdman, 2021)

Proficiency Level: High Intermediate - Bloom's Taxonomy Level 3

Clarify pedagogical purpose for warmer activities

"In general, it is important that ESL students understand why they are doing things, including warmer activities such as brain teasers and 20 questions. This is particularly important for working professionals in Business English classes to gain their buy-in of the value of an activity and build trust.

In a warmer such as 20 Questions, students are told a high-level category of something and take turns asking only Yes or No questions to guess what it is. As an example for Business English students, the teacher might say, "I'm thinking of a well-known multinational company." The challenge for students is to come up with the right questions to ask, using a series of questions that continue to narrow the possible answers. The teacher can provide clues if the answer to a particular question is not clearly a 'Yes' or a 'No.' This type of warmer can be very fun and engaging but has educational value in the Business English classroom for several reasons:

- It reinforces proper question formation (a persistent problem even among many advanced English learners).

- It gets students to learn and practice correct business vocabulary and expressions (for ex., *conglomerate, B2B/B2C, consumer goods*, etc.).

- It builds good listening skills (since previous questions and the associated answers are important to note, you can see if students are carefully paying attention!).

- It reinforces critical thinking skills.

For future warmers, the teacher can assign a student to come up with a category and lead the activity, with all students eventually getting the opportunity to lead. Twenty questions can be used in General ESL classes, perhaps using categories that relate to topics which have been discussed in class. Depending upon the level of the class, the teacher can provide more or less support to the leader and the rest of the students to facilitate the process."

(Ralph Herdman, 2021)

Business English

Sample Course Objective

"To impart knowledge and practical usage of Business English as it is written and spoken, not only in the United States and other English-speaking countries, but also in industrialized and developing societies around the world.

Topics

- Business vocabulary in everyday use
- Business idioms and expressions which are commonly used in the United States, UK, and other English-speaking countries
- Case studies
- Coverage of current business events and articles as highlighted by *The Wall Street Journal, New York Times Business, Financial Times,* and *USA Today*
- Preparation and delivery of business proposals and presentations in a group setting, using PowerPoint, individual stand-up delivery, etc.
- Listening/comprehension activities using authentic business reporting via radio and streaming broadcasts
- Group discussions on such topics as finding solutions to business alliance challenges experienced by two or more countries partnering with one another
- Written critiques of select articles in *Business Week, The Economist*, and other business journals
- In-class debates about current, high-impact business policies, innovative product marketing strategies, etc.
- The growth and development of US business history from 1850-present day
- Role-playing of reality-based business issues affecting US employees in present day

Each student is given an opportunity to develop his or her reading, listening, and speaking skills through interacting with the other students and the instructor. Students gain confidence in speaking in front of a group, and develop research skills through an array of business topics."

(John Artise 2021)

Sample Business English lesson plan

"I recall teaching a session in Business English many years ago in which I introduced a very relevant topic: **Retrieving Lost Articles in Transportation Facilities.**

There were 12 students in the class, and I formed three groups of 4 students in each group.

I asked each group to come up with a method or procedure to locate lost items such as a wallet, a passport, a piece of jewelry, a garment, a book. etc., even a domestic animal.

I told them not to rely on the traditional method of making phone calls to Lost and Found Departments.

I instructed them to rely on BOTH their **memories** of their past experiences AND their **creative imagination** in coming up with a solution.

I allowed 20 minutes for their interactive discussions.

At the end of their discussions, each group chose a spokesperson to report on their own group's proposed solution.

As it turned out, almost all of the students wound up giving their individual ideas, perceptions, and commentary using pertinent vocabulary and expressions in the English Language.

It was enlightening not only to listen to the thoroughness of their ideas, but also to experience their enthusiasm in discussing the issues in English. This session took place several months before the invention of the micro-chip which was eventually used to track lost luggage and runaway domestic farm animals.

The concept and proposition of the micro-chip WAS offered by one of the groups!"

(John Artise, 2021)

Collocations and idioms worksheets

The following worksheets may be used as they are, or they can be adapted, reconfigured, or simply redesigned altogether.

The format follows the idea that an activity should have a task, an example to follow, and collocations or idioms that might be learned in context. Commonality may function as context.

What keeps these worksheets together is one **topic** that should attract the **students' attention** and encourage their **participation** without correcting them too often.

Students can be assigned to work in pairs, small groups, or even larger groups.

Collocations and idioms worksheets

1. **Remember the best bumper sticker you ever saw and share it.**

If you can't remember one, **use your imagination** and make one up.

For example:

If you can read this, thank a teacher.
If you can read this, you are driving too close.
Play rugby! Support your local dentist.
Want to see God? Keep texting while you drive.
If you want to drink and drive, drink milk!
My windows aren't dirty. It's my dog's nose art.
This is not an abandoned car.

Use as many collocations as possible from the list below:

bumper to bumper
day in and day out
day by day
do no harm
designated driver
the devil is in the details
dos and don'ts
dirty little secret
delicate balance
dropped a bombshell
dream come true
faster than a speeding ticket

Proficiency Level: Intermediate − Bloom's Taxonomy Level 3

2. What is your greatest accomplishment?

If you can imagine it, you can possess it.
If you can dream it, you can become it.
If you can envision it, you can attain it.
If you can picture it, you can achieve it.

– William Arthur Ward

"First used in the 15th century, the noun accomplishment derives from the Old French word *acomplir*, meaning 'to fulfill, fill up, complete.' An accomplishment is something you've completed successfully. The word often refers to a goal that you've achieved. If you're a runner, you'd consider completing a marathon a great accomplishment. Gaining a new skill can also be an accomplishment." (www.vocabulary.com/dictionary)

Share a moment in your life when you felt proud you achieved your goal.

Use as many collocations as possible from the list below:

a clean slate
at all costs
eager beaver
to gain ground
to turn over a new leaf
to go the extra mile
to go to great lengths
The sky is the limit.
beyond my wildest dreams
a dream come true

Proficiency Level: Low Advanced – Bloom's Taxonomy Level 5

3. **Write an ad for any of the following items listed below.**

paper clips
dental floss
toothpicks
rubber bands
salt shakers
staples
bottle caps
flash drives
stickies

For example:
Freedom of Choice – French Fries or Onion Rings?

Use some of the following collocations and idioms:

to place an ad

selling points

to carry ads

to go viral

sold on

classified ads

to bring something to the table

front-page ads

to put something on the map

pay-off

Your own:

_____

Proficiency Level: Intermediate – Bloom's Taxonomy Level 3

4. Using computer vocabulary

Challenge your students to check their own knowledge of computer vocabulary by working in pairs and teaching each other specialized computer vocabulary.

For example:

bookmark a site

create an avatar

data management

do a search

hard copy/soft copy

install an application

navigate a website

read an attachment

remote access

search engine

system requirements

zip/unzip a file

For further reading, please check:

Carruthers, E. (2016). *New Word a Day for Kids: Computer Terms.* (n.p.): CreateSpace Independent Publishing Platform.

Ridgon, J. C. (2016). *Dictionary of Computer and Internet Terms.* United States: CreateSpace Independent Publishing Platform.

5. Wishes

How important is **celebrating your birthday** to you?

Birthday parties, presents, friends and family around?

For example:
The good fairy granted them three wishes.

Make a wish and use as many collocations as possible from the list below:

to make wishes come true

to make an exception

to make a deal

a wish for peace

my deepest wish

might as well

wish list

best wishes

I wish you a speedy recovery.

Proficiency Level: Intermediate – Bloom's Taxonomy Level 3

6. **Compose an email to your teacher**. It may be an answer to a previous request, or you may try texting your favorite teacher with a question.

For example:

Dear Teacher,
Greetings from my happy home! Thank you for your prompt response to my previous message. I have another question.

Students may want to use some of the following vocabulary:

to scroll down the page	*to log in*
to italicize	*to join a conversation*
see attachment	*to change passwords*
user name	*prompt response*
to forward	*to highlight*
to change the font	*to cut and paste*

Students should be encouraged to use the correct spelling and punctuation as a sign of respect for their instructors.

Necessary tools:

periods − question marks − exclamation point − the @ symbol

_____

_____

_____

_____

Proficiency Level: High Intermediate − Bloom's Taxonomy Level 6

7. *A slip of the tongue*

From the television show "Parks and Recreation"

Jerry: For my murinal, I was inspired by the death of my grandma.
Tom: You said *murinal*!   [Everyone laughs]
Jerry: No, I didn't.
Ann: Yes, you did. You said *murinal*. I heard it.
Jerry: Anyway, she—
April: Jerry, why don't you put that murinal in the men's room so people can murinate all over it?
Tom: Jerry, go to the doctor. You might have a murinary tract infection.
[Jerry takes down his mural and walks away defeated.]
Jerry: I just wanted to show you my art.
Everyone: Murinal! Mural! Murinal!

Share a moment when you made a mistake in speaking that sounded quite amusing.

For example:
I guess everybody laughed when I said that, but I think they got my drift.

Use as many collocations as possible from the list below:

It is what it is.
If my memory serves me right ...
It comes with the territory.
It slipped my mind.
I thought you'd never ask.
I hear you loud and clear.
It was a slip of the tongue.
If truth be told, ...
If only we could...
I rest my case.

Proficiency Level: High Intermediate – Bloom's Taxonomy Level 3

8. "The only person who can stop you from reaching your goals is you." – Jackie Joyner-Kersee, Six-time Olympic gold medalist

Share a time when you thought you couldn't do something, but you persevered and accomplished the task. How did you feel when it was done?

For example:

I didn't' know how to begin my first essay, but I knew in the end it was going to be a howling success.

Use as many collocations and idioms as possible from the list below:

under the circumstances
to some extent
next to impossible
to set a goal/to work towards a goal
to come a long way
to rise to the occasion
short term/long term goals
with flying colors
to dress for success
a howling success
the sweet smell of victory/success

Proficiency Level: High Intermediate – Bloom's Taxonomy Level 3

> "If you want to make God laugh, tell him your plans." – Woody Allen

9. Share something that happened to you this week or this month that made you laugh.

Share your opinions.

For example:

He pulled a funny face to make us laugh.

Use as many collocations and idioms as possible from the list below:

to have a good laugh/to have the last laugh

just for a laugh

happy/infectious laughter

to make fun of somebody

to laugh out loud/to laugh heartily

to laugh at somebody's expense

a fit of laugher

a laugh a minute

to burst into/to explode with laughter

peals of laughter

Proficiency Level: High Intermediate – Bloom's Taxonomy Level 3

10. If you wrote a book, what would you write about, and what would be the title?

Use as many collocations and idioms as possible from the list below:

from the get-go

in the nick of time

as I recall

in hindsight

If I may say so …

That goes without saying.

that sort of thing

for an instant

in more ways than one

nothing of the kind

in a pickle

I have a gut feeling …

Funny when you come to think of it.

Make no bones about it!

for practical purposes

or so it seemed to me

Proficiency Level: High Intermediate – Bloom's Taxonomy Level 3

11. "You can make more friends in two months by becoming interested in other people than you can in two years by trying to get people interested in you."
 – Dale Carnegie

What qualities do you expect to have in a good friend?   Students interview each other.

A good friend is someone who can help me when I am in a pickle.

Use as many collocations and idioms as possible from the list below:

long standing friendship

deep/firm friendship

a gesture of friendship

there is no obvious way out

in a pinch

a token of your friendship

to start up/strike up a friendship

bonds/ties of friendship

to take somebody at his word

Proficiency Level: Intermediate - Bloom's Taxonomy Level 3

For further reading, please check:

Denworth, L. (2020). *Friendship: The Evolution, Biology and Extraordinary Power of Life's Fundamental Bond. United Kingdom*: Bloomsbury Publishing.

Ray, M. L. (2019). *The Friendship Book*. United States: HMH Books.

12. **What is your favorite expression? Why?**

Try some of the following or share yours with the group:

For example:

We had a very nice conversation yesterday. We talked *about this, that, and the other.*

Use as many collocations and idioms as possible from the list below:

as easy as pie

   the bottom line

      by hook or by crook

         No, it won't wash.

            by fair means and foul

               Keep me in the loop.

                  Look before you leap!

                     this, that, and what not

                        No sweat.

                           Holy mackerel!

                              well put

Proficiency Level: Intermediate – Bloom's Taxonomy Level 3

13. Representing a friend in a debate

Use your imagination and defend a good friend who made a reckless mistake.

For example:

If I am going out on a limb to support you, some people may think it's too risky.

Use as many collocations and idioms as possible from the list below:
on behalf of

on purpose

on the up and up

on to something

once in a blue moon

out of control

out of touch

out on a limb

out of nowhere

on the other hand

Proficiency Level: Intermediate – Bloom's Taxonomy Level 3

14. **Describe your favorite day of the week and then explain why you chose it.**

Sunday the day of the sun

Monday   the day of the moon

Tuesday   Tiw's Day, named after the god of war in Norse mythology

Wednesday   Woden's Day, named after a Germanic and Scandinavian god

Thursday   Thor's Day, after the Norse god of the thunder

Friday   named after the Anglo-Saxon goddess Frigg

Saturday   Saturn's Day, from Latin origins, itself from the god of agriculture

For example: *Sunday is a popular day for picnics and watching movies.*

Use as many collocations and idioms as possible from the following list:

> *Monday morning feeling*
> *from here till next Tuesday*
> *Happy Hump Day!*
> *after the rain on Thursday*
> *a man Friday*
> *Saturday night special*
> *Sunday's best*
> *weekend matinee*

Proficiency Level: Intermediate - Bloom's Taxonomy Level 3

Please check the Appendix for extra worksheets.

Eliciting information from students

Eliciting Effectively in ESL

What **questions** do we need to ask ourselves when we try to elicit information from our students?

1. How do we empower students to say what they already know about a subject rather than the teacher giving the explanation?

2. What makes the combination of teaching and learning the best way of eliciting answers and gaining insight from within?

3. How do we prepare the best questions that work for all students?

4. What happens when students ask their own questions in response?

5. How do we help learners reveal their potential through questioning and arguing?

6. What visual or linguistic prompts are useful?

Things to consider when eliciting:

- Avoid close-ended questions like "Do you understand …?"
- Use synonyms to elicit vocabulary.
- Encourage students to ask their own questions for clarification.
- Consider cultural differences.
- Use flashcards, pictures, mind maps/word clusters.
- Avoid new or difficult vocabulary in your questions.

According to Steve Darn, there are certain things **a teacher should know about eliciting:**

Eliciting is a basic technique and should be used regularly, not only at the beginning of a lesson but whenever it is necessary and appropriate.

Don't try to 'pull teeth.' Prolonged silence or incorrect answers suggest that input is required from the teacher.

Acknowledge or give feedback to each answer with gestures or comments.

Provide sufficient context or information.

Learners can elicit from each other, particularly during brainstorming activities. This helps to build confidence and group cohesion as well as shifting the focus away from the teacher.

At lower levels, more guided questioning is needed. Open-ended questions should be less frequent as the learners are unlikely to have the language to answer them to their own satisfaction.

(Adapted from https://www.teachingenglish.org.uk/article/eliciting)

For additional information about eliciting, please check:

"5 Ways to Elicit Effectively in the EFL Classroom"

https://www.theteflacademy.com/blog/2018/03/5-ways-to-elicit-effectively-in-the-efl-classroom/

"Eliciting Techniques, Questions, Activities & Tips for ESL Teachers"
    https://www.eslactivity.org/eliciting/

Eliciting worksheets

In this section, **each student must have a different answer**.

They should work separately and they are expected to have their own answers.

Each worksheet can also be used by students working in pairs and providing alternate answers.

1. Eliciting information in dialogues

Students provide the missing information in complete sentences in the following dialogues and then compare their answers with a partner:

I.   *A colleague at work drops in your office:*

Colleague: We're having a few friends for dinner next Saturday and I was wondering if you and your friend would like to join us?
You: ...
Colleagues: Oh, well, maybe another time then.

II.   *You are sitting in a crowded open-air café and a person you don't know approaches you:*

Stranger: Do you mind if I share your table?
You: ...
Stranger: I guess I'll just have to wait until someone leaves, then.

III.   *In your school, your colleague and room-mate Bob is off work due to an illness. His student, Etsuko, approaches you:*

Etsuko: Excuse me, do you think I could have Bob's address so I could send him some flowers?
You: ...
Etsuko: Thank you all the same.

(Adapted from Thornbury, 1997, p. 9)

Proficiency Level: Intermediate - Bloom's Taxonomy Level 3

For further reading, please check:

Gorea, L. (2009). *Speak English for Success: ESL Conversations, Topics, and Dialogues*. United States: AuthorHouse.

2. Provide individual responses to each of the following:

Question:	Answer
What's up?	Not much.
Is there anything the matter?	_____
What's the gist of it?	_____
Who's going to get the upper hand?	_____
What's wrong with that?	_____
How's that?	_____
Where do I come in?	_____
What else can I do?	_____
Get it?	_____
What are you hinting at?	_____
How's it going?	_____
What are you ranting about?	_____
No hard feeling?	_____

What in the world are you trying to say? _____

How do you get there? _____

Proficiency Level: High Intermediate - Bloom's Taxonomy Level 3

3. Provide the possible question for the given answer.

Question	Answer
What do you think I need?	*A crash course in how to drive a stick shift.*

Question	Answer
_____	Nothing at all.
_____	I can't put my finger on it.
_____	To get things going.
_____	Go right ahead.
_____	I gave them a piece of my mind.
_____	My heart went out to them.
_____	Nonsense.
_____	Might as well.
_____	When all is said and done.
_____	Suits you to a T.
_____	Just what the doctor ordered.
_____	No ifs, ands, or buts.
_____	We have to go back to the drawing board.
_____	Because I didn't sleep a wink.
_____	Yes, but you have to look on the bright side.
_____	No need to blow things out of proportion.
_____	Way to go!
_____	Good thinking!
_____	Beats me!
_____	Not to my knowledge.

Proficiency Level: High Intermediate – Bloom's Taxonomy Level 3

4. **Paraphrase** the italicized words in your own words
   and then **ask a question:**

For example: The athlete had an Olympic *winning streak.*
              He won an event *in (three) consecutive games.*
              How do you feel about *a winning streak?*

I already *made up my mind.*   _____

We *are in the dark* as much as ever.   _____

Your guess is as good as mine.   _____

His words seem *to have a ring of truth* in them. _____

She *breathed a sigh of satisfaction.*   _____

Let's face it: she won the election *fair and square.* _____

He wouldn't *hurt a fly.*   _____

No need to *blow the whistle*; we knew that all along. _____

We'd *better be off* trying again.   _____

He uttered *a grunt of impatience.*   _____

He stood in the doorway, *devoured with curiosity.* _____

Time flies when you're having fun.   _____

Not bad at all – all things considered. It's *a blessing in disguise.*

_____

The short exercise was *a piece of cake.* _____

Proficiency Level: Advanced – Bloom's Taxonomy Level 3

5. Use the following collocations and idioms in two original sentences. You may want to create a whole context to make the meaning clear. No need to explain or paraphrase if the examples are correct.

by far   *She is by far the best student in the class.*
           Soccer is by far the most popular sport in the world.

under no circumstances   _____

first and foremost   _____

behind the scenes   _____

without a second thought   _____

too many loose ends   _____

the seeds of change   _____

to some extent   _____

at any rate   _____

not in the least   _____

once and for all   _____

like crazy   _____

out of this world   _____

tricks of the trade   _____

through thick and thin   _____

Proficiency Level: Advanced – Bloom's Taxonomy Level 3

6. Guess the meaning from context

For example:

You should trust your intuition first. *the ability to understand something without thinking or the impression based on logical deduction or experience*

We can't wait any longer. We must *leap into action*.

_____

Are you loaded? No, I never drink on the job.

_____

It was his duty *to act as a human sieve* – retaining the grosser matter and passing on the residue to his supervisors.

_____

Your words are very suggestive. They *foster ideas*.

_____

He sticks to his story and he's not *to be heckled*.

_____

Although you *paid through the nose,* you got what you paid for.

_____

I know it's a horror movie, but it still *gives me the creeps*.

_____

She couldn't sleep so she *tossed and turned* in her bed all night.

_____

His *voice shook a little* but he *had full command of himself*.

_____

He said admiringly, "I *take off my hat to you.*"

_____

I haven't told you everything, *not by a long shot*.

_____

No need *to freak out*. First things first.

If you don't sleep for a week, you will *look like a basket case*.

In the world of tennis, **the Williams sisters are** *the cream of the crop*.

This author is so famous his books *are selling like hotcakes*.

With the new equipment we managed *to crank out* the manuscript in no time at all.

Yeah, yeah, and *pigs will fly*.

It's not easy to deal with him because he always *drives a hard bargain*.

We have a final test tomorrow so I will have *to hit the books* tonight.

I know you like music, so I guess this song is *right up your alley*.

What you said was not a good idea. I guess it was *a cheap shot*.

Proficiency Level: Advanced – Bloom's Taxonomy Level 3

7. Ask questions for the italicized words:

For example: The neighbor greeted us *with a nod of the head.*
　　　　　　　　　　　　How did the neighbor greet us?

The breaking news *came out of the blue.* _____

You will never make friends if you always *give them a cold shoulder.*
_____

Now that your friend is in the hospital you should visit her and *cheer
her up.*　　　　　　　_____

This is just *for your ears.* _____

The guy had *a memory like an elephant.* _____

Our party is a secret so *don't let the cat out of the bag.*
_____

Stop yelling and *take it easy*!　　　　_____

She won the race *by a hair.*　　　　_____

No matter what, I will have *to start from scratch.* _____

Her presentation was *head and shoulders above the rest.*
_____

We could not find a solution right away, but now *things are looking up.*
_____

I know I made a big mistake but that's *the way the cookie crumbles.*
_____

He doesn't know that *ranting and raving* will not solve the problem.
_____

Proficiency Level: Advanced - Bloom's Taxonomy Level 3

8. Choose two from the following list of collocations and idioms and use them together in original sentences.

For example: When everything was *done and dusted*, she *heaved a sigh of relief.*

apples and oranges	*on a roll*
back burner	*to pay respects*
ballpark figure	*to push the envelope*
bear in mind	*a piece of the action*
bells and whistles	*quality time*
to sing praises	*to reinvent the wheel*
to bite the bullet	*to rock the boat*
bottom line	*to save money*
breaking news	*sell the sizzle not the steak*
can of worms	*to shoot oneself in the foot*
to catch someone's eye	*to take a chance*
cheap shot	*Take your time!*
to do business	*task force*
for good	*Take it or leave it!*
for keeps	*to throw a party*
for the time being	*time frame*
good as gold	*too close to call*
hard ball	*track record*
to have fun	*in truth*
to have sympathy	*two-way street*
for sure	*under the weather*
low profile	*up in the air*
no brainer	*up to speed*
not a happy camper	*well-endowed*
not to worry	*worried sick*
off the wall	*to zoom in*

For further reading, please check:

McCarthy, M. & O'Dell, F. (2008). *English Collocations in Use: Advanced.* Germany: Cambridge University Press.

Proficiency Level: Low Advanced – Bloom's Taxonomy Level 3

9. Use your imagination to paraphrase proverbs.

Proverb	Paraphrase
An apple a day keeps the doctor away.	_____
April showers bring May flowers.	_____
Better safe than sorry.	_____
A bird in the hand is worth two in the bush.	_____
Birds of a feather flock together.	_____
Don't cry over spilt milk.	_____
Don't put all your eggs in one basket.	_____
The early bird catches the worm.	_____
Every cloud has a silver lining.	_____
A friend in need is a friend indeed.	_____
The grass is greener on the other side.	_____
He who laughs last laughs best.	_____
Look before you leap.	_____
Many hands make light work.	_____
Once bitten, twice shy.	_____
Seeing is believing.	_____
A stitch in time saves nine.	_____

When it rains, it pours.   _____

Where there's a will, there's a way.   _____

You can lead a horse to water, but you can't make it drink.
_____

You can't teach an old dog new tricks.   _____

Your proverbs

_____
_____
_____
_____
_____

Proficiency Level: Advanced – Bloom's Taxonomy Level 3

For further reading, please check:

Moehlenbrock, J. A. (2016). *Proverbs for the Classroom.* (n.p.): CreateSpace Independent Publishing Platform.

Putnam, M. R. (1988). *Using Proverbs and Sayings in the ESL/EFL Classroom.* (n.p.): School for International Training.

10. Dueling proverbs

Choose one of the two proverbs and defend your choice.

Ask no questions and hear no lies. – Ask and you shall receive.

Bird of a feather flock together. – Opposites attract.

Blood is thicker than water. – Many kinfolk, new friends.

Clothes make the man. – Don't judge a book by its cover.

A good beginning makes a good ending. – It's not over till it's over.

He who hesitates is lost. – Look before you leap.

Hold fast to the words of your ancestors. – Wise men make proverbs, and fools repeat them.

If, at first, you don't succeed, try again. – Don't beat a dead horse.

Practice makes perfect. – All work and no play makes Jack a dull boy.

Silence is golden. – The squeaky wheel gets the grease.

Too many cooks spoil the broth. – Two heads are better than one.

There is safety in numbers. – Better be alone than in bad company.

Variety is the spice of life. – Don't change horses in midstream.

Proficiency Level: Low Advanced – Bloom's Taxonomy Level 3

11. Provide the correct form of the gerund:

For example:

What's the advantage of….?

What's the advantage of *waking up early*?
What's the advantage of *having a positive attitude*?
What's the advantage of *eating a balanced diet*?

1. What can we possibly gain by _____?
2. Is he in the habit of _____?
3. Why did she shake her head without _____?
4. Are you sure we have so far succeeded in _____?
5. Did the doctor suggest _____?
6. What's the use of _____?
7. Stop _____ and let's get down to business.
8. If you think you lost your touch, why don't you try

   _____?

9. That's okay but you still have to sweeten the deal by

   _____.

10. Can we try to talk her into _____?
11. Although our plans are up in the air, we still enjoy

   _____.

12. I wouldn't mind _____.
13. Knowing what a pleasant surprise it was for everybody,
    we all felt like _____.
14. Unfortunately, there was no nice way of _____.
15. What's the reason for _____?
16. They should be capable of _____.

Proficiency Level: High Intermediate – Bloom's Taxonomy Level 3

12. Provide the correct form of the infinitive:

For example:
I didn't mean to ___*offend you.*_____ .

1. No one knew what to _____ .
2. I was sorry but I never had a chance to
   _____ .
3. One of the main purposes of this exercise is to
   _____ .
4. They had a very good reason to
   _____ .
5. Under the circumstances, the only choice we had was to
   _____ .
6. When he decided to _____, the others left the classroom.
7. Like everything that helps to _____ ,
   listening would also be an alternative.
8. We were allowed to _____, as long as we finished the task on time.
9. The hosts invited their guests to _____ .
10. The whole idea was to encourage everybody at the party to
    _____ .
11. As soon as we saw the cake, we were tempted to _____ .
12. It all depends on your ability to _____ .

Now try something else:

To be honest with you, _____ .
To illustrate his brand-new idea, he _____ .
To find the right answer, you will have to _____ .
To avoid misleading his readers, the teacher _____ .

Proficiency Level: High Intermediate – Bloom's Taxonomy 3

13. Provide the best answer to these questions:

a. Have you ever **conducted** an experiment in a class? What did you try to understand more deeply? _____

b. What skills are **fundamental** for success in school? In the workplace?

   _____

c. What are some things in your life that need an **upgrade**? Why do you want **to enhance** them? _____

d. Can you spread the flu? Isn't it **contagious**?

   _____

e. Are you interested in learning about international **commerce**? Why is buying and selling important in a society?

   _____

f. What **formula** do you use to learn vocabulary? Explain the steps you use.

   _____

g. Share a **notable** experience you have had in your life. Why was it special or unique? _____

h. Do you often **overlook** the details of a long presentation? Why is it easy to overlook details in general?

   _____

i. In 2007, was the iPhone a **revolutionary** product or was it just like any other phone? Explain your answer.

   _____

j. Do you want **to embark** on a trip around the world when you finish your studies?

   _____

(Peter Campisi, 2020)

Proficiency Level: Low Advanced – Bloom's Taxonomy Level 3

Lessons in Practical Knowledge

Teaching is the communication of experience

Giving advice

Teaching literature

The Road Not Taken by Robert Frost

A teaching lesson from Mark Twain

How can we adapt his idea to our ESL class?

Learning from Benjamin Franklin

Aristotle's words and collocations

Teaching is the communication of experience. Here is just one example of moral values we can provide in the classroom or online by giving advice. Let's use William Shakespeare and John Steinbeck:

And these precepts
  In thy memory
Look thou character. Give
  Thy thoughts no tongue
Nor any unproportioned
  Thought his act.
Be thou familiar, but
  By no means vulgar.
Those friends thou hast
  And their adoption tried,
Grapple them unto thy soul
  With hoops of steel,
But do not dull thy palm
  With entertainment
Of each new-hatched
  Unfledged courage. Beware
Of entrance to a quarrel,
  But being in,
Bear't that the opposed
  May beware of thee.
Give every man thy ear,
  But few thy voice,
Take each man's censure,
But reserve thy judgment.
(…)
(…)
This above all, to thine
  Own self be true
And it must follow as
  The night the day
Thou canst not then
  Be false to any man.

Shakespeare, *Hamlet*, I.3

You know, Suzy, they ain't
no way in the world to get in
trouble by keeping your mouth
shut. You look back at every
mess you ever got in and you'll
find your tongue started it. (…)
That's the second rule: lay off
opinions, because you really
ain't got any. Don't pretend to
be something you ain't and
don't make like you know
something you don't, or sooner
or later you'll fall on your arse.
(…) They ain't nobody was ever
insulted by a question. S'pose
Doc says something and you
don't know what it means. Ask
him. The nicest thing in the
world you can do for anybody is
let them help you. (…) If a guy
says something that pricks up
your interest, why, don't hide it
from him. (…) You got to
Remember you're Suzy and you
ain't nobody else but Suzy. (…)
Don't fight nobody unless
there ain't no other way. Don't
never start a fight, and if one
starts, let it get going good
before you jump in. Best way in
the whole world to defend
yourself is to keep your dukes
down.

Steinbeck*, Sweet Thursday*, p. 120

From the mystery tower of Shakespeare's Elsinore Castle, with voices sounding as if out of dungeons, enchanting and exciting, there is a long way to the southwestern Monterey in California, but John Steinbeck was able to erase the distance in time.

Another very good example of advice comes from Rudyard Kipling. Read the following fragment from one of his poems and pay attention to the verbs:

IF   – Rudyard Kipling

If you can **keep your head** when all about you
    Are losing theirs and blaming it on you;
If you can **trust yourself** when all men doubt you,
    But **make allowance** for their doubting too;
If you can **wait** and **not be tired by waiting**,
    Or being lied about, **don't deal in lies**,
Or being hated, **don't give way to hating**,
And yet **don't look too good, nor talk too wise**.

ESL advice?

Teachers should devise lesson plans keeping in mind the following five steps:

Inspire
Inspire your students to learn from their own life experiences and, at the same time, set an example and inspire others.

Empower
Empower them to emulate their own role models and, if possible, even exceed their own expectations.

Create
Create an emotional attachment to goodness.

Motivate
Motivate students to discover new things and use their power of imagination.

Cultivate
Cultivate the students' desire to learn what is right and useful in life.

Giving advice

Compare the following proverbs and add your own:

English: Don't count your chickens before they're hatched.
Albanian: Don't heat the pan if the fish is still in the sea.
Arabic: Measure how deep the water is before you dive.
Chinese: Don't write a check before depositing money first.
French/Italian: Don't sell the bearskin before you kill the bear.
German: You can't hang people before you catch them.
Hungarian: Don't clink glasses before you catch the bear.
Japanese: Don't count the badger skins before you kill the badgers.
Korean: (Someone who has a rice cake doesn't even think about giving it to you, but) you have already drunk kimchi broth.
Persian: They count chickens at the end of autumn.
Russian: You can't count chickens before autumn comes.
Serbian: First jump and then say "Hop."
Slovak: Don't say "Hop" before you jump.
Spanish: Don't eat the sausages before you kill the pig.
Swahili: Don't curse the crocodile before you have crossed the river.
Swedish: Don't sell the fur before the bear is shot.
Turkish: If you meet a bear while crossing a bridge, address him as "my uncle" until you have crossed to the other side.

Ask your students to work in groups, compare the Ask your students to work in groups, compare the proverbs, and use as many collocations and idioms as possible from the list below:

a piece of advice   a blessing in disguise   sound advice
expert advice/impartial advice   to seek advice
to accept advice − to ignore/reject advice

For example: *I wish (that) I had followed her advice.*

Proficiency Level: Intermediate – Bloom's Taxonomy Level 3

184

Teaching literature in an ESL class

The Road Not Taken
                By Robert Frost

Two roads **diverged** in a yellow wood,	*di(s)*- in two ways
And **sorry** I could not travel both	why *sorry?*
And be one traveler, long I stood	
And looked down one as far as I could	*and* three times?
To where it bent in the **undergrowth**;	shrubs
Then took the other, **as just as fair**,	the idea of equality
And having perhaps the better **claim,**	take ownership
Because it was grassy and **wanted** wear;	lacked
Though as for that the passing there	but
Had worn them really about the same.	
And both that morning equally lay	
In leaves no step **had trodden** black.	Go on foot
Oh, I kept the first for another day!	another chance?
Yet knowing **how way leads on to way**,	how things develop
I doubted if I should ever come back.	
I shall be telling this **with a sigh**	was I sad?
Somewhere **ages and ages hence**:	someday
Two roads diverged in a wood, and I ---	
I took the one less traveled by,	
And **that has made all the difference**.	Was this a good idea?

   Journeying through life, we encounter, like forks in a road, decisions that may lead to quite different destinations. We need to make a choice to find out what lies at the end of the road.

Questions for discussion:
1. Why is a road a good symbol for life?
2. Can you give an example from your own experience of how "way leads on to way?"
3. Did he choose well? How do we know?
4. Why *The Road Not Taken* and not *The Road I Took*?

A teaching lesson from Mark Twain

At the beginning of Chapter 2 in Mark Twain's masterpiece, when Tom Sawyer is asked to whitewash Aunt Polly's fence, he does his best to trick his friends to do it and pay him for the 'privilege.' The first one is Ben Rogers, his friend, who is lured by Tom, and who says:

"Does a boy get a chance to whitewash a fence every day?"

"That," writes Twain, "put the thing in a new light." When Ben asks why, Tom says: "Only an elite painter can be trusted with this careful job. It's got to be done extremely careful. I reckon there ain't one boy in 1,000, maybe 2,000, that can do it the way it's got to be done."

Soon the fence is whitewashed three times, and Tom has a pile of treasures collected from his friends.

"By the time Ben was fagged out, Tom had traded the next chance to Billy Fisher for a kite, in good repair; and when *he* played out, Johnny Miller bought in for a dead rat and a string to swing it with – and so on, and so on, hour after hour. And when the middle of the afternoon came, from being a poor poverty-stricken boy in the morning, Tom was literally rolling in wealth."

What do we learn from this episode?

"Namely, that in order to make a man or a boy covet a thing, it is only necessary to make the thing difficult to attain."

(Twain, 2007, pp. 21-22)

For further reading, please check:

Collie, J., Slater, S., & Swan, M. (1987). *Literature in the Language Classroom: A Resource Book of Ideas and Activities*. Spain: Cambridge University Press.

How can we adapt this idea to our ESL lessons?

Although we sometimes tend to over-teach and display our knowledge and expertise, there is no need to spoon-feed our students. There are many cases when instructors can entice their students to make a mental effort and **discover new ideas** or **new concepts independently**.

Discover
Let the students discover what these words have in common and then they provide their own word in an original sentence.

For example:
prefix   (before)
presume
precede
prepare
Prescribe (your word in a sentence) My doctor *prescribes* aspirin
                                    for cold.

con**sent**   (to feel)
sensation
sensible
sensitive
_____ (your word in a sentence)

companion**ship**   (position held)
owne**rship**
court**ship**
intern**ship**
_____ (your word in a sentence)

to soft**en**   (become)
to fast**en**
to length**en**
to strength**en**
_____ (your word in a sentence)

volunt**eer**   (engaged in something,
engin**eer**   associated with something)
profit**eer**
auction**eer**
_____ (your word in a sentence)

back**ward**   (in a certain direction)
for**ward**
after**ward**
way**ward**
_____ (your word in a sentence)

pres**cription**   (written)
de**scription**
ins**cription**
tran**script**
_____ (your word in a sentence)

trans**port**ation   (to carry)
air**port**
ex**port**
im**port**
_____ (your word in a sentence)

of**fer**   (to bring, or to carry)
pre**fer**ence
re**fer**ence
dif**fer**ence
_____ (your word in a sentence)

wire**less**   (without)
reck**less**
harm**less**
hope**less**
time**less**
_____ (your word in a sentence)

tang**ible**   (able to be)
cred**ible**
neglig**ible**
flex**ible**
_____ (your word in a sentence)

subway   (under)
subterranean
substitution
subconscious
_____ (your word in a sentence)

exhale   (out of)
extinguish
external
exterminate
_____ (your word in a sentence)

mistake   (wrong)
misinterpret
miscalculate
misunderstand
_____ (your word in a sentence

move**ment**   (action or act of)
retire**ment**
establish**ment**
abandon**ment**
_____ (your word in a sentence)

celebrat**ion**   (action or process of)
decis**ion**
revis**ion**
divis**ion**
_____ (your word in a sentence)

Proficiency Level: Intermediate – Bloom's Taxonomy Level 2

189

Memory as love

"My bounty is as boundless as the sea,

My love as deep, the more I give to thee,

The more I have, for both are infinite."

William Shakespeare, *Romeo and Juliet*

Memory as love

Love languages

Pillow Talk

Romeo and Juliet

Beauty and the Beast

Cinderella

La Bohème

High Horse's Courting

1. In pairs, students interview each other.

Topic: Which of the five "love languages" is most important
            to you:

Physical touch – hugs, kisses, etc.

Affirming words – "Well done!"

Acts of service – cooking, driving, helping

Quality time – playing games, listening to music together

Gifts – birthday gifts, Christmas cards, Happy Anniversary cards, etc.

Use some of the following collocations and idioms:

love affair	*to have a crush on*
love letter	*the apple of my eyes*
first love	*to love with all my heart*
fits like a glove	*my one and only*
a match made in heaven	

Proficiency Level: Intermediate – Bloom's Taxonomy Level 3

2. Pillow talk – Conversation with a loved one

When the cat's away ...
Compare the following proverbs and add your own:

English:	When the cat's away, the mice will play.
Chinese:	Cat gone, old rat comes out.
French:	When the cat is absent, the mice dance.
German:	When the cat is out of the house, the mice have a feast day.
Greek:	When the boss is not around, we know a lot of songs.
Italian:	When the cat is out, the mice are dancing.
Korean:	In the valley without a tiger, a rabbit plays the role of a king.
Portuguese:	When the master goes out, there is a holiday in the shop.
Swedish:	When the cat's away, the rats will dance on the table.

Describe **a short conversation with a loved one**.

Use as many collocations and idioms as possible from the list below:

For example: You think *it's just talk*? No, I think it's true.
Snuggle close for some *pillow talk.*

cabin fever
a heart-to-heart talk
arm in arm
very hush-hush
cat's meow
The cat is out of the bag.
cheek to cheek
close call
to come up with
to come clean

Proficiency Level: Intermediate – Bloom's Taxonomy Level 3

193

3.   The story of *Romeo and Juliet*

"The first tale of Romeo and Juliet comes from Italian author Masuccio Salemitano (1410-1475). His *Il Novellino* 'tells of Mariotto and Giannoza, a pair of lovers who come from the feuding families of Maganelli and Saraceni respectively. In this account, their love affair takes place in Siena, Italy, rather than in Verona. [...] Much like Shakespeare's version, Mariotto and Giannoza fall in love and marry secretly with the aid of an Augustine friar. Shortly thereafter, Mariotto has words with another noble citizen [...] and kills the nobleman, resulting in his fleeing the city to avoid capital punishment. Giannoza [...] is comforted only by the fact that Mariotto has family in Alexandria, Egypt and makes a good home for himself there. However, her own father – unaware of her wedding – decides it is time for her to take a husband, putting her in a terrible position. With the aid of the friar who had wed her and Mariotto, Giannoza drinks a sleeping potion to make her appear dead, so she can be smuggled out of Siena to reunite in Alexandria with her husband. Of course, this plan goes terribly awry...' "
                                                            (www.ancient-origins.net)

Several ideas for classroom activities:

1. If the students know the whole story, ask them to come up with a happy **ending.** Is that going to change the perception of the reader?

2. Encourage the students to write a dialogue between the two lovers **before** and **after** they become husband and wife. Does anything change? Why or why not?

3. Going from culture to culture, the students may be able to tell **similar love stories** they have read about or heard about. **Movies** might be another **good source** of information. A good example would be **contemporary** interpretations of old love stories.

4. If the class is ready for individual stories, the students should be asked to present their own life experiences and use some of the following collocations and idioms:

to catch somebody's eye

    first love

        love at first sight

            head over heels (in love)

                to have a crush on someone

                    over the moon

Proficiency Level: Low Advanced – Bloom's Taxonomy Level 4

4.   *Beauty and the Beast*

"A French fairy tale about a beautiful and gentle young woman who is taken to live with a man-beast in return for a good deed the Beast did for her father. Beauty is kind to the well-mannered Beast and pines for her family until the Beast allows her to visit them. Once home, Beauty delays her return until she hears that the Beast is dying without her. She returns to the Beast and brings him back to health. When she agrees to marry him, the evil spell upon him is broken, and he becomes a handsome prince. Beauty and her prince live happily ever after."

(Hirsch, Kett, & Trefil, 2002, p. 31)

Paraphrase the passage using some of the following collocations:

fairy tale

gentle young woman

in return for

pines for

delays her return

back to health

agrees to marry him

the evil spell is broken

a handsome prince

live happily ever after

Proficiency Level: Intermediate – Bloom's Taxonomy Level 3

5. *Cinderella*

"A fairy tale from the collection of Charles Perrault: Cinderella, a young girl, is forced by her stepmother and stepsisters to do heavy work and relaxes by sitting among the cinders by the fireplace. One evening, when the prince of the kingdom is holding a ball, Cinderella's fairy godmother visits her, magically dresses her for the ball, turns a pumpkin into a magnificent carriage for her, warns her not to stay past midnight, and sends her off. Cinderella captivates the prince at the ball but leaves just as midnight is striking, and in her haste she drops a slipper; as the story is usually told in English, the slipper is made of glass. She returns home with her fine clothes turned back into rags and her carriage a pumpkin again. The prince searches throughout the kingdom for the owner of the slipper. Cinderella is the only one whom it fits, and the prince marries her."

(Hirsch, Kett & Trefil, 2002, pp.31-32)

Paraphrase the passage using some of the following collocations:

to do heavy work

is holding a ball

fairy godmother

turns a pumpkin into a carriage

captivates the prince

just as midnight is striking

drops a slipper

the prince searches

throughout the kingdom

the only one

Proficiency Level: Intermediate – Bloom's Taxonomy Level 3

6. *"La Bohème* takes place in Paris and begins in a garret, which immediately confuses the audience: What's a garret? Well, it's **an awful apartment with a great view**, or as New York realtors would say, 'luxury housing.' Living there, cold and broke, on Christmas Eve, are Rodolfo, a poet, and Marcello, a painter. Why are they living in a garret, cold and broke? Perhaps you didn't hear: Rodolfo is a poet, and Marcello is a painter. Into the garret come Colline, a philosopher, and Schaunard, a musician, so you see the prospects are getting worse, but Schaunard has in fact just gotten paid for a job. He's **brought wood for the stove**, food and wine – a feast – and then **a knock at the door**. It's the landlord, and, of course, these guys don't have the rent so they get the landlord drunk and shoo him out and then decide to save their feast and **go on the town**. The audience surely hopes they will too, because the opera has been going for about 15 minutes and so far nothing has happened.

All but Rodolfo head for the café. He stayed behind to write when there was a knock at the door. It's the young woman from the next apartment. **Her candle has blown out,** and she has no match. **A likely story**, you say. Maybe, but at least it's a story. Finally, in fact, it's one of opera's beautiful love scenes. Rodolfo's hand finds hers, and it's so cold, and **she has a bad cough**, although **not so bad as she can sing**. She tells Rodolfo her name is Mimi and, well, **the two fall in love** and it's so beautiful you know they're going to be ruined. Act II is in the Christmas Eve bustle of the Latin Quarter. The four men and Mimi have taken a table outside the café when Marcello spots his ex-girlfriend Musette in the arms of a rich older man, but Marcello ignores Musette's flirtations. He breaks into a song about how charming she is. Marcello **knows this girl is trouble but finds her irresistible**. She's like a Kardashian. Musette **tricks the old man into buying dinner** for all of them and then ditches him and leaves with Marcello. What does it have to do with the plot? Nothing. In Act III, a few weeks later, Mimi comes looking for Marcello because Rodolfo **is trying to break up** with her and she doesn't know why. Mimi hides when Rodolfo enters. He tells Marcello that he wants Mimi to leave the garret because she is getting sicker and she is not going to get well. Her cough betrays her. Rodolfo **rushes to her side,** and they agree in another incredible love scene that it would be best for them to break up, but they just can't do it. In Act IV, we are back in the garret - at least you know what it is now – where Rodolfo and Marcello have broken up with Mimi and Musette and are lying to each other about how glad they are, and then Musette bursts in. Mimi is very sick and wants to see Rodolfo. They bring her up. Her highly advanced tuberculosis retreats long enough for her to join Rodolfo to sing their final duet, and she dies. **Strictly speaking**, not much

happens in *La Bohème*. Boy meets girl, boy gets girl, girl coughs, boy loses girl. **What touches us** in this opera is the beauty and purity of Mimi and Rodolfo's love. Puccini's music makes us hope for them every time **even though our hopes are always dashed**."

[NB: author's emphasis]

(http://(www.wqsr.org/story/3-minute-opera-puccini-la-boheme)

Paraphrase the story using some of the following collocations:

a great view

a knock at the door

go on the town

her candle has blown out

a likely story

a bad cough

fall in love

he finds her irresistible

tricks the old man

is trying to break up

strictly speaking

what touches us

Proficiency Level: High Intermediate – Bloom's Taxonomy Level 3

7. *High Horse's Courting* by Black Elk

"You know, in the old days, it was not so very easy to get a girl when you wanted to be married. Sometimes it was hard work for a young man and he had to stand a great deal. Say I am a young man and I have seen a young girl who looks so beautiful to me that I feel all sick when I think about her. I cannot just go and tell her about it and then get married if she is willing. I have to be a very sneaky fellow to talk to her after all, and after I have managed to talk to her, that is only the beginning.

Well, this young man I am telling you about was called High Horse, and there was a girl in the village who looked so beautiful to him that he was just sick all over from thinking about her so much and he was getting sicker all the time. The girl was very shy, and her parents thought a great deal of her because they were not young anymore and this was the only child they had. So they watched her all day long, and they fixed it so that she would be safe at night too when they were asleep. They thought so much of her that they had made a rawhide bed for her to sleep in, and after they knew that High Horse was sneaking around after her, they took rawhide thongs and tied the girl in bed at night so that nobody could steal her when they were asleep, for they were not sure but that their girl might really want to be stolen.

Well, after High Horse had been sneaking around a good while and hiding and waiting for the girl and getting sicker all the time, he finally caught her alone and made her talk to him. Then he found out that she liked him maybe a little."

Use your imagination and write a paragraph to connect the beginning to the end.

_____

_____

_____

_____

"[He] drove the whole herd right into the village and up in front of the girl's tepee. The old man was there, and High Horse called out to him and asked if he thought maybe that would be enough horses for his girl. The old man did not wave him away that time. It was not the horses that he wanted. What he wanted was a real man and good for something. So High Horse got his girl after all, and I think he deserved her."

(*The Heath Introduction to Literature*, 1996, pp. 36-39)

Proficiency Level: Intermediate – Bloom's Taxonomy Level 5

> "Memory … is an action; essentially, it is the action of telling a story."   – Pierre Janet

Stories

Stories, stories, stories everywhere

Teaching Proficiency through Reading and Storytelling

Vocabulary in stories

Is there another way of telling?

Stories need to be told

How is memory related to stories?

What is a good story?

Unfinished stories

Retell/rewrite in your own words

Stories, stories, stories everywhere ...

Whether they are read, told, or heard, stories are used in advertising, in social interactions, in history lessons, and as such in teaching language. Every time we want to press a point or to defend an opinion, we tell stories in which we play with words, we illustrate or demonstrate, or simply use context for clarification. Every time we read or hear a **story**, we open huge areas of untrodden **paths that activate our conscious minds**.

Stories – informative and entertaining

In this ever-changing society of active, avid readers, writing has become a palpable experience. If we are true to ourselves, we go instinctively for the intensive cultivation of the mind. With little time left for perusing a good source of information, let's say a book, readers are attracted to a literary form that can be easily absorbed and digested. We sometimes look for a shorter format, but simultaneously for something that is appealing, pithy, informative, and **entertaining.** In the middle of our daily routine of jokes, anecdotes, novels, novellas, movies, plays, songs, text messages, memes, we are never satisfied unless or until we can read or hear **a good story**.

Authors create new stories with their own characters through the activity of storytelling. The text of these stories does not describe any real facts, but the message and the lessons we learn will stay with us if and because they engage the audience's imagination. "The story is the product of the author's imagination and the object of an audience's imaginative response." (Salis, 2020, p. 462)

A good story is a human-made artifact created to stir the readers' imagination by using a certain linguistic approach that entails characters and words that have the ability to capture images in our minds. We might go even further and call this an act of mental imagery. Skilled storytellers may be able to translate mental visual images into wonderful narratives.

The English words *story* and *narrative* come toward us through Greek, Latin, and French from two Proto-Indo-European roots – *weid* and *gno*, seeing and knowing. Thus other words related to *story* are *wisdom, vision, wit;* related to *narrative* are *kith, recognition,* and *prognosis.* The etymological messages might be expanded thus – a story is an account of something seen, made visible in the telling. A narrative is an account of something known, especially by the narrator but partially by the audience. [...] both words are defined

202

from the point of view of the teller; the audience is considered only as an object to be "interested or amused." (Price, 1997, pp. 14-15)

In his notes on the origin and life of narrative, Price wondered whether language was originally a divine gift, an imitation of nonhuman sound, a response to pain or intense feeling, natural accompaniment to common acts of labor, or mystic correspondence between sound and sense (pp. 4-5) and went on to say that, if asked or interviewed, people usually include themselves as audience in their answer. Working with his students, the author asked them to express in their own words what they thought of a story, and here are three responses:

> A story is a re-creation of event played out by characters, real or imagined, which unites teller and audience in the recognition of some truth **newly remembered** or known in a new way. [NB: author's emphasis]
> A story is a means of creating communion between two people, a teller and a listener, for the purpose of transmitting some knowledge from the teller to the listener.
> A story is a digression from the listener's life offered by the teller as a gift, serving its purpose through their mutual diversion. (p. 16)

According to Grazer and Fishman (2015), **curiosity is the beginning of our exploration** of the power of curiosity to change our lives. The book itself is a personal account of how curiosity and what the authors call "curiosity conversations" can lead to interesting conclusions. The book is also an invitation for us, the readers, to use our curiosity if we want to lead better lives and be more accomplished as leaders, creators, or managers.

A Curious Mind is quite a treat in itself, with very attractive chapters: "There is no cure for curiosity," "Curiosity is a superhero power," "Every conversation is a curiosity conversation," "The golden age of curiosity," to name just a few. One very appealing idea in the book comes quite unexpectedly when we are led into the concept of storytelling.

> In fact, **storytelling** and **curiosity** are **natural allies**. Curiosity is what drives human beings out into the world every day, to ask questions about what's going on around them, about people and why they behave the way they do. Storytelling is the

act of bringing home the discoveries learned from curiosity. The story is a report from the front lines of curiosity.

Storytelling gives us the ability to tell everyone else what we've learned – to tell everyone the story of our adventure or about the adventures of the people we've met. Likewise, nothing sparks curiosity like good storytelling. Curiosity drives the desire to keep reading the book you can't put down. It's the desire to know how much of a movie you've just seen is true.

[NB: author's emphasis]
(Grazer & Fishman, p. 35)

In the story of the story – no pun intended – researchers are pointing out that, from Gilgamesh to present-day enthusiasts, **a narrative has been an act of communication** skillfully wrought between the teller and the audience. The telling of an oral story automatically implies that somebody will speak and somebody else will listen. This is mainly what we do when we tell children stories before bedtime. If we follow Reynolds Price's introduction, we are pleasantly surprised to read that even songs fall into the same category. The Eskimo hunter Orpingalik says it beautifully:

Songs are thoughts, sung out with the breath when people are moved by great forces and ordinary speech no longer suffices. Man is moved just like the ice-flow sailing here and there out in the current. His thoughts are driven by a flowing force when he feels joy, when he feels fear, when he feels sorrow. Thoughts can wash over him like a flood, making his breath come in gasps and his heart throb. Something like an abatement in the weather will keep him thawed up. And then it will happen that we, who always think we are small, will feel still smaller. And we will fear to use words. But it will happen that the words we need will come of themselves. When the words we want to use shoot up of themselves – we get a new song.   (Bowra, 1962, p. 36)

(Quoted in Price, 1997, p. 18)

"Memories appear in flashes of light, in short scenes, in reflections that can make us laugh or bring us to tears. They might come in on a sneaker wave of grief, or be buoyed up from our past by a certain fragrance in the air, or a sound from afar. "   – Jacqueline Winspear

---

Teaching proficiency through reading and storytelling

Teaching Proficiency through Reading and Storytelling (TPRS) started from the idea that reading has a profound positive effect on language development (Krashen, 1998, 2004; Rodrigo, 2009), that context is a powerful tool for enhancing second language acquisition (Fuller, 2002; Fleishman & Roy, 2005; Krashen, 2002), and that it is much more enjoyable to acquire a language than to learn a language (Krashen & Terrel, 1983).

> TPRS instruction is laden with dozens of strategies that provide an abundance repetition that is highly engaging and comprehensible, but that is not obviously predictable and comprehensible. This allows the teacher to remain in the target language 95-98 percent of the time. The goal is to scaffold language so that it remains completely comprehensible and accessible to students, resulting in successful and relatively rapid acquisition of the language." (Gaab, "Multistory Construction," *Language Magazine*)

To put matters in a more practical context, teachers will resort to no more than 3 Target Language Structures (TLS) for every 60 to 90 minutes of instruction. A TLS can be any word, collocation, phrase, or complete sentence naturally found in oral and written communication, and its structure depends on the age and level of the language learner. In her *Language Magazine* article, Carol Gaab makes the following recommendations regarding new vocabulary and meaning:

- Write the structure in the target language (TL). […]
- Post an illustration or photo that depicts the meaning of the structure.
- Verbally tell the students what the structure means and, when appropriate, explain appropriate contexts or setting for use.
- Use props or realia to convey meaning. Use skits and reenactments to demonstrate meaning.
- Attach a specific gesture (TPR) to make a kinesthetic and a visual connection to the meaning. Use video, technology, and anything else that will help students create their own mental image of the meaning of the structure.

A conversation might be a very useful and practical application in which the teacher and the students go over the structures together. They make sure the communication is focused on the matter at hand and the level of difficulty depends on the proficiency level of the language learners, using *Yes/No, either-or,* and interrogative questions. These are what linguists call 'circling questions.'

> Circling is a scaffolding technique that involves asking systematic questions that progress from low-level to higher-level questions. When done artfully and efficiently, a teacher can achieve 20+ camouflaged repetitions of a TLS by circling all parts of the sentence.

Student input is absolutely necessary to verify their comprehension before a narrative, or a story is read with the whole class.

> The reading may be a concentrated reading specifically based on the curriculum or lesson, a news article, a poem, song lyrics, a fairy tale, story, or any other level-appropriate narrative that focuses on the TLS. The purpose is to provide students with more repetition and exposure to the TLS in another context and format.

(Adapted from:
https://www.languagemagazine.com/multistory-construction/)

For further reading, please check:

Carroll, S. D., & Dailey, S. (1994). *Tales as Tools: The Power of Story in the Classroom.* United States: National Storytelling Press.

Stories for teachers (and students)

Where did the exclamation point (!) come from?

"Turns out, no one really knows the history of the punctuation mark. The current running theory is that it comes from Latin. In Latin, the exclamation of joy was *io,* where the *I* was written above the *o*. And, since all their letters were written as capitals, an *I* with an *o* below it looks a lot like an exclamation point." (https://www.smithsonianmag.com/smart-news/the-history-of-the-exclamation-point-16445416/)

Where did the question mark (?) come from?

"The story accepted by most involved Alcuin of York, an English scholar and poet born in 735, who was invited to join the court of Charlemagne in 781. Once there, Alcuin became one of Charlemagne's chief advisors, and wrote a great number of books, including some works on grammar. In the early Middle Ages, punctuation was limited to a system of dots at different levels. Recognizing the limitations of this system, Alcuin created the *punctus interrogativus* or 'point of interrogation.'"

(https://www.lexico.com/explore/origin-of-question-mark)

"**Both the colon (:) and semicolon (;)** were featured in Gregorian chants with the former as the *punctus elevatas* ('elevated point' in Latin) and the latter as the *punctus versus* (Latin for a 'long pause'). The first usage of the colon dates back to the 1600s to denote a pause time greater than a comma but less than a full stop. The semicolon has a much earlier history with its first written use in 1494. As noted by Lynn Truss in her 2004 book *Eats, Shoots, and Leaves*, a printer by the name of Aldus Manutius the Elder used the semicolon to separate words. Its purpose was to allow the writer to produce new ideas and topics between phrases without producing a new sentence. Originally, the colon was simply an upside down semicolon but the single open inverted comma-like top eroded down to a single point." (Timms, 2016)

(https://unravellingmag.com/articles/history-punctuation-english/)

Vocabulary in stories (1)

Let your students **read** the following passage and try to understand the vocabulary words **without using a dictionary**. They should look very carefully at the context, use their **imagination**, and **decipher their meaning**:

"It was a bright, cold day, the ground covered with a sleet that had frozen so that it seemed as if all the bare trees, the bushes, the cut brush and all the grass and the bare ground had been varnished with ice. I took the young Irish setter for a walk up the road and along a frozen creek, but it was difficult to stand or walk on the glassy surface and the red dog slipped and slithered and I fell twice, hard, once dropping my gun and having it slide away over the ice.

We flushed a covey of quail under a high clay bank with overhanging brush and I killed two as they went out of sight over the top of the bank. Some of the covey lit in trees, but most of them scattered into brush piles and it was necessary to jump on the ice-coated mounds of brush several times before they would flush. Coming out while you were poised unsteadily on the icy, springy brush they made difficult shooting and I killed two, missed five, and started back pleased to have found a covey close to the house and happy there were so many left to find on another day." (Hemingway, 1964, p. 35)

sleet had frozen – leads to – **ground varnished with ice**
the young Irish setter – is explained later – **the red dog**
it was difficult to walk – leads to – **slipped, slithered, slide away**
a covey of quail – must be birds – **because they lit in the trees**
were poised unsteadily – because – **the springy brush was icy**

Further details and explanations:
Slip – You *slip* on a patch of ice/ you lose balance.
Slither – A snake *slithers*.
Slide – You can *slide* down the hill or out of bed.
A covey of quail is like a group or *a flock of birds*.
To scatter – Noise can *scatter* the birds.
Bare trees have no leaves. What can *bare ground* mean?
If you are *poised*, you can stand and keep your balance.
Steadily – A full cup must be carried *steadily*.
If you *flush* birds, they leave their hiding place.

Proficiency Level: High Intermediate – Bloom's Taxonomy Level 3

Vocabulary in stories (2)

"Even at advanced proficiency levels, students often tend to translate every word and heavily rely on dictionaries when reading. It's extremely important to encourage students to use content clues and English-English dictionaries (Oxford, Mariam Webster, etc.) instead. Especially at advanced levels, students should feel confident enough to rely on their previously acquired vocabulary and knowledge as well as to be able to infer from the text.

While teaching a short story by Kate Chopin, *The Kiss*, I put some vocabulary on the board and have students find and underline it in the text. Then, I ask students to identify the meaning of the words by looking at the content as well as morphological and grammatical clues.

> *It was still quite light out of doors, but inside with the curtains drawn and the smoldering fire sending out a dim, uncertain glow, the room was full of shadows. Brantain sat in one of these shadows; it had **overtaken** him and he didn't mind.*
> (Chopin, 2015, p. 124)

Overtake (v) – catch up/ surpass
Overreact (v)
Overwhelm (v)

> *Brantain was enormously rich, and she [Nathalie] liked and required the entourage which wealth could give her.*

Enormously rich (adv + adj) – very wealthy (to use adv + adj combination to emphasize the importance of something)
Extremely talented
Vastly popular

> *The explanation is simple enough and ought to satisfy you that the **misadventure** was **unavoidable**.*

Misadventure (n) – wrong/bad (prefix *mis*- has negative connotation)

Misbehavior
Misunderstanding

Unavoidable (adj) – not/cannot be avoided (prefix *un-* has negative connotation)

Unattainable
Unbelievable

Students should also be encouraged to make up their own sentences with the new vocabulary as well as come up with synonyms following the morphological and grammatical patterns."

(Elina Yasinov, 2020)

Proficiency Level: Intermediate – Bloom's Taxonomy Level 3

Is there another way of telling?

1.   *"By indirections find directions out,*

says Polonius in Act I of *Hamlet* when he gives his son a lot of advice. The use of indirection to seek the truth – as opposed to direct action – was used by the principal characters in the play to achieve their own goals.

2.   *Tell all the truth but tell it slant*
     Success in circuit lies,

says Emily Dickinson in one of her poems, meaning 'let's try to see things from a different perspective, a fresh or refreshing one.'"

(www.online.hillsdale.edu)

If you found yourself doing **one activity** but, in fact**, teaching something else,** you definitely did something quite similar. For example: When **reading** a short passage, students can be taught **pronunciation, vocabulary, word order**, etc. Or, when doing a **dictation**, we can play with **spelling, punctuation**, but also with **intonation, word stress,** or **sentence stress**.

As for **vocabulary**, what if we present an expression like *the lion's share* and, instead of explaining what it means, we just **tell a story**? In this case, one of Aesop's *Fables* might provide a good example of *the lion's share*:

> The lion and the wild ass were hunting, the lion using his strength and the ass his swiftness of foot. When they caught a number of animals, the lion divided them into three lots. "I will take the first one," he said, "because as king I hold the highest rank, and the second one as your equal partner. As for the third one, it will bring you into serious trouble unless you choose to make yourself scarce."
>
> (Adapted from www.//fablesaesop.com)

What better way to teach the moral lesson – *might makes right* – and at the same time use *the lion's share* in a short story!

Within the fable, we might also try to discuss collocations like

> *swiftness of foot*
> *highest rank*
> *equal partner*
> *serious trouble*
> *make yourself scarce.*

Aesop (620 BC – 564 BC) was probably a slave who was famous for his wit and his eloquence. His fables illustrate human virtues and failings in short stories called fables. They crossed centuries and came to us via other famous writers like Jean de La Fontaine (1621 -1605). These very short tales will stay with us because of their wisdom transmitted mostly via oral culture and because they address the adult audience and the younger ones simultaneously. Children might understand one thing, and adults might get a completely different message. This is what happens when you read the same book at different ages. **What makes fables so unique?** Should we say they present the world and its reality in its many facets and bring into action the whole nature, including animals, trees, insects, and humans?

The famous writer Flannery O'Connor (1925 – 1964) once said that **good stories do not need to be paraphrased** because they contain a "primary delight" and as such, we get a powerful message that defies analysis.

This **primary delight** should leave the reader with several questions that they might answer if the writer remembers to provide a takeaway. We often begin writing for ourselves. "We want to see what insights lurk in our hearts and minds, what might be revealed when we prod a memory on the page." (Porter, 2020)

In its June 2020 issue, *The Writer* magazine published an essay entitled *A Truthteller's Toolkit* written by Nicki Porter, Senior Editor. The idea behind writing this essay was the editor's opinion that a good piece of writing should also **incorporate the audience in the narrative.** Here are some ideas the writer can offer a reader in exchange for their time and attention:

1. Humor, which serves as a brief respite from the stresses of our everyday lives
2. A triumph over hardship, in which we learn from the writer's struggles and ultimate success
3. Empathy toward a subject or group of subjects, which encourages us to foster our own empathy in return
4. A heartfelt display of emotion, which lets us access and evoke feelings we might have buried
5. A new way of seeing or expressing a concept, which allows us to view the subject in a fresh light. (p. 37)
(www.writermag.com)

Imagination and Literature

Works of literature (poetry, drama, fiction, and nonfiction) create an imaginary world by **re-creating reality** to attract and enchant the reading population, including students. In some cases, it may be necessary to help students understand point of view, character, setting, plot, conflict, climax, turning point, theme, imagery, symbols, etc. If done properly, the literary analysis may provide students with richer opportunities for interpretation. When talking about the "interpretive richness," Horowitz (2011) resorts to two quotations to support his claim: Fiction "refashions reality in the image of new ideas and new ideals" (Widdowson, 1984b, p. 169), creating a world with "internally coherent meaning." (Gajdusek, 1988, p. 230).

For further information, please check:

Page, M. R. (2016). *The Literary Imagination from Erasmus, Darwin to H.G. Wells: Science, Evolution, and Ecology.* United Kingdom: Taylor & Francis.

How can we connect literature and creative classes with imagination?

There are many ESL students who turned into teachers. Ani Gjika was born in Albania. After learning Italian mostly from TV shows, she majored in Russian in high school. She then managed to get private lessons in English. Her exposure to languages helped her enormously when, at the age of 18, she moved to the United States, where she was forced to study in a language other than her mother tongue.

> Like most people who've had to switch to speaking another language as an adult, I discovered in my early 20s that the language I had begun to speak, think, and write was, slowly but surely, stirring my sense of identity.
>
> I took a semester of ESL before entering college. Like many second-language learners, I was timid to express myself for fear of making mistakes, or of not sounding like a native speaker. I often felt embarrassed, and that feeling followed me for a while, until I became an English major my sophomore year. Taking literature and creative writing classes showed me what it meant to have a voice and express it through words.
>
> (Gjika, 2016)

As an ESL instructor at Massachusetts International Academy, based on the success of a creative writing club she had started previously, Ani Gjika decided to teach an elective class on literary translation. Among her international students were particularly those from China, who had passed the TOEFL (Test of English as a Foreign Language), but whose college professors pointed to their "lack of clarity, evidence of critical thinking, and descriptive language."

In time, she realized that the language barriers she had to overcome as a student led her to "the discovery of the beauty of the language and how malleable and accessible it is when looked at from the inside out, qualities that the process of translation truly exposes."

According to Ani Gjika, one of her best accomplishments was that her students became aware that literal or word-for-word translation should be replaced by a deeper look at the choice of words, which meant understanding the difference between denotation and connotation.
(https://www.publicbooks.org/breaking-esl-students-imagination/)

For further reading, please check:

The Role of Literature in the Language Classroom: Creative Writing and Language Competence in Advanced Classes. (1997). Hungary: ELTE CETT.

Simon, S., (2006). *Teaching Literature in ELT/TESOL Classes.* Delhi: Sarup & Sons.

> "I believe that education must be conceived as a continuing reconstruction of experience; that the process and the goal of education are one and the same thing."   – John Dewey

Stories need to be told

This is how Beth Comstock's shared her life experience and knowledge about making changes in our life that will unlock the unused every person's potential. The title of her book is self-explanatory: *Imagine It Forward: Courage, Creativity, and the Power of Change*):

> In the Middle Ages, wandering troubadours brought news of wars, royal marriages, and religious pronouncements. In Ancient Greece, troupes of actors did the same thing. In the modern world, professional media organizations reported the big stories, first in print and then over the airwaves. Today, digital technology has opened up the field to just about anybody. [...] I believe that everyone [...] has the ability to tell the merits of their own story. Moreover, they have an obligation to do so. If you don't tell your story to the people who are interested, somebody else is bound to do it for you.

Here are tips from Alexander Jutkowits, cofounder of Group SJR, one of the agencies that pioneered brand journalism:

- Digital storytelling is in some senses a race. Speed matters.
- Serialize and atomize. In an age of ephemeral content and short attention spans, the ability to serialize a story and tell it in small pieces over time determines its staying power.
- It's essential to tell stories that can live anywhere and respect the rules and quirks of a particular platform (i.e., Twitter, Facebook, LinkedIn).

(Comstock, 2018, pp. 261-262)

> "I have always imagined Paradise as a kind of library." — Jorge Luis Borges, *Dreamtigers*

"Stories and books have had many forms over the centuries. Humans have written down words on paper, but also on wood, clay, bone, bark, ivory, linen, stone, and the skin of every creature under the sun. Logic dictates that the unwritten words would be the same. But the Unwritten Wing is filled, shelf after shelf, with sturdy leather-bound books. Proper, civilized books. Even the Librarian's Log refers to current collection materials – books, not scrolls. I suppose the log must have some translation magic worked into it, but the Library itself? It puzzled me until I came back to the simple truth: stories want to be told."

(Librarian Claire Hadley, 1990, quoted in Hackwith, 2019, p. 91)

We like to hear and to tell stories. From early childhood, we are enthralled and fascinated by stories our teachers, parents, or grandparents read to us. Here's one from Tara Westover:

> There's a story my father used to tell about the peak. She was a grand old thing, a cathedral of a mountain. The range had other mountains, taller, more imposing, but Buck's Peak was the most finely crafted. Its base spanned a mile, its dark form swelling out of the earth and rising into a flawless spire. From a distance, you could see the impression of a woman's body on the mountain face: her legs formed of huge ravines, her hair a spray of pine fanning over the northern ridge. Her stance was commanding, one leg thrust forward in a powerful movement, more stride than step. My father called her the Indian Princess. She emerged each year when the snows began to melt, facing south, watching the buffalo return to the valley. Dad said the nomadic Indians had watched for her appearance as a sign of spring, a signal the mountain was thawing, winter was over, and it was time to come home.

(Westover, 2018, pp. xv-xvi)

How is memory related to stories?

We all like stories, and we rarely shy away from a conversation that includes a captivating story. Researches tell us that we enjoy hearing stories from early childhood because we use our **imagination** to **visualize** them and **keep** them in our latent **memory** for many years thereafter. Whether stories teach us a life lesson or whether they entertain us, the information they convey strongly affects **our emotions** and **our brain**.

Some researchers argue that there is a **connection between memory and stories** and that there is a link that is tightly woven. One such example would be a quick perusal of Shawn Callahan's blog posted on January 8, 2015, and filed in *Business Storytelling*. The author begins his writing with a historical anecdote that some people deem factual, but stories can be deceiving.

> "Back in the 1870s, the White House wasn't the most comfortable place to relax as the President," Paul Costello begins. "Ulysses S. Grant would often unwind with a whiskey and cigar in the lobby of the [Willard] hotel. Word got around that the President could be found in the hotel foyer so people would arrive seeking favors or just getting the ear of the President. After a time, people became known as lobbyists." Woe, I thought, what a great way for that word to come about. Then Paul said, "but that's just a myth. The term was coined from the gathering of Members and peers in the lobbies of the UK House of Parliament."

(https://www.anecdote.com/2015/01/link-between-memory-and-stories)

After a short interlude in history – when German psychologist Hermann Ebbinghaus performed experiments on himself in 1879 and discovered that we also forget fairly quickly – Callahan went on to point out that people remember things that are **interesting** or **extraordinary**. To prove his point, he admitted to finding very little information to verify the idea that information contained in stories is more memorable than facts alone. However, he says what he found is still quite impressive:

> In 1969 two Stanford professors, Gordon Bower and Michael Clark, set out to test the memorability of words embedded in stories versus a random list of words. Students were asked to memorize and recall 10 sets of unrelated words.

The control group remembered the words in any order they wanted. For the story condition the students constructed a story that contained all the words, one story per set. When asked to recall the words the students that constructed stories were able to remember six to seven times as many words compared to the random set.
(https://www.anecdote.com/2015/01/link-between-memory-and-stories)

In other words, the **context** of a passage or a story – if unique or appealing to the audience – will function as essentially methodological in uncovering the fundamental way of presenting vocabulary and making it viable in real situations.

On the one hand, we are talking about complete sentences. However, on the other hand, short paragraphs or longer passages may function as better vehicles for communicating new words, set phrases, idioms, collocations, etc.

For further reading, please check:

de Caro, F. (2013). *Stories of Our Lives: Memory, History, Narrative.* United States: Utah State University Press.

Schank, R. C. (1995). *Tell Me a Story: Narrative and Intelligence.* United States: Northwestern University Press.

What is a good story?

A good story, because of its simplicity, will stay with us for a very long time. We always go back to the stories we heard when we were young or younger, and we usually expect a nice story when we read a book or watch a movie. Stories are essentially the basic elements of literature and can be used as a joke, as a lesson in humanity, or to illustrate a point during a debate. You don't need to be an orator to tell your audience a nice story. What you need is something that people will understand, follow, and remember for a long time. Most narratives or stories will be adapted or replicated, and some of them will create a trend. Take, for example, the Aesop stories or the love stories of Romeo and Juliet, Eloise and Abelard, to name just a few. What makes them so interesting is the fact that you will find more or less the same story in various cultures, across centuries, and with the same life lessons to be told.

A good example of a story could be how we got the word SINCERE. Its etymology is a story in itself: Long before people used money as a medium of exchange, they gave each other gifts. The legend says that small objects of art, like small stones depicting gods, animals, or birds, were offered as gifts. When such gifts were handed down from generation to generation, because they were broken or had small cracks, the gift givers used to patch up the irregularities with wax (*cera* in Latin). When the present was given, the receivers wanted to make sure that the art object was real or new, so they asked: *sine cera*? In other words, "without wax?" And this is how we got the word SINCERE. In less than ten lines, the reader will remember the etymology or the history of the word.

If you prefer a shorter story, you can try the word *window*. Centuries ago, there were no windows, but most houses had a small opening to let the air in. The people called such an opening *the wind eye*, which in time became *window*.

ESL students may want to share their favorite stories from their culture, family, and childhood.

You can take, for example, the following comparison:

There is no unique name for the @ universal symbol in today's Internet, but it has been associated with the image of animals and in many languages has funny nicknames:

Apestaart – in Dutch, "monkey tail"
dalphaengi – in Korean, "snail"
grisehale – in Norwegian, "pigtail tail"
kissanhnta – in Finnish, "cat's tail"
Klammeraffe – in German, "hanging monkey"
kukac – in Hungarian, "worm"
papaki – in Greek, "little duck"
snabel – in Danish, "elephant horn"
sobachka – in Russian, "puppy"

In Israel the same symbol is often referred to as "strudel," while in Italy, like in Korea, they call it the "snail."

For further reading, please check:

Zafarris, J. (2020). *Once Upon a Word: A Word-origin Dictionary for Kids: Building Vocabulary Through Etymology, Definitions & Stories.* United States: ROCKRIDGE Press.

Unfinished stories (1)

Little is known about Amelia Mary Earhart, except that she was born on July 24th, 1897, and that she was an American aviation pioneer and author. History tells us that she was also the first female aviator to fly solo across the Atlantic Ocean.

We also know that she disappeared on July 2nd, 1937, during a flight over the Central Pacific Ocean near Howland Island. We are left with speculations about her dangerous last flight in her *Lockheed Electra.* Over time, people came out with nothing that could be considered a reasonable explanation of what happened.

On the one hand, we are curious to know what could have happened, but we can only go by facts, and unfortunately, there aren't any. On the other hand, we can **use our imagination** to figure out if she somehow managed to survive and – why not? – even started a new life somewhere in the South Pacific.

Students can be assigned the following task:

Use some of the following collocations and provide an oral and/or written **imaginary account** of her survival.

slowly regained her self-assurance

a test in the practice of patience

to feel at ease in a new environment

went on exploratory walks

the freshness of the landscape delighted her

in harmony with nature

Proficiency Level: Advanced – Bloom's Taxonomy Level 6

For further reading, please check:

Parlin, J. (1991). *Amelia Earhart: Pioneer of the Sky.* United States: Dell Publishing Company.

Unfinished stories (2)

Roanoke İsland was first explored by Captains Philip Amadas and Arthur Barlowe, sent by Sir Walter Raleigh. It is an island off the coast of North Carolina between the Outer Banks and the mainland. There were several unsuccessful expeditions organized by the English in 1585 and 1587, to name a few.

The name Roanoke is thought to have the meaning of "northern people," probably of Algonquin Indian origin. When referring to this place, historians also call it "the place where shell beads are found."

The first settlers inhabited the island between 1587 and 1590, but then disappeared. They only left two words: *Croatoan* and *Cro* etched in a fort's gatepost and a tree, respectively. In 1590, when John White, the colony leader, returned from England, where he had gone for supplies, the place was deserted.

Nobody really knows what happened to the settlers.

Students can be assigned the following task:

Use your imagination and come up with a **possible explanation of what happened to the colony after 1590.** You may want to use as many modal verbs as possible, such as:

would have joined the neighboring Indians...

could have travelled to ....

might have returned ...

may have sailed to ....

Proficiency Level: Advanced – Bloom's Taxonomy Level 6

For further reading, please check:

Harris, N. (2013). *Hidden History of Roanoke: Star City Stories.* United States: History Press.

Unfinished stories (3)

The Maya civilization was one of the dominant societies of what we now know as the Yucatan Peninsula, Guatemala, Belize, the western part of Honduras and El Salvador, plus certain Mexican territories in the states of Tabasco and Chiapas. Historians call this area Mesoamerica.

The earliest Mayan settlements go back to around 1800 B.C. and were mainly agricultural, famous for their crops of corn, beans, and squash. During the first stages of this culture, the Mayans are also known to have built pyramids and similar stone monuments.

Around the year 250 A.D., the Maya civilization reached its peak in cities like Tikal, Copan, Palenque, etc., surrounded by advanced farming communities, where the local population left traces of irrigation and terracing.

Extremely religious, with kings who claimed to be gods, the Mayans worshiped the sun, moon, rain, and corn. Their beliefs can still be found as inscriptions and reliefs carved in stone. Besides mathematics and astronomy, the Mayans are credited with the use of the zero and quite elaborate calendars. They left a rich legacy of codices, written on paper made from tree bark.

Sometime between the late eighth through the end of the ninth century, something happened, and slowly but surely, the cities were abandoned. Whether it was drought or internal violence caused by famine, overpopulation, or other natural causes when the Spaniards arrived, most Mayans lived in villages, but their great cities were already buried under the green rainforest.

(Adapted from www.history.com)

What do you think happened? Use your imagination and find possible explanations.

Proficiency Level: Advanced – Bloom's Taxonomy Level 6

History stories: The Lewis and Clark expedition

In 1803, when the United States acquired the western portion of the country, Thomas Jefferson asked Congress to finance an expedition to survey the lands of the so-called Louisiana Purchase. Very little was known about the vast expanse of land that cost $15 million dollars and covered approximately 827,000 square miles. **The Lewis and Clark Expedition** began in 1804 after President Thomas Jefferson commissioned Meriwether Lewis to explore the territory west of the Mississippi River. Lewis chose William Clark as his companion for the assigned mission.

The whole trip lasted a little bit over two years. It turned to be quite challenging, with unforgiving weather, clashes along the way with Native Americans, and injuries that so many times delayed or impeded the expedition's progress. However, Lewis had prepared for the journey and used his encyclopedic knowledge about medicine, botany, astronomy, and zoology to deal with already existing maps and journals of previous explorers.

In preparation for the journey, Lewis also collected gifts to present the Native Americans along the way: beads, tobacco, knives, mirrors, bright-colored cloth, ivory combs, and similar items that he thought would make himself and Clark welcome.

All in all, the expedition was a success. It was deemed as such when Lewis and Clark shared their experience with President Jefferson in 1806.   (Adapted from www.history.com)

Suggested tasks for our students:

Write a dialogue between Lewis and Clark before the journey.

Ask five questions the Natives might have asked the explorers.

Describe a monument that might have been erected to celebrate the expedition.

Proficiency Level: Advanced – Bloom's Taxonomy Level 6

A story from the *Book of Beasts*

"Aquila the Eagle is called so from the acuteness (*acumine*) of his eyes, for he is said to have such wonderful eyesight that, when he is poised above the seas on a motionless plume – not even visible to the human gaze – yet from such a height he can see the little fishes swimming, and, coming down like a thunderbolt, he can carry off his captured prey to the shore, on the wing.

And it is true fact that when the eagle grows old and his wings become heavy and his eyes become darkened with a mist, then he goes in search of a fountain, and, over against it, he flies up to the height of heaven, even unto the circle of the sun; and there he singes his wings and at the same time evaporates the fog of his eyes, in a ray of the sun. Then at length, taking a header down into the fountain, he dips himself in it, and instantly he is renewed with a great vigor of plumage and splendor of vision."

(The Book of Beasts, 1984, p. 105)

Ask questions for the following collocations in the text:

For example:

wonderful eyesight   *What is the eagle said to have?*

poised above the seas	_____
like a thunderbolt	_____
in search of	_____
the fog of his eyes	_____
in a ray of the sun	_____
at length	_____
splendor of vision	_____

Extra bonus: Why does the passage end with *vision*?

Proficiency Level: Intermediate – Bloom's Taxonomy Level 4

Another history lesson for the classroom

After the Magna Carta was sealed in 1215, King Edward I convened what is now called the first representative parliament. It was November 13th, 1295, and the parliament (etymologically coming from the French word *parler*, meaning "a talk") was composed of those traditionally called on to advise the king: the nobility, the church, and the courts. They were summoned by the king, the representatives of shires and cities and boroughs, or communes ("the commons") at conferences that in time came to be known as *Parliament*.

This is what King Edward I mentioned in his summons:

> *Inasmuch as a most righteous law of the emperors ordains that what touches all should be approved by all, so it evidently appears that common dangers should be met by remedies agreed upon in common.* (www.britannica.com)

In a nutshell, this historical work teaches us a **lesson that we can share with our students:**

"*… what touches all should be approved by all…*"

What do these words mean to us today? Are we to understand that the teacher-student relationship is one of reciprocal respect and understanding?

what	*a specific thing or idea*
touches	*to affect, to relate to*
all	*everybody, each and every one*
should	*a polite form of advice*
be approved	*to be acknowledged, to be accepted*
by	*identifies who performs an action*
all	*everybody in a group*

Students should be asked to paraphrase the whole passage in their own words.

Proficiency Level: Intermediate – Bloom's Taxonomy Level 2

The Story of *The Little Mermaid*

"Outside the palace was a large garden with flame-red and sea-blue trees. The fruit all shone like gold, and the flowers looked like glowing fire among the moving stems and leaves. The ground itself was of the finest sand, but blue as a sulfur flame. A strange blue-violet light lay over everything; you might have thought that, instead of being far down under the sea, you were high up in the air with nothing over and under you but sky.

On days of perfect calm, you could see the sun; it looked like a crimson flower, with rays of light streaming out of its center."

(Andersen, 2014, p. 4)

Check the collocations using color in the story:

flame-red
sea-blue
shone like gold
flowers looked like glowing fire
blue as a sulfur flame
blue-violet light
[the] sun ... looked like a crimson flower

Students should be asked to share the meaning of color in their culture: What do these colors mean to you?

red
blue
violet
crimson

Proficiency Level: Low Intermediate – Bloom's Taxonomy Level 2

For further reading, please check:

St. Clair, K. (2017). *The Secret Lives of Color*. United Kingdom: Penguin Books.

Writing original stories

With a little bit of help and a lot of encouragement, students may be able to construct **original stories**. Short paragraphs might be a good start. If students like the activity, they could develop these **short writings** into **diaries**.

Suggested assignment:

Describe a vacation day you will never forget.

Use as many of the following verb collocations:

go on vacation

rent a hotel room

go shopping/hiking/jogging/swimming, etc.

have a barbecue

take a guided tour

spend hours in the sun

play on the swings/slides

set up a tent

start a fire

buy souvenirs

Proficiency Level: Advanced – Bloom's Taxonomy Level 6

For further reading, please check:

Fedler, J. (2017). *Your Story: How to Write It So Others Will Want to Read It*. United States: Hay House, Incorporated.

Retell/rewrite

To reinforce the subtleties of each vocabulary word with its possible connotations, what if we go one step further and challenge our students to **reconstruct the stories in their own words**?

Rewrite/retell in your own words

1. *The Emperor's New Clothes*

This is "a story by Hans Christian Andersen. An emperor hires two tailors who promise to make him a set of remarkable new clothes that will be invisible to anyone who is either incompetent or stupid. When the emperor goes to see his new clothes, he sees nothing at all – for the tailors are swindlers and there aren't any clothes. Afraid of being judged incompetent or stupid, the emperor pretends to be delighted with the new clothes and 'wears' them in a grand parade throughout the town. Everyone else also pretends to see them, until a child yells out, 'He hasn't got any clothes on!'"

(Hirsch, Kett & Trefil , 2002, p. 33)

Rewrite/retell the story in your own words and use some of the following collocations:

hires two tailors

promise to make new clothes

invisible to anyone

goes to see his new clothes

nothing at all

afraid of

pretends to be

wears them

grand parade

throughout the town

a child yells out

Proficiency Level: Low Advanced – Bloom's Taxonomy Level 3

2. *Pan*

Pan – "the Greek God of flocks, forests, meadows, and shepherds. He had the horns and feet of a goat. Pan frolicked about the landscape, playing delightful tunes. Pan's musical instrument was a set of reed pipes, the *pipes of Pan*. According to legend, Pan was the source of scary noises in the wilderness at night. Fright of these noises was called *panic*."
(Hirsch, Kett & Trefil, 2002, p. 40)

Rewrite/retell the story in your own words and use some of the following collocations:

God of flocks, forests, meadows, and shepherds

horns and feet of a goat

frolicked about the landscape

delightful tunes

a set of reed pipes

according to legend

source of scary noises

wilderness at night

fright was called panic

Proficiency Level: Intermediate – Bloom's Taxonomy Level 3

3. *The Story of Stone Soup*

One day a traveler came into a village. He was **tired from his long journey** and very, very hungry. He asked several villagers if they could **spare some food**, but the answer was always the same. It had been a very hard winter, and they barely had enough food for themselves. The traveler decided that he must do something in order to eat. He **gathered up wood** for a fire and **set it to blaze** in the village square. From his sack, he pulled a large kettle and put it on the fire. He filled it with water. By this time, many of the villagers had come to watch. "What are you doing?" they asked. "Why, I am making Stone Soup," he replied, pulling two large stones from his sack and placing them into the water in the kettle.

After a while, he **stirred his soup** and tasted it. "Very good," he said, "but it really **could use some potatoes**." One of the villagers ran to get him some potatoes. Again he stirred and tasted. "Very good," he said, "but it **could use some vegetables**." The villagers quickly ran to get some of their vegetables. And so it continued until the kettle was **filled to the brim** with everything the villagers could find to place in the kettle. And when the soup was all finished, the traveler **dished it out** to all in the village. And **they all ate their fill.** "This was wonderful," the villagers agreed. And to think it all started from two stones and a kettle of water!

Rewrite/Retell the story by using some of the following collocations:

tired from his long journey	*spare some food*
gathered up wood	*set it to blaze*
stirred his soup	*could use some potatoes*
could use some vegetables	*filled to the brim*
dished it out	*ate their fill*

Proficiency Level: Low Intermediate – Bloom's Taxonomy Level 3

4. *Description of Greece*

"In his second-century *Description of Greece*, the historian Pausanias tells us that a certain Trophonios – perhaps a hero, perhaps a god, but **in any event** a power (the name means 'Nourisher of the Mind') – had an oracle at Labadie. Any man wanting to inquire about the future would descend into Trophonios's cave having first purified himself **for several days**, bathing only in the river Herkyna and making sacrifices. [...] **On the night of** his descent, the petitioner **would be taken** to the river by two young boys who would **wash and anoint him with oil**. Priests would then lead him to **two fountains standing near each other**. From these he **would drink** the Water of Lethe **so as to forget** his past and the Water of Mnemosyne **so as to recall** all he saw during his descent. Dressed in linen, he would then **climb a ladder** down into the chasm, **lie on his back**, thrust his legs feet first into a hole, **the rest of his body** being swiftly drawn in like that of a man **pulled under by the current of a fast-flowing river.**

Later, having learned of the future, he would be swept upward again, his feet darting first out of the same opening. The priests would set him on the Chair of Memory, where, **paralyzed with fear** and **unaware of himself** and his surroundings, he would speak what he had seen and heard. Then he would be given over to his relatives, who would care for him until he recovered **the ability to laugh**." [NB: Author's emphasis] (Hyde, 2019, p. 33)

Rewrite/Retell the whole story in your own words by using some of the following:

in any event – for several days – anoint with oil

so as to forget – so as to recall

climb a ladder

lie on his back – the rest of his body

unaware of himself – the ability to laugh

Proficiency Level: Intermediate – Bloom's Taxonomy Level 3

5. Mining a text for collocations

"Select a text with several striking images, phrases, or vocabulary items. After students have read the text, ask them to write down ten words or phrases they think are particularly striking or colorful on a separate sheet of paper. Then collect back the original texts. They are then asked to construct a new text using the fragments they have 'mined' from the original. You will need to make it clear that they are not to attempt to reproduce the original but to write a completely new text. When they have finished, they compare their texts.

For example:

Ken woke from a confused dream. Gradually his eyes focused. The first thing he noticed was a hand a few inches in front of his face. The fingers were like a bird's claw, stiff, blue with cold. With a shock, he realized that the hand belonged to him. At the same time, he became fully aware of just how cold it was. His bones felt like frozen lead. He remembered an incident from the previous day; he had been hanging about near the kitchen entrance to the Strand Palace Hotel, scavenging for scraps, when a delivery van arrived. The driver had carried in whole sides of beef, the red and white meat refrigerated into hard blocks. He now felt like that frozen meat, his back cold and stiff as a corpse."
(Maley, 1995)

Rewrite/Retell the whole story in your own words by using some of the following:

a confused dream	*a bird's claw*	*blue with cold*
frozen lead	*hanging about*	*scavenging*
stiff as a corpse	*bones frozen meat*	*with a shock*

Proficiency Level: High Intermediate – Bloom's Taxonomy Level 3

6.   In *Canary Row*, John Steinbeck describes the people and the places they inhabit:

"Then Cannery Row whistles **scream** and all over town men and women **scramble** into their clothes and come running down to the Row to go to work. The shining cars bring the upper classes down: superintendents, accountants, owners who disappear into offices. Then from the town pour Wops and Chinamen and Polacks, men and women in trousers and rubber coats and oilcloth aprons. They come running to **clean** and **cut** and **pack** and **cook** and **can** the fish. The whole street **rumbles** and **groans** and **screams** and **rattles** while the silver rivers of fish pour in out of the boats and the boats rise higher and higher in the water until they are empty. The canneries **rumble** and **rattle** and **squeak** until the last fish is cleaned and cut and cooked and canned and then the whistles scream again and the dripping, smelly, tired Wops and Chinamen and Polacks, men and women, straggle out and droop their ways up the hill and into the town and Cannery Row becomes itself again: quiet and magical."

[NB: author's emphasis]
(Steinbeck, 1992, pp. 1-2)

Rewrite/retell the story in your own words and try to use some of the verbs in bold:

scream	**scramble**

clean	**cut**	**pack**	**cook**	**can**

rumble	**groan**	**scream**	**rattle**

Proficiency Level: High Intermediate – Bloom's Taxonomy Level 3

7. **Improvised poetry**

1. Select an appropriate poem.

2. Read; discuss briefly.

3. Direct students to ID words randomly that they like or understand.

4. Underline them. Words should be spread out, but in sequence.

5. Compose them onto a sheet of paper.

6. Students read and compare results. Discover meaning in their results.

7. Repeat process for more fun.
This could be applied to an article, as well.
This provokes and develops language and vocabulary skill as well as literacy practice.
Students create new work from a source creatively reimagined.
Interpretation and meaning are released.

For this adapted plan I'm indebted to Kristin Anderson, NYT, 1/31/21.
(Paul Serrato, 2021)

Proficiency Level: Low Advanced – Bloom's Taxonomy Level 5

Miscellaneous

The Benefits of Our Classroom Experience

Language Learning

Memory and Literature

Memory as History

The Memory of Our Calendar

Memory as Acronyms

The Memory of First Names

What are the benefits of our classroom experience?

Students may have different learning styles and skills and may resort to completely different study methods, but they all have the same classroom or homework assignments. One quick tip for an innovative approach is to attempt to perceive with others' eyes; in other words, teachers (and in many cases students as well) should be able to look at perspectives different from their own. According to Hein (2021), such an effort is the "work of the moral imagination." In his essay entitled *Writing as a Moral Act*, he argues that "excellent thinking and writing always entail a substantial effort."

What do we need to know about moral imagination?

Our everyday life, our life experience, and in our case, the teaching experience might be the best place to foster such ideas through conversations, debates, and similar practical knowledge.

> The richness or the poverty of the moral imagination depends on the richness or the poverty of experience.
> (Guroian, 1998, p. 24)

In other words, moral **imagination** can be kept active because it **motivates us to find meaning**, but it needs nurture and proper exercise. And this brings us back to practice, daily classroom activities where we can resort to good examples of literature.

> There is no shortage of stories […] that challenge, thrill, and excite, and awaken young readers to the potential drama of life, especially to the drama of a life lived in obedience to the highest ideals. Such books have something better than therapeutic reassurance. Like true friends, they encourage us to be our best selves. (p. 6)

Along the same lines, outstanding communication skills in speaking and writing always involve the audience. In Steven Pinker's view, "The form in which thoughts occur to a writer is rarely the same as the form in which they can be absorbed by the reader." (*Wall Street Journal*, September 27, 2014) Dialogues, debates, and other forms of public speaking would be better served when personal experience and clear, concise self-expression are exercised for the benefit of the audience. With excellent teachers guiding the acquisition of skills that require considerable effort, in time, and with well-supported reasoning, students will eventually understand that interlocutors and debate partners are, in fact, the intended audience engaged in the process.

Teaching is how we learn.

The balancing act of initiating a well-crafted argument and, at the same time, thinking about the diversity of opinionated readers or speaking partners will undoubtedly accomplish its task if we remember not to impress but to present a thought-provoking discussion with lots of significant ramifications for those who assert, dispute, and provoke, but also for those at the receiving end who respond, rebuke, and counter-argue.

The big question in such cases will lead us to what might be called self-mastery, which, if appropriately dealt with, can self-produce excellence and simultaneously self-command of the highest order. Unavoidable mistakes might creep into the conversation or pop up in writing when we least expect them. However, practice will deepen the sense of communication with results beyond our imagination. The best choice of a verb or the right adjective that best works for students and teachers come with regular advice and gradual improvement. Students are the ones who will gain not only confidence and competence but also individual self-assurance.

For further reading, please check:

Rose, P. (2014). *The Shelf: From LEQ to LES: Adventures in Extreme Reading*. United States: Farrar, Straus and Giroux.

Skinner, D. (2014). *The Story of Ain't: America, Its Language, and the Most Controversial Dictionary Ever Published*. United States: Harper Perennial.

> "Language is the road map to culture. It tells you where its people come from and where they are going. A study of the English language reveals a dramatic history and an astonishing versatility."   – Rita Mae Brown

What makes human language unique, and how is it related to knowledge?

In 2003 John McWhorter published *The Power of Babel: A Natural History of Language,* in which he dealt with intriguing facts regarding language in general and with languages in particular. From the very beginning, he admitted that from a very early age, he was shocked and mesmerized **by the power of language** and its ability to make us aware of how much we need to know.

> … human language is unique in its ability to communicate or convey an open-ended volume of concepts: we are not limited to talking about exactly where honey is, to warning each other that something is coming to eat us, or to matching vocalizations to fifty-odd basic concepts pertaining to our immediate surroundings and usually focusing on bananas and desire. Neither bees, chimps, parrots nor dogs could produce or perceive a sentence such as "Did you know that there are squid fifty feet and longer in the deep sea? They have only been seen as corpses washed up on beaches." Because animals can only communicate about either things in the immediate environment or a small set of things genetically programmed ("The honey is over there," "A leopard is coming," "Banana!"), they could not tell each other about a giant squid even if they had seen one, nor could they *talk* about corpses even if they had seen plenty. Then there is the specificity for which human language is designed: no animal could specify that the squid have been seen in the past, rather than being seen right now, nor could they communicate the concept of *knowing* in "Did you know…?"
> (p. 5)

What makes a language a language?

Enumerating several types of slang, idioms, baby talk, which some linguists call "function words," we find ourselves connecting to the person we are talking to. On such occasions, we resort of a variety of extra words used loosely or repetitively. In many cases, we may not even be aware of what they sound to an outsider listening to our conversations.

> English is loaded with particles, words and expressions that float up constantly in speech: *like, so, you know, OK, really, actually, honestly, literally, in fact, at least, I mean, quite, of course, after all, hey, [...] sure enough ... know what I mean? Just sayin'*. And it's not only the young who use them. Some particles function as sentence adverbs: *hopefully, surely, certainly*. Some are conjunctions with attitude ("and furthermore..."), conjuring a shaken fist. They keep the conversation going. Although they have no content, they are the soul of the language.
> (Norris, 2019, p. 82)

What happens when we want to express the same idea in spoken language vs. writing?

> Let's hope a quick example will suffice: In conversation, I might say, "So, you know, I was like totally blown away," but in writing I might edit it to the more contained "I was impressed." (p. 83)

This may prove that the way we speak is not exactly the way we write. While spoken English is one thing in plain language, when we express the same idea **in writing, everything unfolds differently.**

How do we go about this type of communication?

We all know, more or less, the story of a young musician going to New York to look for a famous place in Manhattan. The young artist approached a police officer and asked the following question:
"How do I get to Carnegie Hall?
Was this reply a piece of advice or just a friendly reminder:
"Practice, practice, practice..."

What is language learning?

In his 1965 book entitled *Foreign Language Learning*, Robert Politzer addressed students of foreign languages and presented a discussion on how to learn them. In an attempt to create an understanding of language from the point of view of a learner, the author substantiated his assumptions based on scientific research. In his words, these are his convictions:

1. The language learning ability of the mature language learner (high school or older) can be increased by an understanding of the process of foreign language learning and by the creation of specific skills (understanding of patterning, sound-symbol relationship, etc.) which see to underlie the ability to learn a foreign language.
2. There is a definite connection between the understanding of grammar as developed in the native language and the understanding of a foreign language. Until the advent of the new methods and curricula in foreign languages, it was generally felt that grammatical categories of English were directly applicable to foreign languages. Linguists and many language teachers no longer hold this view. Nevertheless, the processes of linguistic analysis, the nature of the sound-symbol relationship, the very nature of language itself are the same for the native and for the foreign language. [...]
3. The important role assigned to foreign language learning in the high school and college curricula is not and should not be based solely on the acquisition of a skill. [...] Elementary language instruction and learning can have subject matter content that goes beyond the acquisition of a skill.
4. Most high school and college students study a specific language without having any assurance that they are studying the language that they will ultimately need in their careers. (Politzer, 1965, p. vi)

What is language awareness?

When linguists like Chomsky analyzed the language "competence," that is, the ability to speak depending on how well they knew the language, they mainly focused on **language awareness** (Thornbury, 1997).

> Language awareness is a person's sensitivity to and constant awareness of the nature of language and its role in human life (Donmall, 1985, p. 7).

Typical activities for native speakers would include the exploration of the difference between written and spoken language. "In second language education, the term has a narrower compass, referring – traditionally, at least – to linguistic knowledge only, and to the teacher's knowledge rather than the learner's. Put it simply, language awareness is the knowledge that teachers have of the underlying systems of the language that enables them to teach effectively." (Thornbury, intro p. x)

From language awareness to language awakening

According to Spiro (2013), methodology reflects the instructor's beliefs and attitudes in the process of language teaching. That concept hasn't changed, but other researchers approached the subject from a different perspective: Kumaravadivelu (2006) went a little further when he signaled a shift in focus and thus coined the term 'post-methods,' whereby he referred to a dramatic change from a single-method approach to what he calls 'pedagogic eclecticism,' giving teachers the power to choose their own methods: grammar-focused tasks (for test takers), communicative games (for using the language hen interacting with others), various other activities (including drama and role-plays).

> Considering the more significant trend-setting shifts that have marked the 1990s, we can claim with some justification that we have now reached a much higher level of awareness. We might even say, with a good measure of poetic license, that we have moved from a state of awareness toward a state of awakening. We have been awakened to the necessity of making methods-based pedagogies more sensitive to local exigencies, awakened to the opportunity afforded by post-method pedagogies to help practicing teachers develop their own theory of practice, awakened to the multiplicity of learner identities, awakened to

244

the complexity of teacher beliefs, and awakened to the vitality of macrostructures – social, cultural, political, and historical – that shape and reshape the microstructures of our pedagogic enterprise. (Spiro, p. 7)

Why is this relevant?

Language instructors have a unique place in education because they can teach their students and learn from them in the process. What works well for the students works well for the teachers.

At the end of the day, both parties must have a feeling of accomplishment. If students acquire new skills, teachers gather valuable information that can ease the burden of preparing future lesson plans.

What basic preparations are we looking for?

Language acquisition should be accessible through practical exercises that follow a curriculum with a syllabus that **matches theory with practice**.

Let's look at various cultures with their specific language traits. We obviously find common ground that can be utilized for the benefit of both teachers and students. For example:

1. The verb TO BE is rarely used in some languages, especially as an auxiliary.
2. Translation of everyday vocabulary does not necessarily convey the same message in the second language.
3. Students in some cultures are more comfortable speaking, while other language learners prefer writing.
4. Correction may not be a useful tool because it inhibits those who are extremely sensitive to changes in their behavior.

If teachers are aware of certain predictable issues depending on the cultural make-up of the class, the outcome can be well expected and therefore overcome.

Any practical suggestions?

 A variety of activity types including (and often in this order):
Identification/recognition tasks: 'Find all examples of X'.
Categorization tasks: 'Classify all the examples of X'.
Matching tasks: Match examples X with definitions Y'.
Explanation/interpretation tasks: 'Explain all the examples of X'.
Evaluation tasks: 'Assess the usefulness of this exercise to practice item X'.
Application tasks: 'Design an exercise to practice item X'.
                                    (Thornbury, intro p. xv)

For further reading, please check:

James, C., Candlin, C. N., & Garrett, P. (2014). *Language Awareness in the Classroom*. United Kingdom: Taylor & Francis.

What is standard English?

Linguists have used this term for years to describe what we now call our written and spoken language. **Why is it necessary to know that?** We are reminded that certain forms of the English language have been adopted as standards and therefore applied in everything we find in books, magazines, newspapers, and other **similar means of communication.**

Why is literacy so important in the modern world?

According to Hirsch (1988), "some of the reasons, like the need to fill out forms or get a job, are so obvious that they needn't be discussed. But the chief reason is broader. The complex undertakings of modern life depend on the cooperation of many people with different specialties in different places. Where communications fail, so do the undertakings. (That is the moral of the story of the Tower of Babel.) The function of national literacy is to foster effective nationwide communications. Our chief instrument of communication over time and space is the standard national language, which is sustained by national literacy. Mature literacy alone enables the tower to be built, the business to be well managed, and the airplane to fly without crashing. All nationwide communications, whether by telephone, radio, TV, or writing are fundamentally dependent upon literacy, for the essence of literacy is not simply reading and writing but also the effective use of the standard literate language." (Hirsch, pp. 2-3)

If we go into the territory of new discoveries, we might say that advanced technology makes it even more pressing that we know **how to communicate with each other** these days. And I mean communicate properly.

Does this apply to ESL?

The primary function of language is communication.

Communication is a BIG WORD today. Teachers must be prepared to empower our students with the tools they need to possess to understand what is written or being said so they can become better thinkers and use the new language accordingly. One very important secret is that words alone are difficult to comprehend. However, it is even more challenging when it comes to using them in original contexts. **A well-spoken person** is usually **better received** in society, and **an educated student** will find **better ways to express** their ideas and thoughts if they have the necessary vocabulary skills.

By the same token, there must be a set of standard rules of correct grammar and vocabulary, which will facilitate the ESL learners in their quest for **accuracy**, and in time, with a lot of practice, the well-deserved **fluency**.

> "You learn more about a person in an hour of play than in a year of conversation."   – Plato

Let's play with words

Teachers like to **play with words,** and this is not a bad habit. If done properly, the same concept can be **learned and practiced** by students, who, in their turn, also like to have a little bit of fun. Lots of ideas come up when we analyze the language of everyday life, and therein we find a plethora of good examples.

If we want to remember a scheduled **event**, we play with the alphabet:

March Madness   *Morning Mozart*
      Midday Monumental Works   *Morning Meditation*
Bach Birthday Bash   *May is Meryl Streep Month More*
      March Music   *The Merry Month of May*

What about **comparisons** or **similes:**

as busy as a bee
as cool as a cucumber
as blind as a bat
as bright as a button
as dead as a doornail
as proud as a peacock

"Old Marley was as dead as a doornail.
Mind! I don't mean to say that I know, of my own knowledge, what there is particularly dead about a doornail. I might have been inclined, myself, to regard a coffin-nail as the deadest piece of ironmongery in the trade. But the wisdom of our ancestors is in the simile; and my unhallowed hands shall not disturb it, or the Country's done for. You will therefore permit me to repeat, emphatically, that Marley was as dead as a doornail."   (Charles Dickens, *A Christmas Carol*)

How about **famous people** or **famous characters**? How do we remember them?

Buffalo Bill
      Byname of William Frederick Cody (1846-1917), US Army scout who dramatized the facts and flavor of the American West through fiction and melodrama.

249

Bugs Bunny
> *Animated cartoon character created in the 1930s by Leon Schlesinger.*

Pied Piper
> *Also called the Pan Piper of Hamelin (in German legend). As the story goes, in 1284, townspeople hired a piper to lure away the rats that had overrun the village.*

Pink Panther
> *The Pink Panther is actually a large pink diamond that received this nickname because there is a flaw in the center that Resembles a leaping pink panther.*

Road Runner
> *Coyote and the Road Runner are two cartoon characters. Hungry Coyote is seen trying to catch the Road Runner, a fast-running ground bird, but is never successful.*

If authors want readers to remember the **titles** of books, they do the same:

> *Sense and Sensibility*
> *Pride and Prejudice*
> *Love's Labor Lost*
> *A Christmas Carol*
> *Nicholas Nickleby*
> *The Posthumous Papers of the Pickwick Club*

Proverbs/sayings

> *Curiosity killed the cat.*
> > *This phrase was originally "care killed the cat" and had nothing to do with the sleuthing abilities of our felines. In time "curiosity" was substituted in the saying to explain that this was sometimes what got cats and people into trouble.*

> *It takes two to tango.*
> > *"Takes two to tango, two to tango*
> > *Two to really get the feeling of romance*
> > *Let's do the tango, do the tango*
> > *Do the dance of love!"*
> > (Hoffman, 1952)

> *There are other dances that need two partners, but tango was preferred because of the alliteration.*

250

Alliterations?
good as gold
power to the people
fish, flesh, and fowl
bed, bath and beyond
best buy
PayPal

Collocations can be another good example:
Bag and baggage
The family went off bag and baggage.
Part and parcel
Traveling was part and parcel
of his sales position.
Safe and sound
We arrived home safe and sound.

How about **internal rhyme**:
simple as a pimple
easy-peasy
fair and square
itsy bits
the latest greatest
our nearest and dearest

For further reading, please check:

Davidow, S., & Williams, P. (n.d.) *Playing with Words: An Introduction to Creative Writing Craft.* United Kingdom: Palgravia Macmillan.

Aristotle's words and collocations

"Every art and every inquiry, and likewise every action and choice, seems to aim at some good, and hence it has been beautifully said that the good is that at which all things aim."

What do these words and collocations really mean to the reader?

Every art   *Art is "something that is created with imagination and skill and that is beautiful."*

every inquiry _____

likewise _____

every action _____

choice _____

seems _____

to aim at _____

some good _____

hence _____

beautifully _____

said _____

the good _____

that _____

at which _____

all things _____

aim _____

Proficiency Level: Low Advanced – Bloom's Taxonomy Level 3

Learning from Benjamin Franklin

According to his autobiography, Ben Franklin sometimes used a little prayer which he took from James Thomson:

> "Father of Light and Life, thou Good supreme,
> O teach me what is good, teach me thy self!
> Save me from Folly, Vanity and Vice,
> From every low Pursuit, and fill my Soul
> With Knowledge, conscious Peace, and Virtue pure,
> Sacred, substantial, never fading Bliss!"
> (Thomson, *The Seasons*, "Winter," lines 218-23)

He designed his daily schedule around the following "Scheme of Employment for the Twenty-four Hours of a natural Day":

The morning		Rise, wash, and address
Question, What Good		Powerful Goodness;
Shall I do this day?	5:00 AM	contrive Day's Business
	6:00	and take the Resolution
	7:00	of the Day; prosecute the present Study: and breakfast?
	8:00–11:00	Work
	12:00	Read, and overlook my
	1:00	accounts, and dine.
	2:00–5:00	Work
	6:00	Put Things in their Places,
	9:00	Supper, Musick, or Diversion, or Conversation, Examination of the Day.
Evening Question, What Good have I done today?	10:00	Sleep

(Adapted from *Ben Franklin's Almanac of Wit, Wisdom, and Practical Advice: Useful Tips and Fascinating Facts for Every Day of the Year*, 1964, p. 154)

Students should be asked to create their own daily routines.

Proficiency Level: High Intermediate – Bloom's Taxonomy Level 5

Intensify/Downplay

We sometimes find ourselves in situations when our ability to use the correct language or apply the best verbiage leaves us baffled or unable to function appropriately. I remember distinctly frustrating moments during some of my college exams or when I was stopped in the street by somebody asking for directions. Job interviews over the years did not turn out to be successful at all when – for example, I did not prepare or formulate the expected answers to the questions presented to me. There were cases when my emotions overwhelmed me, and the vocabulary was ineffective in overcoming such moments that should have been under my control.

In *Language Awareness* (edited by Eschholz, Tosa & Clark, 1978), Hugh Rank developed his schema Intensify/Downplay to help people in their daily communication. In his words. "*All people* intensify (*commonly by* repetition, association, composition) *and* downplay (*commonly by* omission, diversion, confusion) *as they communicate in words, gestures, numbers, etc. But 'professional persuaders' have more training, technology, money, and media access than the average citizen. Individuals can better cope with organized persuasion by recognizing the common ways* how *communication is intensified or downplayed, and by considering* who is saying what to whom, with what intent and what results." (p. 87)

Let's recap:

Intensify by   repetition
                              association
                              composition

Downplay by   omission
                              diversion
                              Confusion

For further reading, please check:

Andrews, S. (2007). *Teacher Language Awareness*. United Kingdom: Cambridge University Press.

Repetition

- "Let it snow, let it snow, let it snow."
- "And miles to go before I sleep, and miles to go before I sleep." – Robert Frost, *Stopping by Woods on a Snowy Evening*
- "A horse is a horse, of course, of course,
  And no one can talk to a horse of course,
  That is, of course, unless the horse is the famous Mr. Ed."
  – Theme Song from *Mr. Ed*, television show

According to Rank (1984), "intensifying by repetition is an easy, simple, and effective way to persuade" (p. 50). Linguists generally do not recommend repetition in the ESL classroom. However, my experience tells me it worked for many other learners and me. Here is a similar opinion from a language school:

> For many students desiring to improve their English fluency, repetition is the key to success. For instance, if you listen to a song or podcast that's in English, maybe you understand most of it. How can you understand the other 20% that at this moment you don't understand? By listening over and over again.
>
> Students want to "own" the new words and phrases they learn in English – they want to really understand the words, recognize them in a way that will make them confident in using the words and phrases.
>
> Repetition is key to remembering things as you learn to speak English. Think about it: if you only listen to a new phrase, word, or say it once, how likely are you to remember? Not very likely.

(www.icchawaii.edu/english-fluency-importance-of-repetition)

Repetition has been used to teach L2 **since 1631**. To be more specific, the most effective way included repetition and imitation of words and sentences, although repetition and drilling have been heavily criticized in recent times. (Larsen-Freeman, 2013)

255

Worksheet for Repetition

1.   Hand out *Here Comes the Sun* (The Beatles)

Here comes the sun.
Here comes the sun and I say,
It's alright.

Little darling, it's been a long, cold, lonely winter.
Little darling, it feels like years since it's been here.
Here comes the sun, here comes the sun and I say,
It's alright.

Little darling, the smiles returning to their faces.
Little darling, it seems like years since it's been here.
Here comes the sun, here comes the sun and I say
It's alright.

Sun, sun, sun, here it comes
Sun, sun, sun, here it comes.
Sun, sun, sun, here it comes.
Sun, sun, sun, here it comes.
Sun, sun, sun, here it comes.

Little darling, I feel that ice is slowly melting.
Little darling, it seems like years since it's been clear.
Here comes the sun, here comes the sun and I say
It's alright.

Here comes the sun.
Here comes the sun.
It's alright.
It's alright.

2.   Play the song, and everybody sings together.
3.   Ask your students to identify and explain *here comes*.
4.   Discuss the difference between
          here comes and *there goes*.

Linguistic association

Associative meaning, also called *linguistic association*, refers to the characteristics of a word beyond the meaning you will find in a dictionary. A word like "nurse" may have (incorrectly) the universal meaning of a woman. Another good example would be the word "pig," somehow related to the idea of a dirty animal.

ESL students coming from cultures in which words mostly have denotative meanings need to be coached into analyzing words in phrases, collocations, or even whole paragraphs. The context might be essential in getting all the aspects of associative meaning.

> A word can sweep by your ear and, by its very sound suggest hidden meanings, preconscious association. Listen to these words: *blood, tranquil, democracy*. You know what they mean literally, but you have associations with those words that are cultural, as well as your own personal associations.
>
> Let's take one word to illustrate my point of meaning in flux: Revolution. *Revolution* enters English in the fourteenth century from the French via Latin. At least that's when it was written. It may have been spoken earlier. *Revolution* means a turning around. That was how it was used. Most often *revolution* was used by astronomers to indicate a planet revolving in space. The word carried no political meaning. (Brown, 2011)

Ask the students to use the following words and **describe what associations** they make when they hear them:

FUN   NAIL   VIDEO CLIP   MEME

Proficiency Level: High Beginning – Bloom's Taxonomy Level 2

For further reading, please check:

Linguistics and the Teacher. (2011). United Kingdom: Routledge

Associative learning

Linguists and researchers consider *The Longman Dictionary of Language Teaching and Applied Linguistics* an indispensable resource for teachers and students alike. With an exhaustive list of terms, concepts, and definitions, the dictionary provides a thorough presentation of what is needed in language acquisition, with a special focus on expanding and broadening students' knowledge which can be extremely useful in curriculum development, teaching methodology, and any other related subject areas. According to the definition presented in the book, associative learning "happens when a connection or association is made, usually between two things:

For example:

a. When someone hears the word *table*, they may think of the word *food*, because it is often used with or near *table*. This is called **association by contiguity**.
b. When someone hears the word *delicate*, they may think of the word *fragile*, because it has a similar meaning. This is called **association by similarity**.
c. When someone hears the word *happy*, they may think of the word *sad*, because it has the opposite meaning. This is called **association by contrast**.

Associative learning theory has been used in studies of memory, learning, and verbal learning." (p. 24)

Suggested classroom activities should include:

1. Encouraging students to use a dictionary and find examples for each type of association.
2. Challenging students to share which association they find more appealing or useful in language learning.

For further reading, please check:

Gagné, R. M. (1985). *The Conditions of Learning and Theory of Instruction.* Japan: Holt, Rinehart, and Winston.

Composition

Play "make up a story" in small groups.

The teacher (or one student) starts with a sentence like this:

One day I decided to be my own master.

Then the next student continues along the same line and adds another sentence around the table until everybody says (or writes something) or until you have a complete story.

Students may want to use some of the following collocations:

first things first

caught me off guard

rush to judgment

It's now or never.

steep learning curve

when push comes to shove

shot myself in the foot

for all intents and purposes

cautiously optimistic

win-win situation

Proficiency Level: Low Advanced – Bloom's Taxonomy Level 5

Omission

"The process of **omission** sometimes leaves out more than can be presented. This type of communication is "limited, is edited, is slanted or biased to include and exclude items. But omission can also be used as a deliberate way of concealing, hiding. Half-truths, quotes out of context, etc. are hard to detect or find."
(Eschholz, Rosa, & Clark, 1997, p. 89)

For example, we can use an ellipsis in the middle of a quotation to signal that we omitted words from the original.

Original sentence:

"Some industries have formal rankings that broadcast the best and brightest workers (e.g., analyst rankings in Institutional Investor), and some organizations provide companywide performance results and publicly recognize top performers."

Correct use:

To make a high-performing employee visible to the community, "some industries have formal rankings that broadcast the best and brightest workers …, and some organizations provide companywide performance results and publicly recognize top performers."
(Call, Nyberg & Thatcher, 2015, p. 629)

(quoted in a blog entitled *Punctuation Junction: Quotation Marks and Ellipses*, by Chelsea Lee, posted on May 27, 2015, in the APA Style Blog.)

Diversion

According to Rank (1978), diversion is "Downplaying by distracting focus, diverting attention away from key issues or important things; usually by intensifying the side-issues, the non-related, the trivial. Common variations include *hairsplitting, nit-picking, attacking a straw man, red herring*; [...] plus things which drain the energy of others: *busy work, legal harassment*, etc. Humor and entertainment (*bread and circuses*) are used as pleasant ways to divert attention from major issues." (p. 89)

Analyze some of these examples used by real estate ads:

"Adorable"   meaning   *small*

"Eat-in kitchen"   *no dining room*

"Handyman's special"   *portion of building still standing*

"By appointment only"   *expensive*

"Starter home"   *cheap*   (p. 90)

Check the ads section of a local newspaper and look for similar words or phrases.

Identify those words or collocations you find in titles or headlines, for example, and explain them in your own words. You can also share your feelings about such phrases.

Proficiency Level: Low Intermediate – Bloom's Taxonomy Level 2

Equivocation

Equivocation: When people deliberately avoid using the exact word or use ambiguous language. A good teacher, however, should always answer questions with clarity, that is, **without equivocation**.

"Using an ambiguous term in more than one sense, thus making an argument misleading." (www.logicallyfallacious.com)

Examples of equivocation:

1. In an episode of *Futurama,* Leela agrees to give her hand to the Robot Devil in exchange for new robotic ears. However, the Robot Devil tricks her – she thinks that she is agreeing to give up one of her physical hands, but in fact, she is agreeing to give the Devil her hand *in marriage*. The Robot Devil is equivocating in his agreement with Leela.
2. In *Star Wars: A New Hope*, Obi-Wan Kenobi tells Luke the Darth Vader "betrayed and murdered your father." [SPOILER:] It turns out that Darth Vader actually *is* Luke's father and that Obi-Wan was speaking metaphorically. Anakin Skywalker, the good man who sired Luke, was betrayed and "killed" by his own vicious impulses and the dark side of the Force and ultimately turned into Darth Vader. Obi-Wan's equivocation is perhaps justified by the fact that the desire for vengeance is what initially sets Luke on his path to becoming a Jedi." (www.literaryterms.net)

I. As an example of equivocation:

For report cards, teachers should avoid harsh expressions:

Avoid	Use instead
Lazy	Needs ample supervision in order to work well.
Cheats	Needs help in learning to adhere to rules and standards of fair play.
Noisy	Needs to develop quieter habits of communication.
Lies (Dishonest)	Shows difficulty in distinguishing between imaginary and factual material.
Steals	Needs help in learning to respect the property rights of others.
Disliked by other children	Needs help in learning to form lasting friendships.

(Eschholtz et al., pp. 53-54)

Let the students discuss the differences between the words/collocations mentioned in **Avoid** and those recommended in **Use instead.**

Your own examples:

_____

_____

For further reading, please check:

Jardine, D. (2020). *A Treatise of Equivocation.* India: Alpha Editions.

Music, memory, and innovation

Can we really innovate the teaching of language by singing?

Does music make some students more comfortable in the classroom?

How can we combine the rhythm and the sound of popular songs with the acquisition of correct pronunciation?

Is it true that singing in chorus makes our students lose their accents?

Why do we remember the lyrics of our favorite melodies?

How about a practical example?

> One of the most exquisite examples of the contributory role of song in the maintenance of memory is portrayed in Bruce Chatwin's description of the Australian Aborigines. The native Australians, faced with the need to travel on foot across vast areas of barren wilderness with few stable landmarks, inherit and retain songs from their ancestors which describe the graphic features of the route and act therefore as an acoustic map, steering the journey-people along the right course. This use of song to prevent becoming lost in the wilderness has a psychological component recognizable in children world-wide who instinctively sing when scared, lost in the dark or faced with the trepidation of having to negotiate themselves through unfamiliar or threatening terrain. (Newham, 1996, p. 73)

For further reading, please check:

Snyder, R., & Snyder, B. (2000). *Music and Memory: An Introduction.* United Kingdom: Bradford Books.

Practicing oral presentation skills

When ESL/EFL students reach a certain level of English proficiency, they should be encouraged to prepare to speak in small groups or even in front of the whole class. Topics may range from cultural aspects of their own country to interesting things in the new learning context or personal reviews of reading material. Voicing their opinions might be a wonderful way to prove how much they have accomplished or simply practice speaking and vocabulary skills in front of their peers. Competition is also a major factor that stimulates argumentation and enhances verbal imagination.

Learning Objectives:
- To present relevant information about an event, a custom, a tradition from a student's point of view.
- To develop student's public speaking ability
- To encourage debate and argumentation techniques.

Tasks: In preparation for the presentation, students will have an opportunity to practice alone/at home or with another student in pairs/small groups. Notes or integral text should be submitted to the teacher prior to the actual presentation to void flawed English.
The presentation may be done with visual (PowerPoint, Prezi, or other) as an aid to understanding. Main ideas together with relevant vocabulary and collocations might add a special touch to the whole event.

Assessment: During the presentation, audience members should be expected to take notes, ask questions if necessary, and provide their own input on the topic at hand. An ideal oral presentation should be accompanied by an audience feedback form which instructors may very well develop in advance, and which may be used to check not only the audience understanding but also the exchange of ideas between the speaker and his colleagues. Such a feedback form should include a summary of the activity and a list of personal questions.

Learning outcomes: – Teachers will get a chance to judge student progress and improvement.
– Presenters will be able to share personal opinions while practicing vocabulary and correct grammar.
– Students will be able to offer their own critique, enrich their vocabulary, and grade each other.

For further reading, please check:

Chen, Y. (2015). *ESL Students' Language Anxiety in In-Class Oral Presentations*. United States: Marshall University.

Onchwari, G. (2017). *Handbook of Research on Learner-centered Pedagogy in Teacher Education and Professional Development*. United States: IGI Global.

Sabbagh, S. A. (2009). *Investigating Oral Presentation Skills and Non-verbal Communication Techniques in UAE Classrooms*. United Arab Emirates: American University of Sharjah.

Hendiadys

How often do we use expressions like *bread and butter, nice and warm, safe and sound?*

Well, these are good examples of hendiadys, a Latinized form of the Greek phrase *hen dia dyoin*, a figure of speech meaning "one through two." It is sometimes called "two for one" or a "figure of twins." What that means is that we use two words connected by a conjunction like *bread and butter*, when, in fact, we mean "buttered bread."

Why do we use such phrases? That is a very good question, and linguists do not have a definite answer. One of the most prevailing explanations would be that once such words become part and parcel (another hendiadys) of the language, people continue to use them for a certain effect, like **sentence rhythm** or **emphasis.**

Mark Forsyth (2013) has a whole chapter dedicated to hendiadys, and here are some of his thoughts:

"When Saint Paul told the Philippians to 'work your salvation with fear and trembling,' it's probably a hendiadys for *fearful trembling*, but it might be a hendiadys for trembling fear. And there's at least the possibility that he really did mean *both with fear and with trembling*, and wasn't using hendiadys at all.

Is *law and order* a hendiadys? It looks damned like it, but I would hate to say for certain. What about *rough and tumble? House and home?* To say for certain that something is hendiadys you have to be certain about what the writer thought in the first place. It may be that God has a glorious powerful kingdom, but Jesus actually said: 'For thine is the kingdom, the power, and the glory.' " (p. 87)

Although this is a translation from Greek, such phrases were common in Ancient Hebrew and maybe even in Aramaic.

"Summertime and the living is easy. But summertime and the living is easy doesn't necessarily have to be hendiadys. It just looks very, very like it. [...]

There's also (some would say) the double verb form where *try and do something* rather than *try to do something* or *go and see somebody* rather than *going to see them.* [...]

In Shakespeare's early works hendiadys barely appears. Maybe popping up once or twice a play. Then, in about 1599, Shakespeare decided that hendiadys was his favorite form. *Hamlet* is the top play, where he averages a hendiadys every 60 or so lines. 'Angels and ministers of grace defend us!' shouts Hamlet, when he really means 'Angelic ministers of grace.' (pp. 88-89) [...]

Hendiadys is hidden all over Shakespeare's great plays. It's in *King Lear* where Edmund says, 'I have told you what I have seen and heard; but faintly, nothing like the image and horror of it'; and, most famously, in *Macbeth*, where life is a tale 'Told by an idiot, full of sound and fury.' Whether Shakespeare was thinking of *furious sound* or *sounding fury* hardly signifies. The point and beauty of hendiadys is that it sets the words next to each other, that it removes the grammar and relation, that it doubles the words out to give breadth and beauty." (p. 90) […]

Mind you, for my money, the greatest use of hendiadys isn't by Shakespeare, but by Leonard Cohen in his song 'Hallelujah':

> *You saw her bathing on the roof.*
> *Her beauty and the moonlight overthrew you."*
>
> (Forsyth, 2013, pp. 90-91)

Similar examples:

nice and hot   body and soul   sick and tired   spic and span

Lord Byron: "She walks in beauty, like the night."

William Shakespeare:
"the grace and blush of modesty"
"the dead vast and middle of the night"
"the whips and scorns of time"

Extra Bonus:

Is this a good example of hendiadys? Why or why not?

Elwood: What kind of music do you usually have here?
Claire: Oh, we got both kinds. We got country *and* western.

(Dan Aykroyd and Sheilah Wells in *The Blues Brothers*, 1980)

Paraprosdokians

"*Paraprosdokian* is a derivative of a Greek word that means 'beyond expectation.' It is a wordplay type of literary device in which the final part of a phrase or sentence is unexpected.

Paraprosdokian is a linguistic U-turn that results in humor or surprise."   (www.literarydevices.net)

Examples:
"If I agreed with you, we'd both be wrong."
                    Sir Winston Churchill
 "War does not determine who is right ... only who is left."
                    Attributed to Bertrand Russell
"Where there's a will, I want to be in it."
                    Anonymous
"If I could just say a few words ... I'd be a better public speaker."
                    Homer in a The Simpsons episode
"Behind every great man, there's a woman, rolling her eyes."
                    Jim Carrey's character in Bruce Almighty
"Human genius has its limits while human stupidity does not."
                    Alexandre Dumas
"The only difference between fiction and reality is that fiction has to make sense."
                    Anonymous

Use your imagination and complete the following with your own ideas:

Beauty is only skin deep _____.
Laugh at your own problems _____.
You can always count on me _____.
Politicians and diapers have one thing in common:

_____.

If I am reading this ad correctly, _____.

Proficiency Level: Intermediate – Bloom's Taxonomy Level 4

Words … words … words …

"We have the same word for falling snow, snow on the ground, snow packed hard like ice, slushy snow, wind-driven flying snow – whatever the situation may be. To an Eskimo, this all-inclusive word would be almost unthinkable: he would say that falling snow, slushy snow, and so on, are sensually and operationally different, different things to contend with; he uses different words for them and for other kinds of snow. The Aztecs go even farther than we in the opposite direction with 'cold,' 'ice,' and 'snow' all represented by the same basic word…."

(Whorf, 216)

The Eskimos use the following words for snow:

Aput	*for snow on the ground*
Qana	*for falling snow*
Pipsirpoq	*for drifting snow*
Qimuqsuq	*for snow drift.*

www.people.brandeis.edu

Group work:

Ask students to compare their native languages and find similar situations when culture created more than one word for the same concept.

_____

_____

_____

The US Island that speaks Elizabethan English

"Ocracoke Island in North Carolina is a very special place where the local native Americans, English sailors, and pirates have created what is nowadays known as the "Hoi Toider" brogue. In other words, people on the island have their way of speaking: a combination of Elizabethan English, to which you might add some Irish and Scottish accents, and then supply a reasonable dosage of pirate slang.

Located 34 miles from the North Carolina mainland, Ocracoke Island is fairly isolated. You can't drive there as there are no bridges, and most people can't fly either as there are no commercial flights. If you want to go there, it has to be by boat. In the early 1700s, that meant Ocracoke was a perfect spot for pirate to hide, as no soldiers were going to search 16 miles of remote beaches and forests for wanted men.

William Howard was one of those outlaws, serving as quartermaster on Blackbeard's ship *Queen Anne's Revenge.* Leaving before Blackbeard's final battle in 1718, Howard made his way to Virginia, eventually taking the general pardon offered by King George I to all pirates. But unlike some, Howard had a plan. For several decades, he dropped out of sight, only to reappear in 1759 when he bought Ocracoke Island for £105 from a man named Richard Sanderson, a justice and later a General Assembly member in mainland North Carolina.

Howard settled down along with some other ex-pirates and started building a community with boat pilots who had been stationed on the island to help guide merchant ships around sandbars in the area. A mainland North Carolina Native American tribe also interacted with the early settlers. The Woccon tribe had set up fishing and hunting outposts on the island, which they called Woccocock. Through misspellings and mispronunciations, it became Wokokon, Oakacock and Okercock, before finally arriving at the current version of Ocracoke in the mid-1700s. So at this point, there were Native Americans, English sailors and pirates from a variety of places all in one location. And that isolated community of just under 200 started blending words and dialects, and eventually building its own way of speaking."

(www.bbc.com/travel/story/20190623-the-us-island-that-speaks-elizabethan-english)

> Language is the finest achievement of culture.

Curiosities about language

"The word **mile** comes from the Latin *mille* – 'one thousand,' referring to a thousand complete paces, left foot and right foot, of the legion's formal parade step, approximately 5,200 feet, the regular Roman way of measuring distance between towns."

(Berlitz, 2005, p. 17)

"Dialogue (sometimes spelled **dialog**) is a reciprocal conversation between two or more entities. The etymological origins of the word in Greek διά (*diá*, through) + λόγος (logos, word, speech) concepts like *flowing-through meaning*) do not necessarily convey the way in which people have come to use the word, with some confusion between the prefix διά- (diá- through) and the prefix δι-(di-, two) leading to the assumption that a dialogue is necessarily between only two parties. A dialogue as a form of communication has a verbal connotation. While communication can be an exchange of ideas and information by non-verbal signals, behaviors, as the etymology connotes, dialogue implies the use of language. A dialogue is distinguished from other communication methods such as discussions and debates. While **debates** are considered **confrontational, dialogues** emphasize **listening and understanding."** (**www.newworldencyclopedia.org**)

"During the battle of Copenhagen in 1801, the flagship commander signaled to Lord Nelson that he should stop attacking the Danish fleet and retreat. Nelson held a telescope to his blind eye and said, 'I do not see the signal.' Having disobeyed the order, Nelson continued to attack and won the battle. This incident has come to be known as *turning a blind eye.*"   (Archer, 2021)

"In medieval times, doctors used astrology because they believed that people's health was affected by the movement of stars. The word *influenza* comes from a Medieval Italian word meaning 'the influence of the planets.'" (https://www.bbc.co.uk/bitesize/guides/zyscng8/revision/)

"The Teutons called the Celts *wealas* – foreigners – and it is from this word that we get the modern name *Wales*. The Celts first called their new oppressors *Saxons*, then *Angles*. King *Aethlbert* was known as *Rex*

Anglorum, the country known as *Anglia*, and the words *Engle, Englisc*, and *Englaland* all slowly crept into common currency, until by the eleventh century the nation in the making was formally known as *England*."   (Winchester, 2003, p.5)

"The history of the '&' sign (also called the ampersand) dates back to 63 B.C. when it was invented by Cicero's slave Tyrone. In the 19th century, it was the 27th letter of the English alphabet."

(www.speakwiz.com)

"Our deep relationship with the forest is echoed in language. The book you are holding in your hands reveals an early connection. I don't mean my book in particular but the word 'book.' If you trace its origin, you come to the Brothers Grimm of fairy tale fame. In a dictionary of the German language that they published in 1860, they mention that old German characters were scratched onto wooden boards. And because these boards often came from beech trees (*Buche* in German), the name for such writing tablets was transferred from the tree to the functional object – *Buch*, the book. […] Take the word 'true.' It, too, has to do with trees, specifically the oak. The wood of oak trees is hard and resistant to weathering, just as human relationship should be, figuratively speaking. The original word in Indo-European is *dru*, which means *oak*. In English it turns up as 'true,' and in words such as 'trunk,' a wooden chest in which important things are kept safe."

(Wohlleben, 2021, pp. 111-112)

Good to know!

1. Why did collecting of books come to be so important in the American fight in World War II? The answer lies in the very nature of books and printed texts, and in the particular character of the war. Books serve readers in many different ways: as sources of useful information, as forms of communication, and as material manifestations of knowledge and cultural tradition. In a total war, these general attributes became terrains of battle. To fight the enemy required the mobilization of knowledge, which produced a sweeping commitment to intelligence gathering, including the 'open source' intelligence gleaned in publications.

(Peiss, 2020, p. 7)

2. In the original Sherlock Holmes stories, Sherlock never says "Elementary, my dear Watson." He only ever says this in movies and on television.

(Haddon, 2003, p.
74)

3. *To butter someone up* meaning "to praise or flatter someone, usually to gain a favor," is said to have originated in ancient India, where a customary religious act included throwing butter balls at the statues of gods to seek fortune and their favor. (Adapted from https://www.inklyo.com/english-idioms-origins/)

4. The Library of Alexandria was the first time humanity attempted to bring the sum total of human knowledge together in one place at a time. Our latest attempt? **Google.**
(Brewster Kahle, entrepreneur and founder,
The Internet Archive)

The Memory in Literature

Tennessee Williams (1911 -1983) is considered among the three foremost playwrights of the 20th –century American drama. His famous plays include *A Streetcar Named Desire, Cat on a Hot Tin Roof, The Rose Tattoo, Sweet Bird of Youth, The Night of* the *Iguana,* and his semi-autobiographical masterpiece entitled *The Glass Menagerie,* **a memory play**.

The action of the play centers around the tragedy of the Wingfield family and its members: Tom, his sister Laura, and his mother, Amanda. There is another character, Jim O'Connor, who appears later in the play.

Here is part of the beginning:

Tom: "The play is memory. Being a memory play, it is dimly lighted, it is sentimental, it is not realistic. In memory everything seems to happen to music. That explains the fiddle in the wings. I am the narrator of the play, and also a character in it. The other characters are my mother, Amanda, my sister, Laura, and a gentleman caller who appears in the final scenes. He is the most realistic character in the play, being an emissary from a world of reality that we were somehow set apart from. But since I have a poet's weakness for symbols, I am using this character as a symbol; he is the long delayed but always expected something that we live for. There is a fifth character in the play who doesn't appear except in this larger-than-life photograph over the mantel. This is our father who left us a long time ago. He was a telephone man who fell in love with long distances; he gave up his job with the telephone company and skipped the light fantastic out of town … The last we hear of him was a picture post-card from Mazatlan, on the Pacific coast of Mexico, containing a message of two words – 'Hello – Goodbye!' and an address. I think the rest of the play will explain itself …. "

(The Hearth Introduction to Literature, 1996, pp. 882-883)

W. Somerset Maugham (1874 – 1965) is considered one of the most popular novelists of the twentieth century. He was also a playwright and a short-story writer. *Of Human Bondage, The Moon and Sixpence, The Razor's Edge* are among his best-known novels. He is also known for his story-telling technique and wonderful descriptions of people and places. Here is one of them:

I often think of the little village from which I come, with black and white cows in green pastures, and of Copenhagen. The houses in Copenhagen with their flat windows are just like smooth-faced women with large, short-sighted eyes, and the palaces and the churches look as if they had come out of a fairy tale. But I see it all like a scene in a play, it is very clear, and amusing, but I don't know what I want to step on to the stage. I am quite willing to sit in my dark seat in the gallery and watch the spectacle from far away.

[…] life is what you make it. I might have been a clerk in an office, and then it would have been more difficult, but here, with the sea and the jungle, and **all the memories of the past** crowding in upon you, and these people, the Malays, the Papuans, the Chinese, the stolid Dutch, with my books and as much leisure as it were a millionaire – good heavens, what can **the imagination** want more?

[…] What does one do things for? Of course one has to work a certain amount to earn one's living, but after that, only to satisfy **the imagination**. Tell me, when you saw those islands from the sea and your heart was filled with delight, and when you landed on them and found them a dreary jungle, which was the real island? Which gave you most, and which are you going **to treasure in your memory?**

[N. B.: Author's emphasis]
(*The Narrow Corner*, 2009, pp. 141-142)

Rabindranath Tagore (1861-1941) was the first non-European poet and lyricist who received the most coveted of the international awards, the Nobel Prize for Literature in 1913, "because of his profound, sensitive, fresh and beautiful verse, by which, with consummate skill, he has made his poetic thought, expressed in his own English words, a part of the literature of the West." (www.nobelprize.org) While Tagore is recognized today mostly for his poetry, he also wrote essays that reveal another facet of his personality. It is his philosophical thought that he distinguished himself as a language innovator. His meditation on the power of words is thought-provoking and inspiring:

> When we continue to derive joy by comprehending the vast significance of literature, then every word with its independent identity does not obstruct our minds any more. Every word reveals just the meaning and not merely the word itself. Then it is as if the very word loses its own independence. [...]
>
> When the realization of the significance of a poem becomes deep, becomes illuminating to us, only then the fruition of each of its words becomes particularly beautiful to us due to the sweetness of that entire emotion. At that time, when we look back, we see that no word is meaningless, the essence of the whole is being revealed in every word itself. Then, every word of that poem becomes the cause of particular joy and amazement to us. The as its words help us in the realization of the whole instead of obstructing us, they become immensely valuable to us.

(*Detachment*)   (27 February 1909)

(Bhattacharyya, M. (2020) *Rabindranath Tagore's Śāntiniketan Essays,* Routledge, pp. 90-93)

Lawrence Durrell (1912 – 1990), born in India to British colonial parents, is best known as the author of *The Alexandria Quartet*, a series of four interconnected novels, in which he describes Alexandria as a sophisticated, dazzling place, where art and love are used to define the human quest for expression.

The sea is high again today, with a thrilling flush of wind. In the midst of winter, you can feel the inventions of spring. A sky of hot nude pearl until midday, crickets in sheltered places, and now the wind unpacking the great planes, ransacking the great planes ….

I have escaped to this island with a few books and the child – Melissa's child. I do not know why I use the word "escape." The villagers say jokingly that only a sick man would choose such a remote place to rebuild. Well, then, I have come here to heal myself, if you like to put it that way ….

At night when the wind roars and the child sleeps quietly in its wooden cot by the echoing chimney-piece I light a lamp and limp about, thinking of my friends – of Justine and Nessim, of Melissa and Balthazar. I return link by link along **the iron chains of memory** to the city which we inhabited so briefly together: the city which used us as its flora – precipitated in us conflicts which were hers and which we mistook for our own: beloved Alexandria!"

[NB: Author's emphasis]
(*Justine*, p. 13)

278

Vladimir Nabokov (1899 -1977), Russian-American novelist

Originally published in 1951 by Harper & Bros., New York, *Speak, Memory* was **Vladimir Nabokov's** autobiography. In 1989, approximately 12 years after the author's death, Vintage International printed his work with the subtitle, *An Autobiography Revisited.*

Nabokov had planned to entitle his British edition *Speak, Mnemosyne*, but was told that "little old ladies would not want to ask for a book whose title they could not pronounce." After considering other titles, the author finally decided that it would be *Speak, Memory.*

His good sense of humor was obvious in his *Foreword,* where he acknowledged his own conundrum:

> Among the anomalies of a memory, whose possessor and victim should never have tried to become an autobiographer, the worst is the inclination to equate in retrospect my age with that of the century. This led to a series of remarkably consistent chronological blunders in the first version of this book. I was born in April 1899, and naturally, during the first third of, say, 1903, was roughly three years old; but in August of that year, the sharp *3* revealed to me (as described in "Perfect Past") should refer to the century's age, not to mine, which was *4* and as square and resilient as a rubber pillow. Similarly, in the early summer of 1906 – the summer I began to collect butterflies – I was seven not six as stated initially in the catastrophic second paragraph of Chapter 6. Mnemosyne, one must admit, has shown herself to be a very careless girl. (p. 13)

If we continue reading his autobiography, we find Nabokov debating between memory and imagination, only to realize that "Imagination, the supreme delight of the immortal and the immature, should be limited. In order to enjoy life, we should not enjoy it too much." (p. 20)

We all treasure the childhood moments that we recall later on in life, and here is a marvelous example from Vladimir Nabokov:

> One night during a trip abroad, in the fall of 1903, I recall kneeling on my (flattish) pillow at the window of a sleeping car (probably the long-extinct Mediterranean Train de Luxe, the one whose six cars had the lower part of their body painted in umber and the panels in cream) and seeing with an inexplicable pang, a handful of fabulous lights that beckoned to me from a distant

hillside, and then slipped into a pocket of black velvet: diamonds that I later gave away to my characters to alleviate the burden of my wealth. [...] Nothing is sweeter or stranger than to ponder those first thrills. They belong to the harmonious world of a perfect childhood and, as such, possess a natural plastic form in one's memory... (pp. 24-25)

Doris Lessing (1919 – 2013), a British-Zimbabwean novelist, was born in Persia in 1919. Her British parents moved to South Rhodesia and then to England in 1949. Doris Lessing is the author of books, stories, reportage, poems, and plays. When her autobiography came out, the readers could see the sensitive side of a wonderful sense of humor and compassion for the human character.

The first volume of **Doris Lessing**'s autobiography that begins with her childhood in Africa and ends with her arrival in London in 1949 has been hailed as distinctive and challenging. Critics and reviewers thought that the autobiography revealed the writer's mind, and the readers could not agree more. Here is a short passage from her book:

> When you write about anything – in a novel, an article – you learn a lot you did not know before. I learned a good deal writing this. Again and again I have had to say, "That was the reason was it? Why didn't I think about this before?" Or even, "Wait … it wasn't like that." **Memory** [our bold] is a careless and lazy organ, not only a self-flattering one. And not always self-flattering. More than once I have said: "No, I wasn't as bad as I've been thinking," as well as discovering that I was worse.
>
> And then – perhaps this is the worst deceiver of all – we make up our pasts. You can actually watch your mind doing it, taking a little fragment of fact and then spinning a tale out of it. No, I do not think this is only the fault of story-tellers. A parent says, "We took you to the seaside, and your built a sandcastle, *don't you remember?* – look, here is the photo." And at once the child builds from the words and the photograph a memory, which becomes hers. But there are moments, incidents, real memory, I do trust. This is partly because I spent a good part of my childhood *fixing* moments in my mind. (Lessing, 1994, p. 13)

These words carved out of her verbal landscape will provide a touching introspect into her storytelling mind:

> There are memories that have about them something of the wonderful, the marvelous. A man, a gardener – Persian – stands over stone water channels that come under the brick wall into the garden, bringing water from the snow-mountains, and he is pretending to be angry because I am jumping in and out of the delicious water, which splashes him too. I am sent by my parents into the kitchen to tell the servants that dinner may be served, and that is Tehran because I have my brother by the hand, and I look up, up, up at these tall dignified men and see that their faces are grave under their turbans, but their eyes smile. (p. 34)

Sir Kazuo Ishiguro was born in Nagasaki, Japan, in 1954, but his parents moved to England in 1960. Famous for his literary accomplishments, Kazuo Ishiguro became an international sensation after the publication of his novels, of which we should mention *The Remains of the Day*, which was also made into a movie starring Anthony Hopkins and Emma Thompson. In 2017, when it was announced that Kazuo Ishiguro was awarded the Nobel Prize for literature, the academy said that the author was selected for his "novels of great emotional force" that have "uncovered the abyss beneath our illusory sense of connection with the world."

In *Nocturnes* (2009), Kazuo Ishiguro's exploration of his past unfolded his individual perception of the sentiment of love by way of music and left the reader with another example of the writer's ability to delve into his memory:

> When I first took up English teaching after university, it seemed a good enough life – much like an extension of university. Language schools were mushrooming all over Europe, and if the teaching was tedious and the hours exploitative, at that age you don't care too much. You spend a lot of time in bars, friends are easy to make, and there's a feeling you're part of a large network extending around the entire globe. You meet people fresh from their spells in Peru or Thailand, and this gets you thinking that if you wanted to, you could drift around the world indefinitely, using your contacts to get a job in any faraway corner you fancied. And always you'd be part of this cozy, extended family of itinerant teachers, swapping stories over drinks about former colleagues, psychotic school directors, eccentric British Council officers.
>
> In the late '80s, there was talk about making a lot of money teaching in Japan, and I made serious plans to go, but it never worked out. I thought about Brazil too, even read a few books about the culture and sent off application forms. But somehow I never got away that far. Southern Italy, Portugal for a short spell, back here to Spain. Then before you know it, you're forty-seven years old, and the people you started out with have long ago been replaced by a generation who gossip about different things, take different drugs and listen to different music. (p. 40)

St. Augustine (354 – 430) was a theologian, philosopher, and the bishop of Hippo Regius in Numidia, Roman North Africa. He is famous for his literary output of approximately 5.4 million words and his excellent historical and philosophical scholarship.

> I arrive in the fields and vast mansions of memory, where are treasured innumerable images brought in there from objects of every conceivable kind perceived by the senses. There too are hidden away the modified images we produce when by our thinking we magnify or diminish or in any way alter the information our senses have reported. There too is everything else that has been consigned and stored away and not yet engulfed and buried in oblivion … The huge repository of the memory, with its secret and unimaginable caverns, welcomes and keeps all these things, to be recalled and brought out for use when needed; and as all of them have their particular ways into it, so all are put back again in their proper places … This I do within myself in the immense court of my memory, for there sky and earth and sea are readily available to me, together with everything I have even been able to perceive in them, apart from what I have forgotten.
>
> (*The Confessions*, 2012, p. 273)

The memory of places

> **Peter Fleming** (1907-1971), the elder brother of Ian, creator of the 007 novels, was a prolific travel writer, whose volume *Brazilian Adventure* described his expedition to find the lost explorer Percy Fawcett.
> (*Great Cities through Travelers' Eyes*, 2019)

"Looking back, I cannot remember very clearly what I expected from Rio, or why I was disappointed. It is, as they say, a fine city. Make no mistake about that. It is one of the places (for all I know, one of several places) where Brazil's national motto, Order and Progress, has not that rich flavor of irony which is too often, alas, the chief recommendation of public watchwords. Its streets are clean and wide and (when possible) straight. Its taxicabs purr majestically and go like the wind. Its tram service is indefatigable. Its cinemas are numerous, its gardens a delight, and all the male inhabitants wear collars. Its buildings boast – and in Brazil this is something to boast about – the usual offices. But above all, I should like to praise its statuary." (p. 259)

In 1842, **Charles Dickens** (1812-1870) spent three weeks in New York, where he visited, among other places, not only the big attractions but also penitentiaries, orphanages, and asylums.

"Was there ever such a sunny street as this Broadway! The pavement stones are polished with the thread of feet until they shine again; the red bricks of the houses might be yet in the dry, hot kilns; and the roofs of those omnibuses look as though, if water were poured on them, they would hiss and smoke, and smell like half-quenched fires. No stint of omnibuses here! Half a dozen have gone by within as many minutes. Plenty of hackney cabs and coaches too; gigs, phaetons, large-wheeled tilburies and private carriages – rather of a clumsy make, and not very different from the public vehicles, but built for the heavy roads beyond the city pavement. […]

Are there any amusements? Yes. There is a lecture room across the way, from which that glare of light proceeds, and there may be evening service for the ladies thrice a week, or oftener. For the young gentlemen, there is the counting house, the store, the bar-room; the latter, as you may see through the windows, pretty full. Hark! to the clinking-sound of hammers breaking lumps of ice, and to the cool gurgling of the pounded bits, as, in the process of mixing, they are poured from glass to glass."

(Dickens, 2019, pp. 227-229)

Mark Twain and his definition of a nation

"A nation is only an individual multiplied," wrote **Mark Twain,** and he knew very well that the special nature of America is to be found in its emphasis on the individual and the particular.

> This emphasis finds at least part of its cause in the diversity of cultural heritages that have come to call the United States home. This diversity, and the individual's relationship to it, combine to produce a kind of cultural confusion that may well be singularly American: there is no easily identifiable or 'official' culture that the individual can automatically feel a part of; there is no really consistent cultural framework.
>
> (Benedict, 1981, introduction)

James Fenimore Cooper (1789 – 1851) spent his childhood in Cooperstown, now known ironically as the home of baseball's Hall of Fame. His 1823 tale entitled *The Pioneers* provides a touching tableau of his wandering places:

> Near the center of the State of New York lies an extensive district of country whose surface is a succession of … mountains and valleys. It is among these hills that Delaware takes its rise; and flowing from the limpid lakes and thousand springs of this region, the numerous sources of the Susquehanna meander through the valleys, until, uniting their streams, they form one of the proudest rivers of the United States … Beautiful and thriving villages are found interspersed along the margins of small lakes, or situated at those points of the streams which are favorable for manufacturing; and neat and comfortable farms, with every indication of wealth about them, are scattered profusely through the vales, and even to the mountain tops. (p. 3)

Born in Greenwich Village in 1843, **Henry James** was somehow attached to *Washington Square*, a name which he popularized as the title of his narrative where he shares his fondness of this lovely place:

> I know not whether it is owing to the tenderness of early associations, but this portion of New York appears to many persons the most delectable. It has a kind of established repose which is not of frequent occurrence in other quarters of the long, shrill city; it has a riper, richer, more honorable look than oy other of the upper ramifications of the great longitudinal thoroughfare – the look of having had something of a social history…

> (*The Wayfarer in New York*, 1909, p. 135)

Hamlin Garland and his *Main Travelled Roads*

Main-Travelled Roads is a collection of short stories written by an American author named **Hamlin Garland.** The book was first published in 1891, and its stories are set in what the author calls the Middle Border, the prairie states of Wisconsin, Nebraska, Iowa, Minnesota, and South Dakota. However, what left an indelible mark on his memory was the metropolis on the western shore of Lake Michigan:

> Chicago has three winds that blow upon it. One comes from the East, and the wind goes out to the cold gray-blue lake. One from the North, and men think of illimitable spaces of pinelands and maple-clad ridges which lead to the unknown deeps of the arctic woods.

> But the third is the West of the Southwest wind, dry, full of smell of unmeasured miles of growing grain in summer, or ripening corn and wheat in autumn. When it comes in winter the air glitters with incredible brilliancy. The snow of the country dazzles and flames in the eyes; deep blue shadows everywhere stream like stains of ink. Sleigh bells wrangle from early morning till late at night, and every step is quick and alert. In the city, smoke dims its clarity, but it is welcome.

> (Quoted in Benedict, 1981, p. 102)

Vachel Lindsay and his townsmen

The vision of a new America came, not surprisingly, from a poet named **Vachel Lindsay** (1879-1931), who rediscovered his childhood home when he returned from his early years of wanderings. He came to realize that, "This is a year of bumper crops, of harvesting festivals. Through the mists of the happy waning year, a new village arises, and the new country community, in visions revealed to the rejoicing heart of faith. And yet it needs no vision to see them. Walking across this land I have found them, little ganglions of life, promise of thousands more. The next generation will be that of the eminent village. The son of the farmer will be no longer dazzled and destroyed by the fires of the metropolis. He will travel, but only for what he can bring back. Just as his father sends half-way across the continent for good corn, or melon seed, so he will make his village famous by transplanting and growing this idea or that. He will make it known for its pottery or its processions, its philosophy or kits peacocks, its music or its swans, its golden roofs or its great union cathedral of all faiths." (Lindsay, *On the Building of Springfield*)

Vachel Lindsay also envisioned a future for his townsmen when he composed this little poem:

> "Let not our town be large ... remembering
> That little Athens was the muses' home,
> That Oxford rules the heart of London still,
> That Florence gave the Renaissance to Rome.
> Some city on the breast of Illinois
> No wiser and no better at the start
> By faith shall rise redeemed, by faith shall rise
> Bearing the western glory in her heart."
> (Lindsay, *On the Building of Springfield*)
> (Quoted in Benedict, 1981, p. 115)

California, one of the most diversified American states, can be ranked next to New York because it can exist alone. Unlike other similar states, California is unique in its self-supporting attributes. It has everything you would like to see in an American state – industry, agriculture, business, commerce, and the vital asset of having a 1, 054-mile coastline.

We need to go back to **Rudyard Kipling** (1865-1936), who put it extremely well when he said this:

> Remember that the men who stocked California […] were physically, and as far as regards certain tough virtues, the pick of the earth… It needs no little golden badge … to mark the native son of the Golden West. Him I love because he is devoid of fear, carries himself like a man, and has a heart as big as his boots.

> (Kipling, 1899, p. 44)

Dr. Buscaglia and his visit to Cambodia

Today, **Felice Leonardo "Leo" Buscaglia, Ph.D. (1924-1998)**, is remembered as Dr. Love. His informative books and lectures speak for themselves. However, one stands out: *Living, Loving & Learning*, a collection of writings assembled between 1970 and 1981.

It all started when Buscaglia was interviewed by the Dean at the School of Education in California. Having left the job as Director of Special Education in a large district in California, he decided that he wanted to go back to the classroom. When asked what he was planning to do in the future, Buscaglia simply said he would teach a class in LOVE. Two years later, he found himself teaching such a class that started with 20 students but ended up with 200 and a waiting list of 600 students.

When he began his teaching career, Buscaglia looked at both sides and had to acknowledge what other people, for example, Carl Rogers, had to say about education:

> You know that I don't believe that anyone has ever taught anything to anyone. I question the efficacy of teaching. The only thing that I know is that anyone who wants to learn will learn. And maybe a teacher is a facilitator, a person who puts things down and shows people how exciting and wonderful it is and asks them to eat. (Buscaglia, 1982, p. xv)

His book came out in 1982, but seven years before its publication, the author sold almost everything he had, collected a small amount of money, and spent two years traveling around the world. Those years of traveling put him in contact with cultures completely different from the Western cultures, and what struck him was the variety of feelings describing how people lived, thought, and felt.

"I learned something really unique when I was in Cambodia. I was in Angkor Wat looking at the wonderful Buddhist ruins. They're fantastic – great tremendous Buddha heads being devoured by Banyan trees, and monkeys swinging in the air, everything wild and open and beautiful, ruins such as you never dreamed of – a completely new world for us. There, I met a French woman who stayed on after the French had left Cambodia. She said, 'You know, Leo, if you really want to experience Cambodia, don't sit here in the ruins. This is all well and good, but get out and see the people. Find out what they're doing. And you've come just at a good time because the Monsoons are coming, and the way of life changes.' And then she said, 'Go down to the Tonle Sap,' (If you

293

remember in your geography, it's a great lake that makes up most of Cambodia) 'because the people are now involved in a very interesting thing. When the Monsoons come, the great rains wash away their houses and take away everything they have. Then these people get on communal rafts, several families together. The rains come, the rafts raise, and they go right on living, but now communally.' I thought, wouldn't that be beautiful if six months out of every year some of us could live together? I can see you thinking – Who the hell wants to live with my neighbor? But maybe it would be a beautiful thing to live with a neighbor and find out what it is again to be dependent upon people and how beautiful it is to be able to say to someone, 'I need you.' "

(pp. 16-17)

> "Books have always had a secret influence on the understanding; we cannot at pleasure obliterate the ideas: he that reads books of science, though without any desire fixed on improvement, will grow more knowing; he that entertains himself with moral or religious treatise will imperceptibly advance in goodness; the ideas which are often offered to the mind will at last find a lucky moment when it is disposed to receive them." – Samuel Johnson

Memory as history

What is the forgotten quest to create the greatest library of the Renaissance?

We are somewhere at the peak of the Exploration Period after Columbus completed his journeys to the New World. There is a story recently told about his illegitimate son, Hernando Colon, who wanted to equal or even surpass his father's quest in unchartered territories.

Edward Wilson-Lee's *Catalogue of Shipwrecked Books* (2018) lays claim that Hernando had a secret project to "lift Columbus's discoveries above the petty cost-benefit calculations on which many of the courtly debates were centered, framing them instead as events in a grand religious narrative of history...." (p. 59)

Hernando assembled a plethora of information in a manuscript as evidence of what those times discovered to accomplish his goal.

> The manuscript in which he compiled his evidence now survives as eighty-four leaves of badly damaged paper, sporadically filled with writing in a number of different hands. Each sheet of paper, originally made in Italy, is water-marked with a splayed hand below a six-pointed star. The work was initially given the rather bland, descriptive title of "Book or collection of *auctoritates* [authoritative writings], saying, opinions, and prophecies..." Hernando was to rename it *The Book of Prophecies*, and the role he played in its creation is the first evidence of his growing genius for ordering. (p. 59)

Unfortunately, the collection was lost during a maritime disaster in 1522. Our history missed a monumental opportunity to record what could have been a library of universal knowledge. We know this from

Edward Wilson-Lee, who related the incident in his *Catalogue of Shipwrecked Books*. He planned to produce a book to include things that people do not really treasure: ballads, erotic poems, romances, fables, newsletters, etc.

In Part III, entitled *An Atlas of the World*, Edward Wilson-Lee tells us a story about **Albrecht Durer**'s visit on August 27, 1520, to the Town Hall in Brussels, where he saw several objects brought to Europe from the coast of Mexico, with armor, weapons, shields, sacred costumes, bed coverings and other interesting artifacts from far-away places. Among other things, **Albrecht Durer** came into contact with what was then known as Aztec Culture. Two exhibits attracted his attention: "…two disks each six feet broad: a 'sun' made of pure gold and a 'moon' of pure silver, of the type thought to have served the Mexicans as calendars. Hernando would already have seen such objects in Spain, perhaps when they were first displayed at Valladolid in March earlier that year." (p. 201)

Although Hernando could not prove that his father was the first to discover the New World, at least he managed to make his valuable contribution to the world of knowledge. His image should be very close to his father's.

When the Central Library in Los Angeles burned in 1986, everything in the Fiction section from A to L was lost, including all the books by Ray Bradbury. However, that did not destroy in any way the legacy left to posterity.

As a young man, **Ray Bradbury** spent long hours in the library, whether it was this library or that library. For a while, he worked in a room in the basement of UCLA's Powell Library, where he rented a typewriter and wrote a short story about a book burning that he originally entitled "The Fireman." In time, the short story turned into a novel about the fear that people might destroy or burn books one day.

Susan Orlean, the award-winning *New Yorker* reporter and *New York Times* bestselling author, started her story from the moments when the fire alarm sounded in Los Angeles on April 29, 1986, for what some said it was a false alarm. The fire burned for hours and destroyed four hundred thousand books. In *The Library Book* (2018), she assembled her thoughts and research on the facts of those days in 1986, and the crucial role books and libraries play in our lives.

When approaching Ray Bradbury's short story turned novel, Susan Orlean takes us to the moment when Ray Bradbury was not so sure about the title of his work.

When he finished writing the book, Bradbury tried to come up with a better title than "The Fireman." He couldn't think of a title he liked, so one day, on an impulse, he called the chief of the Los Angeles Fire Department and asked him the temperature at which paper burned. The chief's answer became Bradbury's title: *Fahrenheit 451*. (Orlean, 2018, p. 105)

What is *The Landscape of Memory*?

In 1987 Milton Meltzer explored the complexities of memory in his thought-provoking book entitled *The Landscape of Memory*. The book opens with several paradoxes, of which one needs to be mentioned here: "Scientists estimate that in a lifetime the brain can store a million billion items of information. (That's 1,000,000,000,000,000 items.) It amounts to a thousand new bits of information per second of a life lived from birth to seventy-five years of age. And still, if you live that long, you'll have used only a fraction of what the memory could store." (p. 5)

Each of the eleven chapters of *The Landscape of Memory* starts with quotations from famous personalities who have something to say about memory and its uses:

"Everything fades, save memory."

Albert Camus

"Memories lurk like dust balls at the back of drawers."

Jay McInerney

"A liar ought to have a good memory."

Apuleius

"The opposite of history is not myth. The opposite of history is forgetfulness."

Elie Wiesel

What is *The Memory Palace*?

In Milton Meltzer's (1987) opinion, **memory is the greatest asset of the human mind** and in Chapter VII, entitled "The Memory Palace," the author reviews historically how we have built systems to increase the power of memory. For thousands of years, the ideas have been the same: we tend to construct images, and the systems in question mainly resort to "intense concentration at the moment of memorization" - which also imply steady practice. After reviewing Matteo Ricci's "memory palace" which also gives the chapter its name, Meltzer goes back in our history to support his views about mnemonics, the science of memory:

> A mnemonic can be any method that helps you to remember something. Before printing was invented and books became easily available, the memory of people had to carry knowledge from place to place and from generation to generation. The handwritten journal of Jasper Danckaerts, a Dutchman who traveled to New York in 1679, tells how the local Indians, without writing, relied on memory to pass the contents and contracts down through the generations. As the Indians negotiated with the white settlers for land sales, for each article of an agreement taken up, one of the Indians would hold a different shell in his hand. When agreement was reached, the specific meaning of that shell-marker was repeated in words.

> Danckaerts's journal goes on to note of the Indians: 'As they can neither read nor write, they are gifted with a powerful memory. After the conclusions of the matter, all the children who have the ability to understand and remember it are called together, and then they are told by their fathers, sachems, or chiefs how they entered into such a contract with these parties. [The children] are commanded to remember this treaty and to plant each article in particular in their memory.' The shells were tied together with a string, put in a bag, and hung in the house of the Indian chief. He adds that the young people were warned to preserve the memory 'faithfully so that they may not become treaty-breakers, which is an abomination' to the Indians, he said.
>
> (Meltzer, 1987, pp. 60-61)

The memory of our calendar

January   from *Janus*, the Roman god of beginnings and entrances, gates, transitions, doorways, passages.

Students can be asked to interview each other and talk about New Year's resolutions or about celebrating the New Year in other cultures.

February   from the Latin *februo*, "to purify through sacrifice."
Students may want to talk about Groundhog Day or similar celebrations.

March   from *Mars*, the Roman god of war; it was originally the first month of the Year. It is a month of firsts: the first daffodil, robin, earthworm.

Dialogues between students might be able to talk about firsts or spring events in their own culture.

April   from the Latin word *aperire*, meaning "to open or bud." Naturalist Hal Borland wrote: "April is a promise that May is bound to keep."

Question for our students: Do they have an April Fool's Day?

May   from *Maya*, the Roman goddess of fertility, who ruled over the growth of plants.

Here's an easy way to teach the months of the year in a joke:
       Can February march? If not, April may.

June   named for the Roman goddess *Juno*, patron of marriage and women. It is the time for weddings and feasts.

Students should be encouraged to talk about the longest day of the year or about outdoor activities.

 July   Julius Caesar named July after himself when he reorganized the old Roman calendar.

The Fourth of July can be the start of student conversations.

August   named for Augustus Caesar. The Romans changed the name of the month from *Sextilius* to *August* to **honor** him for changing the calendar.

"One of the finest pleasures of August is this: On a clear night between the 11th and 13th, put a blanket on the lawn, invite someone you like to join you, and lie down to watch the sparkling Perseid meteors streak across the sky."

(Ben Franklin's *Almanac*, 2003, p. 227)

Do people in other cultures have similar traditions or customs?

September was the seventh month (from *septem* in Latin) in the old Roman calendar. When Julius Caesar decided to start the year with January instead of March, September kept its name.

September is famous for the Full Moon Harvest rising, and other cultures may have similar celebrations.

October When the Julian calendar changed October (the eighth) to the tenth month of the year, people tried to rename it after famous Roman gods, but to no avail.

Pumpkins and Halloween costumes are now becoming popular all over the world. Anything similar or different in other places?

November from *novem* in Latin, meaning the ninth month in the Roman calendar.

Thanksgiving is a typical American holiday, followed by Black Friday, which is now so infamous in other places.

December has lost its meaning of "ten" (*decem* in Latin) and now people associate it more with "decorate" for the holidays.

"During the Vietnam War, H. Ross Perot decided he wanted to do something for American prisoners of war who were being held in North Vietnam. He arranged for Christmas presents to be purchased, wrapped, and sent to Hanoi on a fleet of Boeing 707s. When the North Vietnamese refused to allow the presents to be delivered, Perot had the parcels flown to Moscow and sent to Vietnam from the central post office, one at a time, as regular mail. The Packages arrived on time and were delivered to the POWs."

(Ben Franklin's *Almanac*, 2003, p. 359)

Topics for classroom discussions:
How do you choose the best gift for a loved one?

Memory as ACRONYMS

> "Americans, as a rule, employ abbreviations to an extent unknown in Europe. Life, they say is short and the pace is quick; brevity, therefore, is not only the soul of wit, but the essence of business capacity as well. This trait of the American character is discernable in every department of the national life and thought..." (John S. Farmer, *Americanisms – Old and New*, London, 1889) (Quoted in *Dickson's Word Treasury*, 1992)

When Paul Dickson collected and published his *Word Treasury* in 1992, acronyms were already widely used and even proliferated, especially after 1940.

> The term *acronym* (from *akros*, meaning tip, plus *onym*, name) was first introduced to scholars in a 1943 issue of *American Notes and Queries*, which traced it back to Bell Telephone Laboratories, which had created the word as a title for a pamphlet written to keep workers abreast of the latest initialized titles for weapons systems and agencies. Acronyms are best described as pronounceable formations made by combining the initial letters or syllables of a string of words. (p. 5)

Here are some of his examples of acronyms that are now treated as new words:

ABBA Swedish pop group, whose name is an acronym made from the first names of the group members: **A**gnetha, **B**enny, **B**jorn, and **A**nni-frid.

AWOL **A**bsent **W**ith**O**ut **L**eave. Armed Forces

CABAL There is a legend that this word is an acronym for the names Clifford-Ashley-Buckingham-Arlington-Lauderdale, who conspired in the court of Charles II. It actually derives from the Hebrew *cabala* ('full of hidden mystery'), but makes a nice story anyhow.

COBOL **CO**mmon **B**usiness **O**riented **L**anguage

FORTRAN **FOR**mula **TRAN**slation

JEEP   Name derived from GP for General Purpose

LEGO   Building-block toy that got its name from the Danish *leg godt* for 'play good.'

SNAFU   Situation **n**ormal: **a**ll **f**ouled **up**

ZIP   The Zip in Zip Code stands for **Z**one **I**mprovement **P**lan

DISCOVER: Ask the students to find out what these acronyms mean:

SoHo
NoHo
TriBeCa

If possible, local **acronyms from places of interest** might be a good topic.

> "A man's life proceeds from his name, the way that a river proceeds from its source."

The memory of first names

Like many other things related to the beginning of early linguistic history, first names occupy a relatively important seat of debate. Some researchers consider the oldest surviving personal name to be **En-lil-ti**, which was found on a Sumerian tablet from around 3300 B.C.. However, there is no consensus related to this name, mostly because some other linguists think it represents the name of a deity.

Another possible first name could be **Narmer**, the Father of Men, who is thought to be the first Egyptian pharaoh who lived around 3150-3100 B.C. Some historians argue that Narmer was the one who founded the First Dynasty and even unified Egypt.

> Among various linguistic theories about the origin of names, the most valid states that people were named for physical characteristics. Put simply, a small man might be called "the Short One," a light-complexioned woman "the White One," and so on. [...]
>
> The descriptive quality of names became more specific as civilization advanced. The Romans alone gave such graphic names as Agrippa, "born feet-first"; Dexter, "right-handed"; Seneca, "old"; Cecil, "dimwitted"; Lucius, "light"; and Livvy, "bluish."
>
> (Panati, 1984, p. 62)

The next kind of names came to indicate surnames related to occupation or location: *Angelo* for "messenger" and *Morgan*, Welsh for "dweller of the sea." (p. 63)

The most common family names in English are derived from occupations: Barber, Baker, Taylor, Gardner, Farmer, Shepherd, etc. A good example would be the name **Smith** and here are the equivalents in other languages:

Le Fevre, La Farge, La Forge, Fernand	French
Ferrari, Fabbri, Fabroni, Ferraro	Italian
Herrera, Herrero, Hernandez, Fernandez	Spanish
Ferreiro, Ferreira	Portuguese
Schmidt, Schmied	German

Smed	Swedish
Kuznetsov	Russian
Kovac	Czech
Kovacs	Hungarian
Kowak, Kowalski	Polish
Covaci	Romanian
Hadad	Lebanese and Syrian Arabic
Magoon	Irish

(Compiled from Charles Berlitz, *Native Tongues*, 2005, p. 170)

What can we do with first names in an ESL classroom?

> Most ESL students know where their names come from or how their parents chose those names.
>
> In pairs or small groups, each student can talk about their family, their first names, and how the meaning of their names might affect their lives.

Appendix 1

Collocations and Idioms Worksheets

1. *Against all odds*:

"Odds literally means the likelihood of success, given a specific set of numbers. The origin of the idiom *against all odds* can be traced to the origin of the word *odd,* which was first used in a wagering sense by none other than the great William Shakespeare in his 1597 work *Henry IV.* The pluralization of *odd* to *odds* did not happen until the 19th century, so it's likely that this idiom was coined after the word *odds* instead of *odd* came into common use. Who said it? No one really knows." (www.gingersoftware.com)

Students should be asked to use some of the following collocations/idioms and **speak about a memorable event** in their lives as teenagers.

For example, *I sometimes think of the best memorable events in my life with nostalgia.*

Use some of the following collocations and idioms:

at first glance
a glorious summer
a typical day for me
blessed event
at one time or another
against all odds
second to none
worth its weight in gold
an emotional event
on second thought

Proficiency Level: Low Advanced – Bloom's Taxonomy Level 4

2. *Blood, sweat, and tears*

"Winston Churchill, the Prime Minister of the United Kingdom during World War II, first uttered the phrase that turned into the popular 'blood, sweat, and tears' during a speech in 1940. Many scholars say that the phrase dates back to before Churchill's time. Various translations of the Bible mention Jesus 'bathed in his own blood, sweat, and tears' or praying while his sweat and blood drip down."
(https://writingexplained.org/idiom-dictionary/blood-sweat-and-tears)

Students should be asked to work in pairs or small groups and describe a **dear member of the family**.

For example:
My next-door neighbor has always been a member of our extended family.

You may use some of the following collocations and idioms

back in the day
a close-knit family
a nuclear family
family ties
bear in mind
beyond a shadow of a doubt
success runs in the family
blood, sweat, and tears
a breath of fresh air
bottom line
the support of family and friends
to start a family

Proficiency Level: Low Intermediate – Bloom's Taxonomy Level 3

3. Compose an email message to a good friend. Imagine you have to make a **big decision about a sensitive issue** and you definitely need help from somebody you trust.

You may want to use some of the following collocations, but you can also use any other words or phrases of your own choice.

in my humble opinion
to talk openly
to fight bravely
tears of happiness
to satisfy curiosity
to build a relationship
to feel at ease
to love unconditionally
no wonder
shocking news

Dear Abby,

_____
_____
_____
_____
_____
_____
_____

Proficiency Level: Low Advanced – Bloom's Taxonomy Level 5

4. Anecdotes

"Today, *anecdote* refers to any brief, often humorous tale. Walter Johnson, who pitched for the Washington Senators from 1907-1927, once had two strikes on a batter. The batter started walking away when the umpire called him back. 'What's the use,' responded the batter, 'you can't hit what you can't see.' The anecdote emphasizes the speed of Johnson's fastball."

(Popkin, 1988, p. 89)

Share an anecdote and use as many collocations as possible from the list below.

Example: *I can tell you a lot of fact-related anecdotes.*

to bear in mind/to keep in mind/to call to mind

to share anecdotes

to recount/tell/relate anecdotes

to exchange/swap anecdotes

an amusing anecdote/a telling anecdote

if you'll pardon my French

entertaining/amusing anecdote

a personal anecdote

research based on anecdote, not fact

inspiring anecdotes

Proficiency Level: Low Advanced – Bloom's Taxonomy Level 5

5. *(Strictly) for the birds*

"Strictly for the birds originated in U.S army slang during the Second World War. The earliest instance [...] is from *Blitz Hits Army Talk*, a glossary of U.S. army slang, by Corporal Jimmy Cannon, published in the *St. Louis Star-Times* (St. Louis, Missouri) of Monday 10th, 1941; however, the phrase had a different sense, that of **unpleasant news**:

*Unpleasant news 'is **strictly for the birds.'***

The second-earliest occurrence [...] of **strictly for the birds** is used in its current sense; it is from *Camp Adair Version Tells How to Make Friends in Africa* published in the Corvallis Gazette-Times (Corvallis, Oregon) of Tuesday 9th February 1943:
*Don't kill snakes and birds. Some Arabs believe that the souls of departed chieftains dwell in them. (The editor believes this is **strictly for the birds**.)* (https://wordhistories.net/2018/11/08/strictly-birds/)

Share a piece of information about something that has happened recently.

For example:

For the life of me, I don't know what they were talking about.

> *for the birds*
> *front page news*
> *excellent/fantastic news*
> *great/positive/wonderful news*
> *devastating/tragic news*
> *breaking news/a piece of news*
> *to share/spread the news*
> *up-to-the minute news*
> *global/international/local*

Proficiency Level: Low Advanced – Bloom's Taxonomy Level 5

6. *To grasp at straws*

The idiom refers to a drowning man trying to save himself by grabbing or catching any floating object, even a straw. Thomas More first used it in *A Dialogue of Comfort against Tribulation* (1534).

Share a moment in your life when you tried something with little hope of succeeding.

For example:

His weak ideas will tell you that he is just grasping at straws.

Use as many collocations and idioms as possible from the list below:

to clutch at straws

to get out of hand

get a grip on yourself

to strive for

to get wind of something

getting away with murder

to go with the flow

giant leap forward

to give one another chance

going forward

Proficiency Level: Low Advanced – Bloom's Taxonomy Level 5

7. Apology

"In classical Greek, 'a well-reasoned reply'; a 'thought-out response to the accusations made,' as that of Socrates. The original English sense of 'self-justification' yielded a meaning 'frank expression of regret for wrong done,' first recorded 1590s, but this was not the main sense until 18c. Johnson's Dictionary defines it as 'Defense; excuse,' and adds, '*Apology* generally signifies rather excuse than vindication, and tends rather to extenuate the fault, than prove innocence,' which might indicate the path of the sense shift. The old sense has tended to shift to the Latin word *apologia* known from early Christian writings in defense of the faith."

(www.etymonline.com/word/apology)

Share a moment when you had to apologize.

For example:
 I was expected to submit a written apology.

Use some of the following collocations and idioms:

I'm awfully sorry
my bad/my mistake
I'm awfully sorry
hear me out
half-hearted apology
my sincere apologies
to owe an apology
to issue an apology
to demand an apology
a letter of apology

Proficiency Level: Low Advanced – Bloom's Taxonomy Level 5

8. Self-deprecating

The jig is up – "a dishonest plan or activity has been discovered and will not be allowed to continue."

For example: "They all laughed when I said I'd become a comedian. Well, they're not laughing now." – Bob Monkhouse, *Crying With Laughter: My Life Story*

Share a moment when you laughed at yourself:

For example*:*
As usual, I had to use my self-deprecating humor.

Use as many collocations as possible from the list below:

The jig is up.

Laugh it off!

LOL, right?

dark humor

a sense of humor

good humor

to jump for joy

jealous bone

to jump through hoops

just as bad, if not worse

Proficiency Level: Low Advanced – Bloom's Taxonomy Level 5

9. Confessions: *Lost my marbles*

"*To lose one's marbles* is to lose one's mind. In the 1954 film, *The Caine Mutiny,* Humphrey Bogart likened insanity with marbles when he showed his character, the demented Lt. Cmdr. Queeg restlessly jiggling a set of metal balls under stress in court. [...] The expression has now been shortened to simply *losing it.*"

(www.phrases.org.uk)

No need to explain what the expression means. The best idea would be to create a quick example and let the students paraphrase it in their own words:

For example:
My grandma lost her marbles after she had a stroke.

Share a moment when you had to make a confession and use some of the following expressions:

You may want to start by saying: *I have a confession to make.*

Laid eyes on you.
a true confession
to force a confession
to hear a confession
a shy confession of love
Let bygones be bygones.
Listen up!
Lo and behold!
Let nature take its course.
Look the other way.

Proficiency Level: Low Advanced – Bloom's Taxonomy Level 5

10. *Nip it in the bud*

"Well, you know, I was thinking I'd just nip it in the bud, before it gets worse, because they were talking about it in health class, how pregnancy, it can lead to ... an infant."

(Juno in Juno, The Movie)

Share with the rest of the group an incident when you had **to stop a problem before it started**.

For example:

It's never easy to confront a problem with someone you love.

Use as many collocations as possible from the list below:

to nail down

neither confirm nor deny

Never say never!

Nip it in the bud!

no dice

no offense

No pun intended.

Not my cup of tea.

Nothing short of a miracle.

Proficiency Level: Low Advanced – Bloom's Taxonomy Level 5

11. *A quick fix* – "an easy and expedient solution or remedy, especially one producing results that are temporary, illusory, or counterproductive."

(*Webster's New World College Dictionary*, 4th Edition. Copyright © 2010 by Houghton Mifflin Harcourt)

For example:
There are no quick answers and quick fixes.

Share with a partner a moment when you looked for *a quick fix*.

Use as many collocations as possible from the list below:

for quite some time

speaking quite frankly

effective/efficient solution

a satisfactory solution

a practical/convenient solution

quite the best/worst

a lasting/long-term solution

a way to solve the problem

a quick fix

Proficiency Level: Low Advanced – Bloom's Taxonomy Level 5

12. "Courage is being scared to death and saddling up anyway."
– John Wayne

Interview each other and ask the following question:

Do you think courage is important these days?

For example:

You should always have the courage of your convictions.

Use as many collocations as possible from the list below:

a tall order

Tell you what!

Take it or leave it!

to demonstrate courage

Take it for granted!

That speaks volumes.

tremendous courage

through and through

too hot to handle

a story of incredible physical courage

Proficiency Level: High Intermediate – Bloom's Taxonomy Level 4

13. "Success is never final; failure is never fatal; it is courage that counts."   – Winston Churchill

In small groups or pairs, share your greatest test of courage.

For example:
What he did was an act of courage.

Use as many collocations as possible from the list below:

confident of success
chance of success
a runaway success
the key to success
a notable success
degree of success
great success
a symbol of one's success
to run a risk
if at first you don't succeed, try again

Proficiency Level: Intermediate – Bloom's Taxonomy Level 4

14. 'Sleight of hand'

"The phrase 'sleight of hand' is a translation of a French expression: *léger de main,* 'light of hand.' The French expression refers to the performance of tricks in which nimble action with fingers deceives the eye of the beholder. The French expression exists in English spelled as one word: *legerdemain.*"

(www.dailywritingtips.com)

Share a moment in your life when you had to use good humor in a difficult situation.

For example:
What a surprise to see you in this neck of the woods!

You may want to use some of the following collocations:

an elaborate joke

a practical joke

a humorous touch

a light-hearted and humorous look

wickedly humorous

humorous asides

lame jokes

a funny joke

visual jokes

Proficiency Level: Low Advanced – Bloom's Taxonomy Level 5

15. "A person is what he thinks about all day."
– Ralph Waldo Emerson

What occupies most of your thoughts during the day?

Language reflects our daily preoccupations, and there are several ways to express this concept. For example, if you find yourself **in a difficult position**, you may want to use a collocation like this:

I found myself between a rock and hard place.

Use as many collocations as possible from the list below:

between the devil and the deep blue sea

up in the air

up-and-coming

under the circumstances

under the weather

up to it

up to snuff

up close and personal

up to no good

too close to call

between Scylla and Charybdis

Proficiency Level: Low Advanced – Bloom's Taxonomy Level 5

16. You can't always express what you feel in words, but you still have to press your point.

Share a moment when you had to insist on your own idea.

For example:
That day, I had to raise my voice.

Use as many collocations and idioms as possible from the list below:

to get to the point

point of view

more to the point

to raise one's voice

to reach a turning point

at this point in time

to voice an opinion

the point of no return

point taken

to press a point

Proficiency Level: Low Advanced – Bloom's Taxonomy Level 5

17. Would you **describe yourself as a private person or an outgoing person**?

At a party or a school function, do you prefer **to talk with a few friends or a lot of people, even strangers?**

For example:
My best friend is never shy to speak out in front of a large audience.

Use as many collocations as possible from the list below:

brutally honest
speak your mind
set high standards
have a sense of humor
have a way with word
wait-and-see attitude
strong personality
outgoing personality
burning ambition
risk taker
good at keeping secrets
have a vivid imagination

Proficiency Level: Low Intermediate – Bloom's Taxonomy Level 2

The longest word in English? **Smile**s Why? Because there is a mile between the first and the last letter.

18. Laughter feels so good and is so good for us!

"Shakespeare is a well-spring of characters which are saturated with the comic spirit; with more of what we will call blood-life than is to be found anywhere out of Shakespeare; and they are of this world, but they are of the world enlarged to our **embrace by imagination**, and by great poetic imagination."

[NB: author's emphasis] (Comedy, 1956, p. 11)

We all love stories, especially if they are funny. In his essay entitled *Laughter*, Henri Bergson resorted to basic definitions of what the comic can do to make us laugh and argued that man is "an animal which laughs." To produce an effect on us, "the comic demands something like a momentary anesthesia of the heart. Its appeal is to intelligence, pure and simple." (quoted in *Comedy*, pp.63-64.) Starting from the premise that our laughter is always the laughter of a group, he tells us what happened one day, when a man was asked why he did not weep at a sermon when everybody else was shedding tears, he replied: "I don't belong to the parish!" (p. 64)

There is another story of a teacher who was lecturing about grammar. He was trying to impress his students with his extensive knowledge and commented that in some languages, a double negative makes a positive. However, he said, two positives cannot make a negative – to which a student replied: "Yeah…. yeah…"

Students should be asked **to share a funny story or a joke** and use some of the following collocations and idioms:

good for a laugh   *take it with a pinch of salt*   *raise a smile*
pardon my French   *spill the beans*
pull one's leg   *Cat got your tongue?*

Proficiency Level: Low Advanced – Bloom's Taxonomy Level 5

19. *Fit as a fiddle*

"Nowadays, *fit* means *healthy*. However, in the past *fit* meant *fitting*, as in something that is well suited for a particular purpose. *Fiddle* means *violin*, but in the past, it also had the connotation of being something very positive. Therefore, in the past, comparing something to a fiddle was a way to compliment it. The expression *fit as a fiddle* was a way to say that something was correct or proper. It first started appearing around the year 1600. Over time, the meaning changed to its current form today."

(www.https://writingexplained.org)

Does music make the world go round?

For example:
Getting an extra bonus? That's music to my ears.

Share your opinions with a partner and try to use as many of the following idioms:

all that jazz

to blow your own trumpet

clean as a whistle

fine tuning

play by ear

with bells on

like a broken record

to face the music

bells and whistles

Proficiency Level: Intermediate – Bloom's Taxonomy Level 3

20. *Barking up the wrong tree*

"The origin of the idiom *barking up the wrong tree* dates back to early 1800s America, when hunting with packs of dogs was very popular. The term was used literally at first, when wily prey animals such as raccoons would trick dogs into believing they were up a certain tree when in fact they had escaped. Thus, dogs barking at the base of an empty tree were said to be *barking up the wrong tree*." (www.gingersoftware.com)

Share a moment when somebody or you made the wrong choice, asked the wrong person, or followed the wrong course.

Create a whole context following the example from Agatha Christie:

It was a hoax all right. Nothing doing. One broken shop window – kid throwing stones – and a couple of drunk and disorderlies. So just for once our Belgian friend was barking up the wrong tree.
(Christie, 1963, p. 20)

You may want to use some of the following expressions:

on the fence
> *vote with your feet*
>> *dig your heels in*
>>> *split hairs*
>>>> *no strings attached*
>>>>> *light at the end of the tunnel*
>>>>>> *stick to your guns*
>>>>>>> *up in arms about*

Proficiency Level: Low Advanced – Bloom's Taxonomy Level 6

21. How are you feeling today? Share with the group your feelings today by using the graph below.

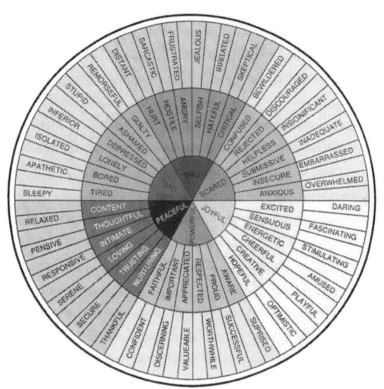

(https://325424.com/2015/08/13/emotions-and-feelings-charts/)

22. "When our remote ancestors first invented systems of counting, they unwittingly took a tremendous step toward the development of communication, writing, and the storing of information – eventually leading to our technically developed world civilization."

(Berlitz, 2005, p. 99)

Expand the following:

For example:

Count one's blessings *I remember to count my blessings every day.*

Lose count   _____

Every minute counts   _____

Body count   _____

At the last count   _____

But who's counting?   _____

Count one's pennies   _____

It's the thought that counts _____

Count me in   _____

Proficiency Level: Low Advanced – Bloom's Taxonomy Level 5

23. Mum's the word

"Mum's the word has become a popular name for baby product shops and nursery services, but the 'mum' in this phrase isn't mother. Nor has *mum* anything to do with Egyptian mummies, despite their prolonged taciturn disposition. That *mummy* derives from *mum* being an alternative name for the bitumen used for embalming. The *mum* of *mum's the word* is *mmm* - the humming sound made with a closed mouth, indicating an unwillingness or inability to speak. The word is of long standing in the language and first appeared in print in William Langland's Middle English narrative poem *Piers Plowman*, circa 1376."

(www.phrases.org.uk)

Share a curiosity from your language or culture and use as many collocations/idioms as possible from the list below:

> *from a mile away*
> *up close and personal*
> *constructive dialogue*
> *a nimble wit*
> *that's that*
> *for the life of me*
> *day in and day out*
> *to no avail*
> *unintended consequences*

Proficiency Level: Low Advanced – Bloom's Taxonomy Level 5

24. What means of learning are most stimulating to you?

I remember extremely well how I started my education. I was 6 years old, and we were gathering to meet our teacher, who greeted us with a big smile. It was then I realized how important it was to have a good start, or better say, start on the right foot. I also treasure the time we began each new school year afresh.

> Although – like every child – I hated to see the summer end, the beginning of school held a sense of promise: a fresh chance at playing myself, with the live option to try on new personae – those brittle masks we mold to our skin, that eventually become indistinguishable from what new call the self, that many-faceted figuration we present to the world. There was also the chance to reinvent my relationship to the rest of the class: to make old friends new, to discover which classmates I might have overlooked or overestimated. It meant recalculating my place within the group, making adjustments and being adjusted by others. (Parini, 2005, p. 3)

Not everyone learns in the same way. Some people like math; others hate it. Most kids prefer to play games and learn from the spirit of initiative or from becoming self-sufficient. What we all like – although we rarely say it – is the idea that we compete with each other, and we want to be the best.

Ask your students to share with their peers **what means of learning are most stimulating to them. What makes them stay on their path to learning?**

Some of the following collocations might become useful:

effective learning	*distance learning*	*infectious enthusiasm*
to acquire knowledge	*to gain support*	*to be inquisitive*
to make progress	*study habits*	*to play hooky*

Proficiency Level: Low Advanced – Bloom's Taxonomy Level 4

25. What makes you feel good?

There are moments in life when we solve problems because we have the right attitude. There are days when positive things stimulate our minds, and there are cases when we meet people of normally affectionate and kindly disposition.

Words cannot describe a good feeling when you win an argument or make intelligent deductions from the facts presented to you. It is very hard to control your feelings in extreme situations, and it doesn't matter if you have the mental power or the proverbial luck. However, good results usually come when hard work and dedication come to fruition and make everyone **intensely happy**.

The common thread in our daily routine?
Just listen carefully to what is said when we feel gifted with abundant energy and respond properly to seemingly impossible challenges. In most cases, we automatically resort to collocations that include the word *good* or the ideas that it implies.

Describe a situation when such words would be appropriate:

Good news!	*Good heavens!*
to do good	*a good fit*
good-doers	*good-natured*
good feeling	*good breeding*
good luck	*as good as gold*
good humor	*quite good*
as good as it gets	*a pretty good job*

Proficiency Level: Intermediate – Bloom's Taxonomy Level 4

26. Swimming

For some of us, swimming is an addiction, and I would simply describe it as **a competition with yourself**. It is definitely more addictive than coffee, but it is also a skill that implies sustained effort and concentration.

> We can learn something of the nature of swimming competition from its origin as a wartime art. The ability was held in high rega rd in ancient civilizations from the Egyptians to the Greeks; to be ignorant of "either letters or swimming," Plato declared, was to lack a proper education. Herodotus described the Greeks as expert swimmers and thus able to make their escape to shore when their ships were destroyed in battle with the Persians. (Tsui, 2020, p.155)

Are we talking about a skill that is an experience but also an adventure? Absolutely! Isn't that more or less what teachers and students do when they talk about skills?

It's much easier to teach such collocations as chunks and encourage students to do the same. Here are some words and collocations that might be good for a conversation about competitions/swimming:

to go swimming	*how about a quick swim?*
to hold/stage a competition	*to go for a swim*
competition between	*competition for*
fair competition	*a competitive encounter*
fierce competition	*interesting matchup*
dead heat	*photo finish*
contender	*antagonist*

Proficiency Level: Low Advanced – Bloom's Taxonomy Level 5

Appendix 2

The Irregular Verb Chart

AAA

bet	bet	bet
burst	burst	burst
cost	cost	cost
cut	cut	cut
fit	fit	fit
hit	hit	hit
hurt	hurt	hurt
let	let	let
put	put	put
quit	quit	quit
set	set	set
shut	shut	shut
slit	slit	slit
split	split	split
spread	spread	spread
wet	wet	wet

ABA

become	became	become
come	came	come
run	ran	run

ABB

awake	awoke	awoke
bend	bent	bent
bind	bound	bound
bleed	bled	bled
bring	brought	brought
build	built	built
buy	bought	bought
catch	caught	caught
creep	crept	crept
deal	dealt	dealt
dig	dug	dug
feed	fed	fed
feel	felt	felt
fight	fought	fought
find	found	found
flee	fled	fled
fling	flung	flung
hang	hung	hung

have	had	had
hear	heard	heard
hold	held	held
keep	kept	kept
kneel	knelt	knelt
lay	laid	laid
lead	led	led
leave	left	left
lend	lent	lent
light	lit	lit
lose	lost	lost
make	made	made
mean	meant	meant
meet	met	met
pay	paid	paid
read	read	read
say	said	said
seek	sought	sought
sell	sold	sold
send	sent	sent
shine	shone	shone
shoot	shot	shot
sit	sat	sat
sleep	slept	slept
slide	slid	slid
spend	spent	spent
spin	spun	spun
stand	stood	stood
stick	stuck	stuck
sting	stung	stung
sweep	swept	swept
swing	swung	swung
teach	taught	taught
tell	told	told
think	thought	thought
understand	understood	understood
win	won	won
wring	wrung	wrung

ABC

arise	arose	arisen
be	was, were	been
bear	bore	born
begin	began	begun
blow	blew	blown
break	broke	broken
choose	chose	chosen
do	did	done
draw	drew	drawn
drink	drank	drunk
drive	drove	driven
eat	ate	eaten
fall	fell	fallen
fly	flew	flown
forbid	forbade	forbidden
forgive	forgave	forgiven
forget	forgot	forgotten
freeze	froze	frozen
get	got	gotten
give	gave	given
go	went	gone
grow	grew	grown
hide	hid	hidden
know	knew	known
lie	lay	lain
prove	proved	proven
ride	rid	ridden
ring	rang	rung
rise	rose	risen
see	saw	seen
show	showed	shown
shrink	shrank	shrunk
sing	sang	sung
sink	sank	sunk
spring	sprang	sprung
stink	stank	stunk
swim	swam	swum
wake	woke	woken
wear	wore	worn
write	wrote	written

The 10 ESL Commandments

1. All good stories have **a hook** to capture the reader's interest. Good lessons are the same.
2. **Praise** students in public. Criticize in private.
3. Make all your lessons as **multicultural**, inclusive, and gender-fair as possible. Good teaching leaves no one out.
4. Help students **get organized** and **stay organized**.
5. Make room for **fun**. A quick joke always helps!
6. Don't rule out memorization. What's **worth remembering** is **worth memorizing**.
7. When you see students who are 'natural teachers,' encourage them. They are **tomorrow's miracle workers.**
8. Think like a child. **Act** like an adult.
9. Pay attention to complaints. **Critics** can be teachers too.
10. Don't just give students something to do. Give them **something to think about**.

(Adapted from Robert D. Ramsey, *501 Tips for Teachers*, 2003)

Final thoughts

From objects of art, or from nature, or even from our past recollections, we develop a new order of thought that awakens the mind and stirs our imagination. It is not only the exercise of imagination, but also what it involves through a continued succession of thoughts that trigger an infinite variety of new ideas. The trains of thought, in turn, generate in us the desire **to remember what is good and what is useful** but also **to learn** how **to imagine**.

For the teachers who are avid readers in search of knowledge, writing may be considered meditation in ink. What we intend to do as instructors (when we read and absorb knowledge) may be an attempt to give full weight to the most inclusive understanding of **education as a place of wonder and entertainment**. We may find our **memory as a repository of knowledge** that would satisfy the students' curiosity and thirst for invention and creativity. **Information seeking creatures** will always find happiness in a world where they can discover "the joy of elevated thoughts."

We are still wondering whether **the goal** is more important than **the journey**, which gives us a measure of unease. However, what makes the classroom/online experience a moving and rapturous experience may very well supply our imagination and creative thinking with lasting impressions and rewards that will stay with us for a long time.

And maybe, just maybe, besides the goal and the journey**, the company we keep** when we engage in the process of teaching and learning might provide us with the unexpected thrill and challenge.

References

Anagnostou-Laoutides, E. (2018). *Dreams, Memory and Imagination in Byzantium.* Netherlands: Brill.

Alford, S. (2017). *London's Triumph: Merchants, Adventurers, and Money in Shakespeare's City.* United States: Bloomsbury Publishing.

Alison, A. (1790). *Essays on the Nature and Principles of Taste.* Edinburgh: J. Hutchison.

Aquinas, T. (2015). *De Memoria et Reminiscentia.* Aeterna Press, eBook.

Archer, J. (2021). *To Turn a Blind Eye.* St. Martin's Press.

Austin, J. L. (1962). *How to Do Things with Words.* The William James Lectures delivered in Harvard University in 1955. Oxford: Clarendon Press.

Labaree, L. W., Fineman, H. H., Boatfield, H. C., Franklin, B., & Ketcham, R. L. (1964). *The Autobiography of Benjamin Franklin.* United Kingdom: Yale University Press.

Baddeley, A. D. (1997). *Human Memory: Theory and Practice.* Psychology Press.

Bate, J. (2009). *Soul of the Age. A Biography of the Mind of William Shakespeare.* New York: Random House.

Battelle, J. (2005). *The Search. How Google and Its Rivals Rewrote the Rules of Business and Transformed Our Culture.* London: The Penguin Group/Portfolio.

Bauer, S. W., & Wise, J. (2016). *The Well-Trained Mind: A Guide to Classical Education at Home.* United Kingdom: W.W. Norton.

Ben Franklin's Almanac of Wit, Wisdom, and Practical Advice: Useful Tips and Fascinating Facts for Every Day of the Year. (2003). Ireland: Yankee Books.

Benedict, S. (1981). *The Literary Guide to the United States.* Vol. 3. Facts on File.

Berlitz, C. (2005). *Native Tongues.* Edison, NJ: Castle Books.

Bhattacharyya, M. (2020). *Rabindranath Tagore's Śāntiniketan Essays. Religion, Spirituality and Philosophy.* London & New York: Routledge.

Bloom, H. (2002). *Genius. A Mosaic of One Hundred Exemplary Creative Minds.* New York: Warner Books.

The Book of Beasts: Being a Translation from a Latin Bestiary of the Twelfth Century. (1984). United Kingdom: Alan Sutton.

Bower, G.H., & Clark, M.C. "Narrative Stories as Mediators for Serial Learning." *Psychonomic Science* 14 (1969): 181-182.

Bowra, C.M. (1962). *Primitive Song*. New York: World Publishing Company.

Bridgman, R. (2006). *1000 Inventions and Discoveries*. London: Dorling Kindersley.

Bronowski, J. (1978). *The Origins of Knowledge and Imagination*. United Kingdom: Yale University Press.

Brown, R. M. (2011). *Starting from Scratch: A Different Kind of Writers' Manual*. United Kingdom: Random House Publishing Group.

Burke, E. (1767). *A Philosophical Enquiry into the Origin of Our Ideas of the Sublime and Beautiful*. London: J. Dodsely.

Burke, J., & Van Heusen, J. (1940). *IMAGINATION*. New York: ABC Music Group Corp.,

Buscaglia, Ph.D., L. (1982). *Living, Loving & Learning*. New York: Fawcett Columbine.

Cain, S. L. How to Use Art Activities to Illustrate ESL Vocabulary. https://www.fluentu.com/blog/educator-english/art-vocabulary-esl/
(Retrieved March 22, 2021)

Call, M. L., Nyberg, A. J., & Thatcher, S. M. B. (2015). "Stargazing: An integrative conceptual review, theoretical reconciliation, and extension for star employee research." *Journal of Applied Psychology*, 100, 623-640.

Callahan, S. (2015). *The Link between Memory and Stories*. https://www.anecdote.com/2015/01/link-between-memory-and-stories

Cather, W. (2006). *My Antonia*. Oxford: Oxford University Press.

Chatwin, B. (1987). *Songlines*. London: Picador.

Chopin, K. (2015). *The Dover Reader*. Dover Thrift Editions.

Christie, A. (1963). *The ABC Murders*. New York: The Black Dog & Leventhal Publishers.

_____, (1970). *Passenger to Frankfurt*. New York: Dodd, Mead & Company.

Collins, D. (2020). "The Importance of Imagination/Phantasia for the Moral Psychology of Virtue Ethics" in *Imagination and Art: Explorations in Contemporary Theory*. Leiden and Boston: Brill. 174-205.

Collins English Dictionary. (2015). United Kingdom: Collins.

Comedy. (1956). New York: Doubleday Anchor books.

Comstock, B. (2018). *Imagine It Forward. Courage, Creativity, and the Power of Change*. New York: Currency.

The Confessions. (2012). United States: NEW CITY Press.

Coreil, C. (1985). *Asking Questions*. English Language Center. Faculty of Arts & Humanities, King Abdulaziz University. Jeddah, Saudi Arabia.

Costa, A. L. (1992). *The School as a Home for the Mind*. Arlington Heights, Illinois: SkyLight.

Cox Gurdon, M. (2019). *The Enchanted Hour. The Miraculous Power of Reading Aloud in the Age of Distraction*. New York: Harper Collins Publishers.

Creativity in Language Teaching: Perspectives from Research and Practice. (2015). United Kingdom: Taylor & Francis.

Dewey, J., & Dewey, E. (1915). *Schools of To-morrow*. New York: E. P. Dutton & Company.

Dewey, J. 1916 (2008). "Democracy & Education" in *The Collected Works of John Dewey*. Carbondale: Southern Illinois University Press.

Dickson, P. (1982). *Dickson's Word Treasury*. New York: John Wiley & Son, Inc.

Doidge, N. (2007). *The Brain That Changes Itself*. London: Penguin Books.

Donmall, B. G., Ed. "Language Awareness." National Congress on Languages in Education Assembly (4th, York, England, July 1984). NCLE Papers and Reports 6.

Dor, D. D. (2015). *The Instruction of Imagination: Language as a Social Communication Technology*. United States: Oxford University Press.

Dörnyei, Z. (2001). *Teaching and Researching Motivation*. England: Pearson Education Limited.

Dörnyei, Z., & Csizér, K. (1998) "Ten Commandments for Motivating Language Learners: Results of an Empirical Study." *Language Teaching Research*, 2(3), 203-29.

Dos Passos, J. (2010). *The Ground We Stand on. The History of Political Creed*. New Brunswick, New Jersey: Transaction Publishers.

Eagleman, D. (2020). *Livewired: The Inside Story of the Ever-changing Brain*. United States: Pantheon Books.

Egan, K. (2013). *Imagination in Teaching and Learning*. London: Routledge.

Elster, C. H. (2000). *Verbal Advantage: Ten Easy Steps to a Powerful Vocabulary*. United States: Diversified Publishing.

Encyclopedia of Creativity. (2020). United States: Elsevier Science.

341

Engel, W. E. (2016). *The Memory Arts in Renaissance England: A Critical Anthology*. United Kingdom: Cambridge University Press.

Epstein, J. (2018). *The Music of the Grand American Show*. Claremont Review of Books.

Eschholz, P., Rosa, A., & Clark, V. (Eds.). (1997). *Language Awareness*, New York: St. Martin's Press.

Fagell, P. L. (2019). *Middle School Matters*. New York: DaCapo Press.

Findlay, M. S. (1998). *Language and Communication: A Cross-cultural Encyclopedia.* Abc-Clio Inc.

Fleischman, M., & Roy, D. (2005). "Intentional Context in Situated Natural Language Learning." *Cognitive Machines*. The Media Laboratory. Massachusetts Institute of Technology.

Flesch, R. (1974). *The Art of Readable Writing*. New York: Harper & Row.

Fogler, J., & Stern, L. (2005). *Improving Your Memory. How to remember what you're starting to forget*. Baltimore: The John Hopkins University Press.

Forsyth, M. (2014). *The Elements of Eloquence: Secrets of the Perfect Turn of the Phrase.* New York: Berkley Books.

Frost, R. (2010). *The Road Not Taken, Birches, and Other Poems*. Claremont, California: Coyote Canyon Press.

Fuller, R. Ph.D. (2002). *The Power of Context; Creating Meaning in Language and Thought. How to Use It to Teach Reading.*

Gajdusek, L. (1988). "Toward wider use of literature in ESL; Why and how." *TESOL Quarterly, 22*. 227-257.

Gawain, S. (2002). *Creative Visualization. Use the Power of Your Imagination to Create What You Want in Your Life*. Novato, California: New World Library.

Gelb, M. J. (2002). *Discover Your Genius*. New York: Harper Collins Publishers.

Gerard, A. (1759). *An Essay on Taste*. London: A. Millar, A. Kincaid, and J. Bell.

Gjika, Ani. (2016). "Breaking the ESL Student's Imagination." https://www.publicbooks.org/breaking-esl-students-imagination/ (Retrieved July 12, 2021)

Gray, R. (2000). *Grammar Correction in ESL/EFL Writing Classes May Not Be Effective*. Boston: Pearson.

Grazer, B., & Fishman, C. (2015). *A Curious Mind. The Secret to a Bigger Life*. New York: Simon & Schuster.

Great Cities Through Travelers' Eyes. (2019). United Kingdom: Thames & Hudson.

Great Ideas Today. (1987). Chicago: Encyclopaedia Britannica, Inc.

Hackwith, A. J. (2019). *The Library of the Unwritten*. Penguin Random House.

Haddon, M. (2003). *The Curious Incident of the Dog in the Night*. New York: Vintage Books.

Hadfield, J., & Dörnyei, Z. (2017). *Motivating Learning*. United Kingdom: Taylor & Francis Group.

Hemingway, E. (1964). *The Snows of Kilimanjaro and Other Stories*. New York: Scribner.

Hirsch, Jr. E.D. (1988). *Cultural Literacy*. New York: Vintage Books.

Hirsch, E. D., Kett, J. F., & Trefil, J. (2002). *The New Dictionary of Cultural Literacy*. United States: Houghton Mifflin.

Memory: Histories, Theories, Debates. (2010). United States: Fordham University Press.

Horowitz, D. (2013). "Fiction and Nonfiction in the ESL/EFL Classroom: Does the Difference Make a Difference*?" Landmark Essays on ESL Writing.* Edited by Tony Silva and Paul Kei Matsuda. 109-116.

Howells, W. S. (1941). *The Rhetoric of Charlemagne and Alcuin*. Princeton: Princeton University Press.

Hunter, J. (1848). *Text-Book of English Grammar: A Treatise on the Etymology and Syntax of the English Grammar*. London: Longman, Brown, Green, and Longmans.

Huyssen, A. (1995). *Twilight Memories*. New York: Routledge.

Hyde, L. (2019). *A Primer for Forgetting. Getting Past the Past*. New York: Farrar, Strauss & Giroud.

Janet, P., & Paul, C. (1925). *Psychological Healing*. New York: Macmillan.

Johnston, K. R. (1998). *Wordsworth. Poet. Lover. Rebel. Spy*. New York: W. W. Norton & Company.

Kilpatrick, W., Wolfe, G., & Wolfe, S. M. (1994). *Books That Build Character. A Guide to Teaching Your Child Moral Values Through Stories*. New York: Simon & Schuster.

Kind, A. "Introduction: Exploring Imagination," [in] Amy Kind, ed. *The Routledge Handbook of Philosophy of Imagination*. (New York: Routledge, 2016). 1-11.

Kipling, R. (1899). *American Notes*. Boston: Brown and Company.

Kipling, R. (1978). *Just So Stories*. New York: Shocken Books.

Kirkpatrick, E. A. (1920*) Imagination and Its Place in Education*. Boston: Ginn and Company.

Konstan, D. "Imagination and Art in Classical Greece and Rome," *Imagination and Art: Explorations in Contemporary Theory*. 2020. Leiden/Boston: Brill Rodopi. 35-49.

Krashen, S. (1998). "Teaching Grammar: Why Bother?" California English.

_____. (2002). *Second Language Acquisition and Second Language Learning* (internet version), University of Southern California .

_____. (2004). *The Power of Reading*: Insights from the Research.

Krashen, S. D., & Terrell, T. D. (1983). *The Natural Approach: Language Acquisition in the Classroom*. United Kingdom: Alemany Press.

Kumaravadivelu, B. (2006). *Understanding Language Teaching. From Method to Postmethod*. Mahwah, New Jersey: Lawrence Erlbaum Associates, Publishers.

Ladurie, E. L. R. (1967). *Histoire du climat depuis l'an mil*. Flammarion.

Landmark Essays on ESL Writing: Volume 17. (2013). United States: Taylor & Francis.

Lanir, L. "Teachers: Are Your Teaching Methods Stimulating the Senses?") https://languagelearningdifficulties.com/2020/09/30/ (Retrieved July 27, 2021)

Larsen-Freeman, D. & Anderson, M. (2013). *Techniques and Principles in Language Teaching*. 3rd Ed. Oxford: Oxford University Press.

Lee, C. "Punctuation Junctions, Quotation Marks, and Ellipses." *The APA Style Blog*, May 27, 2015.

Lerner, F. (1998). *The Story of Libraries. From the Invention of Writing to the Computer Age*. New York: Continuum.

Lessing, D. (1994). *Under My Skin. Volume One. My Autobiography to 1949*. New York: HarperCollins Publishers.

Longman Dictionary of Language Teaching and Applied Linguistics. Pearson Education Limited.

Madoc-Jones, G. & Egan, K. "On the Educational Uses of Fantasy." *The Journal of the Imagination in Language Learning and Teaching*, Volume VI, 2001, 8-15.

Maley, A. "Creativity with a Small 'c' ". *The Journal of the Imagination in Language Learning and Teaching*. Volume IV, 1997, 8-16.

Martinez-Alba, G. (2017). *English U.S.A. Every Day*. Hauppauge, NY: Barron's.

Mastropieri, M. & Scruggs, T. E. "Enhancing School Success with Mnemonic Strategies"

http://www.ldonline.org/article/5912 (Retrieved July 26, 2021)

May, R. (1994). *The Courage to Create*. New York: W.W. Norton & Company.

Mayfield, M. (2014). *Thinking for Yourself*. Boston: Wadsworth.

McGowen, K. "Fantasy Books: There's a Whole Other World Out There," *Yale National Initiative.* https://teachers.yale.edu/curriculum/viewer/initiative_06.03.08
(Retrieved July 26, 2021)

McWhorter, J. H. (2003). *The Power of Babel: A Natural History of Language*. New York: Times Books.

Meltzer, M. (1987). *The Landscape of Memory*. Brattleboro, Vt.: The Book Press.

Monkhouse, B. (2012). *Crying with Laughter: My Life Story*. United Kingdom: Random House.

Moser, K. & Sukla, A. Ch. (Eds) *Imagination and Art: Explorations in Contemporary Theory*. 2020. Leiden/Boston: Brill Rodopi.

Moskowitz, G. "Humanistic Imagination: Soul for the Language Class." *The Journal of the Imagination in Language Learning and Teaching*. Volume II, 1994, 8-17.

Mueller, L. & Reynolds, J. D. (1992). *Creative Writing. Forms and Techniques*. Lincolnwood (Chicago): National Textbook Company.

Murphy, L. (2018). *The Prodigal Tongue. The Love-Hate Relationship between American* and *British English*, New York: Penguin Books.

Nabokov, V. (1989). *Speak, Memory. An Autobiography Revisited*. New York: Vintage International.

Nation, I. S. P. (2001). *Learning Vocabulary in Another Language*. Cambridge: Cambridge University Press.

Newham, P. "Making a Song and Dance: The Musical Voice of Language." *The Journal of the Imagination in Language Learning*. Volume III, 1995-1996, 66–74.

Norris, M. (2019). *Greek to Me. Adventures of the Comma Queen*. New York: W.W. Norton & Company.

Orlean, S. (2018) *The Library Book*. New York: Simon & Schuster.

Osborn, A. F. (1963). *Applied Imagination: Principles and Procedures of Creative Problem-Solving*. Revised edition. New York: Charles Scribner's Sons.

Ostler, N. (2005). *Empires of the Word. A Language History of the World*. New York: Harper Perennial.

Panati, C. (1984). *Browser's Book of Beginnings. Origins of Everything under, and Including the Sun*. Boston: Houghton Mifflin Company.

Parini, J. (2005). *The Art of Teaching*. Oxford: Oxford University Press.

Peiss, K. (2020). *Information Hunters. When Librarians, soldiers, and spies banded together in World War II Europe*. New York: Oxford University Press.

Pennycook, A. (2007). "The rotation gets thick. The constraints get thin": Creativity, re-contextualization, and difference. *Applied Linguistics*, 28 (4), 679-596.

Pinker, S. (2003). *The Language Instinct: How the Mind Creates Language*. United Kingdom: Penguin Books Limited.

Politzer, R. L. (1965). *Foreign Language Learning*. Englewood Cliffs, NJ: Prentice Hall, Inc.

Popkin, D. (1988). *Vocabulary Energizers*. Hada Publications.

Porter, N. "A Truth-Teller's Kit." *The Writer*, June 2020, 32-37.

Price, R. (1997). *A Palpable God*. New York: The Akadine Press.

Rajamanickam, M. (2007). *Modern General Psychology*. Second Edition. Ashok Kumar Mittal. Concept Publishing Company.

Ramsey, R. D. (2003). *501 Tips for Teachers*. Chicago: Contemporary Books.

Rank, H. (1984). *The Pep Talk: How to Analyze Political Language*. United States: Counter-Propaganda Press.

Robinson, K. (2013). *Finding Your Element. How to Discover Your Talents and Passions and Transform Your Life*. London: Viking.

Encyclopedia of Creativity. (2020). United States: Elsevier Science.

Sawyer, R. K. (2006). *Explaining Creativity. The Science of Human Innovation*. Oxford: Oxford University Press.

Schachter, D. L. (1996). *Searching for Memory*, New York: Basic Books.

Schmitt, N. (2000). *Vocabulary in Language Teaching*. Cambridge: Cambridge University Press.

Schmitt, N. & Carter, R. (2000). "The lexical advantages of narrow reading for second language learners." *TESOL Journal, Spring*, 4-9.

Shuman, M. "Back Stage Behaviorism," *Psychology Today*, June 1973, 51-54.

Schuman, M. (2015). *Confucius and the World He Created*. New York: Basic Books.

Senge, P. M. (1990) *The Fifth Discipline. The Art and Practice of the Learning Organization*. New York: Doubleday.

Shakespeare, W. (1992). *Hamlet*. New York: Simon & Schuster.

Sökmen, A. J. (1997). "Current Trends in Teaching Second Language Vocabulary." In *Vocabulary: Description, Acquisition and Pedagogy*. Schmitt, N., & McCarthy, M. (eds.) 237-257. Cambridge: Cambridge University Press.

Spiro, J. (2013). *Changing Methodologies in TESOL*. Edinburgh University Press.

Steinbeck, J. (1992). *Cannery Row*. New York: Penguin.

Stevick, E. W. "Imagination and Memory: Friends or Enemies." *The Journal of the Imagination in Language Learning*. Volume I, 1993, 8-19.

Symonds, P. M. "Implications of fantasy for education," *The Elementary School Journal*, Volume 49, Number 5, Jan., 1949, 273.

Thornbury, S. (1997). *About Language: Tasks for Teachers of English*. Cambridge: Cambridge University Press.

Timms, A. "A History of Punctuation in English." *Unravel Magazine*. December 28, 2016.

(https://unravellingmag.com/articles/history-punctuation-english/)
(Retrieved July 13, 2021)

Truscott, J. (1996). "The Case Against Grammar Correction in L2 Writing Classes." *Language Learning* 46:2, June 1996, 327-369. National Tsing Hua University.

Tsui, B. (2020). *Why We Swim*. Algonquin Books of Chapel Hill.

Twain, M. (2007). *The Adventures of Tom Sawyer*. Oxford: Oxford University Press.

Urmson, J. O., & Austin, J. L. (1962*). How to Do Things with Words*. United Kingdom: Harvard University Press.

Verene, D. P. (1987). *Vico's Science of Imagination*. Ithaca and London: Cornell University Press.

Vico, G. (1982). *Vico: Selected Writings*. Edited and translated by L. Pompa. Cambridge: Cambridge University Press.

Warnock, M. (1978). *Imagination*. Berkeley and Los Angeles: University of California Press.

The Wayfarer in New York. (1909). Introduction by Edward S. Martin. New York: The Macmillan Company.

Webster's New World College Dictionary. 4th Edition. (2010). Houghton Mifflin Harcourt.

Westover, T. (2018). *Educated. A Memoir*. New York: Random House.

Whately, R. (1841). *Elements of Rhetoric*. London: B. Fellowes.

Whorf, B. L. (1956). *Language, Thought and Reality*. Cambridge, Massachusetts: The MIT Press.

Widdowson, H. G. (1984a). "Reference and representation as modes of meaning." In H. G. Widdowson, *Explorations in Applied Linguistics 2* (pp. 160-173). Oxford: Oxford University Press.

Winchester, S. (2003). *The Meaning of Everything*. Oxford: Oxford University Press.

Winspear, J. (2020). *This Time Next Year We'll Be Laughing*. New York: Soho Press, Inc.

Wohlleben, P. (2021). *The Heartbeat of Trees. Embracing Our Ancient Bond with Forests and Nature*. Vancouver: Greystone Books.

Wolf, C. (2006). *Basic Library Skills*. Jefferson, North Carolina and London: McFarland & Company, Inc.

Wolf, M. (2018). *Reader, Come Home. The Reading Brain in a Digital World*. New York: Harper Collins.

Worden, B. (2013). Book review on the inside cover of *The Pleasures of the Imagination*. London and New York: Routledge.

Wulf, A. (2016). *The Invention of Nature. The Adventures of Alexander von Humboldt. The Lost Hero of Science*. London: John Murray.

Index

By The Same Author

Articles

"The Quest for Knowledge." (2022). *Journal of Practical Studies in Education*, *3*(2), 12-15
https://doi.org/10.46809/jpse.v3i2.44

"Experience Magic: Read!" (2021). *Trends in Humanities and Social Sciences*. *1*(1), 3-4 https://publons.com/journal/1003200/trends-in-humanities-and-social-sciences/

"The Magic and Mysteries of Teaching ESL." (2021). *Middle Eastern Journal of Research and Social Sciences*. Vol. 2, Issue 3
https://bcsdjournals.com/index.php/mejrhss

"Testing by Any Other Name. Nuance in Language." (2020). *ELT Society*. https://eltsociety.org/testing-by-any-other-name/

Book reviews:

Bhattacharyya, M. (2020). Rabindranath Tagore's Śāntiniketan Essays: Religion, Spirituality and Philosophy. London & New York: Routledge. *Journal of Practical Studies in Education, 2*(3), 12-15
https://doi.org/10.46809/jpse.v2i3.25

Collins, P. (2009). The Book of William. How Shakespeare's First Folio Conquered the World. Bloomsbury. *Journal of Critical Studies in Language and Literature.2(*1), 22-23
https://doi.org/10.46809/jcsll.v2i1.49

Flanders, J. (2020). A Place for Everything. The Curious History of Alphabetical Order. New York: Basic Books. *Journal of Critical Studies in Language and Literature*, *2*(5), 11-15
https://doi.org/10.46809/jcsll.v2i5.80

Moser, K. and Sukla, A. Ch. (Eds). (2020). Imagination and Art: Explorations in Contemporary Theory. Brill. *Journal of Critical Studies in Language and Literature, 2*(2), 30-32
(https://doi.org/10.46809/jcsll.v2i2.56

Wulf, A. (2015). The Invention of Nature. The Adventures of Alexander von Humboldt. The Lost Hero of Science. John Murray Publishers. *Journal of Practical Studies in Education*, 2(4), 1-4 https://doi.org/10.46809/jpse.v2i4.26

Made in the USA
Middletown, DE
18 December 2022

19022642R00210